The IMS/VS Expert's Guide

The IMS/VS Expert's Guide

Lockwood Lyon, CDP, CSP

VNR Van Nostrand Reinhold
New York

Library of Congress Catalog Card Number 90-12510
ISBN 0-442-23977-7

Printed in the United States of America

Van Nostrand Reinhold
115 Fifth Avenue
New York, New York 10003

Van Nostrand Reinhold International Company Limited
11 New Fetter Lane
London EC4P 4EE, England

Van Nostrand Reinhold
480 La Trobe Street
Melbourne, Victoria 3000, Australia

Nelson Canada
1120 Birchmount Road
Scarborough, Ontario M1K 5G4, Canada

16 15 14 13 12 11 10 9 8 7 6 5 4 3 2 1

Library of Congress Cataloging-in-Publication Data

Lyon, Lockwood.
      The IMS/VS expert's guide / Lockwood Lyon.
            p.   cm.
      Includes index.
      ISBN 0-442-23977-7
      1. Data base management. 2. IMS/VS (Computer system)   I. Title.
      II. Title: IMS/VS expert's guide.
   QA76.9.D3L96   1990
   005.74--dc20
                                                                    90-12510
                                                                    CIP

Contents

Preface

During the past two decades I have spent a lot of time doing IMS database design, application design, and programming. As part of my first job, in 1972, I attended an in-house class on introductory IMS programming, taught by one of the systems programmers. The class lasted two weeks, at the end of which I was as mystified as ever. Why did one need IMS? What did it buy you? Could you not do the same things with regular OS/VS files and ISAM? Why all the confusing function codes, status codes, command codes, processing options, search arguments, and so forth? Why use *get*, rather than *read*, and *insert* instead of *write*?

For the next several years I coded as I had been taught, learning the answers to these questions along with much other intermediate-level IMS knowledge. When I had questions, I was forced to ask my peers or the local guru. There was little training available in many of the intermediate IMS concepts, and no reference materials worth reading. The IBM IMS manuals of the time seemed to be written as conventional reference manuals—great for reference, but not so great for training. The assumption behind these manuals seemed to be that you had to know what you were looking for if you were to find it. Some of these concepts, such as checkpoint/restart, initial database loading, user and system abends, and database access methods, became increasingly significant to know as IMS applications grew in complexity and importance.

Over the years I became an analyst, then a database designer. Still, no good reference or training materials on intermediate IMS concepts had become available. Some introductory books did appear, though, such as *IMS Programming Techniques (2nd ed.)*, by Kapp and Leben (Van Nostrand Reinhold, 1986).

Some companies came out with advanced classes on IMS database internals, performance tuning, and the like, but no substantial books, manuals, or texts appeared. By this time most of my peers and I had collected our bags of IMS *tricks*, scrawled on yellow legal paper and kept in three-ring binders for future reference. Some of them read like this:

■ An AC status code ("hierarchical error in SSAs") can be caused by a misspelled segment name in the PSB.

■ A U261 ("invalid parameter in IMS call") may mean that the program ENTRY statement and PCB list do not match.

■ After a get hold call (GHxx), multiple replaces (REPL) against the same segment are allowed without additional hold calls.

Wait as we might, no one published a book of these tricks, known as *heuristics*, although the idea seemed to be sitting there for anyone to use. From project to project and employer to employer, the books of tricks differed substantially. Then when VSAM and DB2 appeared, the number and intricacy of these tricks increased manyfold.

At present there still seems to be a lack of such books. IMS users want to know these things, but where can they learn them? From IBM reference manuals? For IMS/VS alone, the manuals' total page count is in the tens of thousands, so this seems unlikely. From other practitioners? Possibly. From experience? Maybe.

The Purpose of This Book

This book combines most of my seventeen years of IMS and DB2 experience, in both the classroom and the workplace. I have collected information, tricks, anecdotes, war stories, and even some fairy tales that taught me *why* IMS applications simply had to do certain things.

But there is a more important purpose for this book. In the past few years, several new developments have taken place that have radically changed the way we now develop software.

For one, the microcomputer revolution has invaded the workplace. PCs now exist in the United States in the tens of millions. PC-based development is now more the rule than the exception. Over 100 third-party PC software tools exist to assist the application developer in the various steps of the systems development life cycle (SDLC).

Another development is that relational databases have come into vogue. Originally only a tool for data modeling, relational data structures and relational database management systems (RDBMSs) are now replacing traditional hierarchic and network systems. The most prominent mainframe RDBMS is IBM's DATABASE 2 (DB2).

As companies grow and diversify they decentralize, become international, and provide more and more services for their customers. These services are often computer-assisted. Some examples are airline reservations systems, automated teller machines, automobile problem diagnostic hardware, air traffic control systems, manufacturing process control systems, and electronic data interchange software. More and more, a business enterprise's data are spread geographically. Such so-called *distributed systems* are becoming commonplace.

How will these new developments in data processing affect the way we design new systems and applications? In particular, how will we develop IMS and DB2 applications? One industry group estimates that worldwide there are more than six thousand IMS licenses and over four thousand DB2 licenses. With these numbers growing almost daily, and with more and more distributed relational systems being designed with PCs, future systems practitioners should have an organized view of the new way things will be done:

- Future applications will be written in, or interface with, one or more relational database management systems.

- Company growth will spur the need for distributed systems.

- Microcomputers will be used by analysts and programmers to design, code, test, and implement complicated systems.

With all these changes transpiring, what will happen to IMS applications? Managers and database administrators must plan to maintain these applications and interface them with newer, relational distributed systems.

The Audience

This book will be of interest to IMS and DB2 analysts and programmers. In addition, managers overseeing development projects that must interface with IMS or DB2 systems will also gain insight into the latest design and development techniques. Professionals who want to stretch their knowledge of IMS and DB2 will also find this book helpful.

Novice IMS programmers may initially find some of the topics in this book to be beyond their comprehension. Do not worry — keep reading! Many gurus remain unaware of these things too. In any event, there is a comprehensive glossary of IMS and DB2 terms.

The Products

The products mentioned throughout this book exist on several release levels in the industry. Most of the topics in this book refer to features common in the latest releases. For convenience these release levels are summarized below. When a characteristic of a different release is being highlighted it will be referred to using a specific version and release.

CICS/VS Version 2, Release 1
DATABASE 2 Version 2, Release 2
IMS/VS Version 2, Release 2
QMF Version 2, Release 3

Many versions of IMS have come and gone. As noted, this book covers topics from IMS/VS Version 2, Release 2. This version will be referred to herein simply as IMS. IBM has recently introduced a new version of IMS called IMS/ESA Version 3. This version, made available in March 1990, has not yet been widely accepted, partly because it is new and partly because it requires MVS/ESA. Chapter 11 of this book reviews some of the features of IMS/ESA.

As always, those wishing a more thorough review of the material contained herein are directed to the appropriate IBM manuals.

Organization

The Introduction reviews where we stand today in applications development, particularly in regard to IMS environments. It also presents some ideas for the future, on how the systems development life cycle is evolving, and about where IMS will most likely fit in.

The first section concentrates on the IMS environment. It describes the types of IMS application programs and database access methods that are possible and compares the various alternatives. In addition, it contrasts IMS databases with DB2 tables and VSAM files, then compares performance and access characteristics. This section ends with a comparison of IMS data communications, CICS, and TSO.

The second section focuses on IMS applications. It covers specifically database load, checkpoint/restart, deadlock, recoverability, and maintainability. A full chapter is devoted to various frequently encountered problems, including common abends and debugging. There is also a chapter on utilities.

The third section highlights the distributed and relational data considerations mentioned earlier, including linking to other systems, DB2/SQL techniques, and such special IMS/DB2 problems as performance, cursor processing, and referential integrity. The final chapter summarizes features of IMS/ESA Version 3, Release 1.

This book is not meant to be a substitute for appropriate software reference manuals, nor should any facts presented herein be taken at their face value. To paraphrase an acquaintance of mine, "One manual is worth a thousand professional opinions." To get the actual truth, consult the relevant manual.

Acknowledgments

My thanks to Barbara, who inspired this book, and to the staff at Van Nostrand Reinhold, who put up with me throughout the entire process. A special note of thanks to Dave Seibert, who provided technical editing assistance.

Anyone having questions or comments about this book may direct them to the author on CompuServe™ [71600,2673], or in writing in care of the publisher.

Part 1

The IMS Environment

Introduction

IMS in a Distributed, Relational World

There have been many technical topics in the news of the past few years that will affect the way we design, code, test, install, and maintain data processing systems in the future. Let us review some of these issues, paying particular attention to the effects they may or may not have on the way we will build application systems using IMS.

MICROCOMPUTERS

Some experts estimate that more than 50 million microcomputers have been sold in the last decade. This would seem to indicate that microcomputers are more than just a passing fad. Now, as they have invaded the office environment, microcomputers have changed the way we do business, the way people interact, and the way we develop systems. Computers are now as common as office furniture; indeed, in some cases they *are* office furniture.

Dataquest, a San Jose, California, market research firm, periodically releases surveys of microcomputer sales. They found that in 1988 the total market grew by about 13 percent, to about 9.9 million machines. Apple Computer had the largest share of the market in 1988 with 12.9 percent, compared with IBM's 12.5 percent share.

As hardware firms continued to crank out more and faster machines, software vendors developed programs to match. In the beginning (IBM began shipping its first PCs in 1981) much of the software available for PCs was either educational or for entertainment. Later, as PCs became faster and more powerful, business software appeared. Small businesses could now afford to purchase packages to solve business problems.

Still later, as the hardware and software both matured, various program development tools became available for the PC. With the arrival of networking software, companies could connect their PCs into local area networks (LANs). This setup permitted file sharing, easy transfer of data among workstations, and off-loading of work from mainframes. For the first time, systems could now be developed to run entirely on microcomputers, without requiring the brute computing power of mainframe hardware.

These advances have now made it possible to simulate a mainframe database management environment on one or more microcomputers. Indeed, one large software development firm, Compuware Corporation, has developed several complete IBM mainframe-compatible systems entirely on PCs. These systems, which were written in COBOL, involved IMS, CICS, and DB2 application programs that were coded and tested on micros before they were "ported" to the mainframe. IMS databases and DB2 tables were created centrally on file servers, and accessed locally by the PCs. Developing software in this fashion allowed Compuware and its clients to avoid using expensive CPU cycles on clients' mainframes during prime hours. In addition, use of expensive DASD for system software and database storage was not required, and clients' production systems were insulated from system failures during testing.

SYSTEMS DEVELOPMENT TOOLS

Origins

The term *software engineering* in Computer-Assisted Software Engineering (CASE) was first used at a 1968 NATO conference. This was the era of the *software crisis*, when developers had begun to worry about an increasing backlog of unfinished applications. Software engineering seemed the answer to this problem: it would mold mathematics, engineering, and management science into a single exquisite software development process.

As with most new ideas, it took some time for this concept to catch on. The systems development life cycle (SDLC) became in various forms a template for software engineering. Subsequently, as the field of data processing matured, various software tools were developed to assist analysts, designers, programmers, and maintainers with their work. Thus was CASE as a concept born.

Apart from simply automating repetitive tasks, CASE tools, tool kits, and workbenches allow applications developers to leverage their resources. With CASE, applications managers can allocate staff effectively, increase overall efficiency, and minimize errors. Documentation from the analysis phase of the SDLC can be used as input for the design phase, and design specifications may be fed into code generators. Testing and debugging tools speed the acceptance testing of software. And data modeling documentation aids in maintenance.

There are now two general categories of such tools: analysis and design tools, often called front-end or upper-case tools; and prototyping and testing tools, also called back-end or lower-case tools (see Figure A).

Tool Categories

Certain categories of tools fit best in different portions of the systems development life cycle. Let's review these categories briefly in the order in which they are usually performed.

Requirements Definition. This category includes all manner of strategic planning, data modeling, and pre-analysis tools.

Feasibility Study. Under this category are tools for system description, prototype analysis, feasibility assessment, as well as some initial logical design tools.

Logical Design. This category includes such workbench tools for analysts as diagramming, screen design, documentation, and prototyping.

Physical Design. In this category are included tools for DASD space analysis, selection of access methods, database and file definition, and initial performance measurement.

Coding. Workbench tools for programmers, including editors, syntax checkers, general-purpose query facilities, and application generators are in this category. A subset of this area includes various in-house productivity tools and standards for required fields, screen layouts, program boilerplates, security, help facilities, and mail/messaging capabilities.

Testing. Here are included test data generators, on-line debuggers, performance monitors, log and audit processing, and abend aids.

Implementation. This category includes system performance monitors, user-training tools, and documentation aids.

Maintenance. In this category are system performance monitors, documentation aids, and data modeling tools.

Prototyping. This category includes temporary definition of inputs, processing, calculations, and outputs, as well as graphics and system emulation.

Successive Approximation. This category is usually merged with prototyping.

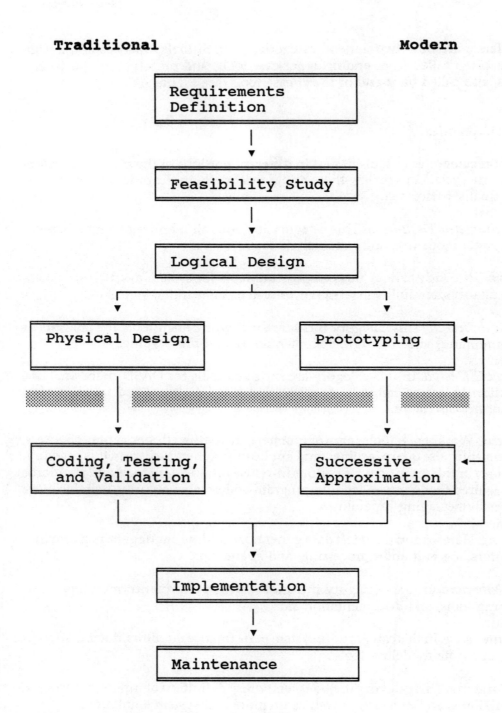

Figure A. The systems development life cycle (SDLC).

It refers to a process of iteration performed jointly by the user and the application designer. Beginning with the prototype, the user suggests changes to output formats, input availability, and processing logic. The designer then makes the requested changes and presents the user with the latest version. This process is repeated until the application finally meets the user's criteria.

The New SDLC

The explosive growth of software engineering products has changed the way developers view the SDLC. It can now be viewed as a set of parallel paths traversed by the development team (see Figure B).

Metrics. Metrics are methods of measurement and estimation, including those for estimating programming tasks and testing. This path is one of the fuzziest, with a lack of definition that gives analysts the most headaches. Such questions arise as how long will it take to design a database, code a program, or test a string of applications? Do we measure work in hours, lines of code, tested paragraphs, or by some other standard? The tools that assist the designer in developing metrics for task estimation are most useful in the requirements and design phases. They are frequently used to determine the costs, benefits, or feasibility of a proposed system. Metrics also come into play during maintenance as changes and enhancements to the system need to be prioritized.

Process Flow and Data Flow. These techniques are methods of designing, analyzing, and diagramming the flow of processes and data. Structured analysis and design methodologies usually espouse one or the other. Designers and analysts use this documentation for describing the flow of data through a system and defining how data are processed. These results may then be verified by the user. Some examples of diagramming methodologies include Yourdon, Warnier/Orr, Jackson, HIPOs, Gane and Sarson/Stradis, and Chen diagrams. These diagrams are probably the most important single set of documents produced during the early phases of a development project. Process flow documents are usually the basis for program specifications, whereas data flow diagrams form the elements of records, files, and databases. Unfortunately, during the later stages of a project, especially during maintenance, these documents are all too often ignored.

Project Management. This stage is a combination of project tracking, forecasting, and control systems. Managers use various methods, such as PERT and GANTT charts, to track work hours spent, compare actual to planned hours, monitor budgets, reallocate resources, and forecast dates for deliverables. In general, projects become more difficult to manage as the number of people

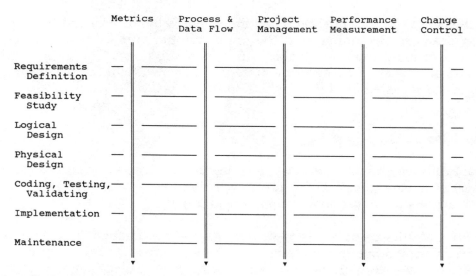

Figure B: Paths in the SDLC matrix.

assigned to them increases. The transition from the design phase step to those of coding and testing is the most likely period for project staffing to reach its maximum. At this point, methods of tracking, controlling, and allocating resource use become essential.

Performance Measurement. A number of methods of measuring system performance may be required at one stage or another to verify design correctness or efficiency. Some of the measurements are transactions processed per minute, on-line screen response time in seconds, required database reorganizations per week/month, percentage of available free space, and DASD usage statistics. Unless a project involves enhancing an existing system, it is almost impossible to measure performance early in the requirements or design phases. In later phases, as tested programs become available, developers can use performance measures to tune the system. These measures form a great part of the enhancements (defined below) made during maintenance.

Change Control. This path involves a methodology for controlling system changes. Typically security or audit features, these systems are used to verify that changes to a system are controlled, tested, verified for accuracy, and audited. Although the greatest number of changes to a system (usually called enhancements) come during maintenance, such changes cost the designer much less if discovered earlier. The single greatest cost saving for a system designer is to be able to detect system changes in the requirements phase so that they may be incorporated into the system design from the beginning. Any changes made later may affect programs already coded or database designs.

It is clear that certain phases and paths through the SDLC are more affected than others by the availability of software engineering tools. Each path has its own unique requirements in staff experience and expertise. Many software tools exist to assist the developer, implemented in either mainframe or micro-computer versions.

THE RELATIONAL MODEL AND RELATIONAL DATABASES

The Relational Model

The relational model presents a way of looking at data — that is, a prescription for how to represent data and how to manipulate that representation. More specifically, the relational model is concerned with three aspects of data:

- Data structure
- Data integrity
- Data manipulation

A relational system is simply a system constructed in accordance with the principles of the relational model. The relational model was first described by E. F. Codd in 1969. He has since expanded and extended this model several times. A complete treatment may be found in his recent book *The Relational Model for Database Management: Version 2* (Codd, 1990).

The most widely known mainframe relational database management system is IBM's DATABASE 2 (usually referred to as DB2). With several thousand DB2 installations in use worldwide, many new application systems are being designed specifically for relational environments. Some industry pundits have predicted the demise of IMS, but many application developers are finding the conversion from hierarchical and network DBMSs to DB2 to be a long, complex task. Meanwhile, users keep generating requirements for new systems, and current systems must continue to be maintained.

Implementing DB2

The most common scenario in major corporate data processing departments is to merge DB2 into current IMS and CICS applications. Sometimes this process causes problems, as DB2 is not yet widely known for good performance in on-line transaction processing environments. Indeed, one of the original selling points for relational systems in general was that they were to be an ad hoc processing environment. Relational systems lend themselves to set-level processing, the asking of "what if" questions, and situations not handled well by procedure-oriented languages such as COBOL.

Data Integrity

Perhaps the most important concept of the relational model is that of *data integrity*, a combination of *entity integrity* and *referential integrity*. Entity integrity deals with the allowable values of the primary key for an occurrence of a row. Referential integrity deals with occurrences of rows in tables having keys that exist in rows in other tables. Analysts dealing with data integrity in relational systems have learned that these requirements for data integrity were handled automatically in hierarchical systems. In IMS, for example, data integrity is enforced by requiring unique non-null keys for segments and by implementing parent-child relationships in the database structure. Relational systems do not have these features and thus must implement data integrity either through their process of data definition or with application logic. DB2 at present (Version 2, Release 2) does not fully implement data integrity, although it expands upon that which is available in IMS. This situation sometimes requires the application designer and programmer in the DB2 world to include additional program logic.

DISTRIBUTED PROCESSING

Distributed Relational Data

To make easier the implementation and portability of functions through different systems, IBM introduced a concept called Systems Application Architecture (SAA). SAA is a set of software interfaces, conventions, and protocols known as an application interface architecture. It is intended to serve as the basis for developing compatible applications across both the current and future offerings of the three major IBM computing environments: System/370, AS/400, and PS/2. These interfaces, conventions, and protocols are designed to provide enhanced consistency in the programming interface, user access, and communications support areas.

In September 1988 IBM described how distributed relational systems would interface with other such systems, in a document titled "Introduction to Distributed Relational Data" (GG24-3312). This explanation was followed that December by "Concepts of Distributed Data" (SC26-4417). In these documents IBM defined four levels of what it called distributed relational data access as part of SAA. These levels are:

1. *Remote request.* A local application can send a single database request to a remote site for execution. The request is processed entirely at the remote site. The application can then send another request to the same remote site, or any other one, whether or not the first request was successful.

IBM's Enhanced Connectivity Facility (ECF) allows a microcomputer user to perform SQL operations on data stored on a mainframe. ECF is a set of products that collectively permit a microcomputer to download host data from DB2 tables, IMS databases, VSAM files, and other sequential files. In addition, host resources such as DASD and printers can be accessed as though they were connected directly to the microcomputer. ECF supports remote requests.

2. *Remote unit of work.* A local application can send several database requests to a single remote site for execution. These requests may be logically related (a transaction). The remote site processes the requests, but the local site decides whether or not to commit or roll back the entire transaction.

3. *Distributed unit of work.* A local application can send several database requests in a given transaction to one or more remote sites for execution. Each database request is then executed entirely at a single remote site. Again, the local site decides whether or not to commit or roll back the transaction.

4. *Distributed request.* A local application can send several database requests in a given transaction to one or more remote sites for execution. In addition, each database request may span multiple sites. As before, the local site decides whether or not to commit or roll back the entire transaction.

Note that only the remote unit of work and the distributed unit of work are supported in DB2 V2.2, and then only partially.

Advantages of Distributed Systems

Fully distributed databases have many advantages over site-dependent ones. Among them are the following:

■ *Application portability.* Developers can create applications that do not depend either upon their running on a particular machine or using special hardware. They may then be run on any machine attached to the distributed DBMS network.

■ *Capacity.* The size of the database network and the traffic volume can increase without affecting the application design. Network nodes can be added, replaced, or removed transparently to the user. Examples would include nodes that are primarily processors, such as CPUs, and nodes used to store data.

■   *Productivity.* Applications act against the distributed database as if it were entirely local. Therefore, analysts and programmers need very little additional knowledge or expertise to design distributed applications or formulate queries.

■   *Local autonomy.* Local sites maintain control of local data, for ease administration and increased security.

■   *Location transparency.* Data can be moved from site to site without difficulty, because applications do not need to know where the data are stored.

■   *Performance.* Fluctuations in network traffic volume do not affect the way application programs are written.

■   *System independence.* Applications and users can function independent of the hardware, network, and languages used in the distributed system.

DB2 V2.2 provides a few of these advantages. Later releases of DB2 and a full implementation of Systems Application Architecture will provide more of them. (For a more detailed discussion of distributed processing, see Chapter 9.)

Relational Databases and DB2

The major feature of DB2 Version 2, Release 2 is that it provides a degree of support for distributed databases. Specifically, V2.2 supports the SAA concepts of distributed unit of work and remote unit of work for transactions at local sites, as follows:

■   Access is DB2-to-DB2 only. For example, a single distributed transaction cannot access both DB2 and SQL/DS data.

■   Within a given transaction, each database request must be wholly executed at a single DB2 site.

■   All updates in a transaction must be performed at the same site.

■   If the transaction is executing under IMS or CICS, the single site at which updates are performed must be the local site.

■   No data manipulation statement is allowed to span sites.

■ A foreign key at one site cannot reference a primary key at another site.

■ Database requests for remote data are always processed by dynamic bind at run time.

A new component of DB2 called the Distributed Data Facility provides distributed database support to DB2 V2.2. It operates in its own address space. Communication between sites is performed using VTAM, with each DB2 site acting as a VTAM logical unit.

To take advantage of the new distributed processing features, applications must take into account the factors that follow.

Authorization

If a local user is permitted to operate on data belonging to a remote user, then the local user must somehow make itself known at the remote site. Doing so allows the owner of the data at the remote site to grant the appropriate privileges. DB2 V2.2 uses its SYSUSERNAMES table to map local authorization IDs to IDs at remote sites, to link the local ID with its remote pseudonym.

When a database request is submitted to the remote site, the system will send the mapped ID (the pseudonym) along with the request as the authorization ID. Authorization checking is then done at the remote site. Authorization checking for remote requests is always done at run time.

Data Naming

Tables in DB2 V2.2 are defined with globally unique names consisting of the *location, authorization ID,* and *local name*. The location is the site at which the table was created, the authorization ID, an authorization ID at that site, and the local name the table's unqualified name.

To refer to a table, applications can now use an *alias,* a public name for a table at a local site. One is created with a CREATE ALIAS statement. Applications can now become independent of the locations of tables by referring to them by using the alias.

Cursor Processing

When fetching rows using a cursor, V2.2 now uses *block FETCH* wherever possible. In this process, rows are batched into blocks of about 100. Block fetch is used when no UPDATE CURRENT or DELETE CURRENT operations are being done for the cursor. This is done transparent to the user or application.

THE IMPLICATIONS FOR IMS SYSTEMS AND APPLICATIONS

Microcomputers and IMS

Application developers are no longer tied to the mainframe. IMS, CICS, and DB2 application programs written in COBOL can be coded and tested on a PC. As workstations, PCs can be networked together, allowing file and resource sharing. With the development process being off-loaded from the mainframe, mainframe applications can now perform more efficiently, since they will no longer be competing for CPU and virtual memory with test systems. Large DASD "forests" will no longer be required to store test databases or tables. Users wishing to do CPU-intensive tasks with data can download production data from the mainframe to a microcomputer, work with the data there, and upload the results when finished. (IBM's Enhanced Connectivity Facility product does this now.)

In general, the maturation of the PC and PC software will increase an enterprise's return on its investment, insulate the production environment from that of development, and enhance the productivity of the workforce.

CASE Tools and IMS

The IMS application developer's biggest challenge comes when alterations to a company's business data model require regenerating all of the IMS/VS database definitions for the system. This step is likely to require extensive programming changes. Converting old database definitions to new ones can be complicated and lengthy and may require having experienced personnel in the systems department.

In this arena the most cost-effective CASE tools are those that help define and refine the business data model as early as possible in the SDLC. This would mean that the system design life cycle process would take the data flow path in the analysis and design phases as shown previously in Figure A. During these phases, software engineering tools lower the probability of massive design changes later in the SDLC. The disadvantage (if one could call it that) is that a great deal of time must be spent early on planning and organizing the logical and physical data structures. Staffing schedules may preclude this, as programmers may have to wait idly by for completed analysis and design.

In general, then, CASE tools will assist a business in organizing its information so as to enhance the application development process. This will pay great dividends in that an organization's full understanding of its business data model is a prerequisite to productive application development.

Distributed Relational Systems and IMS

Although it is sometimes possible to simulate some relational database structures in IMS, true distributed relational database management is beyond IMS's capabilities. Only by integrating current IMS application systems with a fully relational DBMS such as DB2 may soon become will an organization be able to keep pace with its competitors in the information processing world of the next decade.

COMING OF AGE IN A RELATIONAL WORLD: A PARABLE

The widespread implementation of relational database technology has ushered in a new climate for data processing applications development. The emergence of fourth- and fifth-generation languages, CASE tools, prototyping, and a wealth of PC-based software has changed the nature of the way in which we analyze and design software. How are these changes reflected in our organizations and our people? What new problems have arisen, and how must managers, supervisors, and analysts deal with them?

Consider the following hypothetical story. This parable is an amalgamation of several true stories involving real data processing installations, their staffs, and their application environments. The problems the protagonist must cope with are actual ones that arise in the modern DP world. Although this particular story deals with a CICS environment, the lessons illustrated apply in any modern applications environment.

Monday, 8:00 A.M.

"Well, here I am!"

With these words George Programmer introduced himself to his new boss, Linda Leader. George, fresh from DB2 programming classes in the ABC Company's Education division, has just been transferred. Previously a senior analyst, he was "promoted" from his job in CICS Applications Maintenance to a position in the new Applications Development Center.

"Sit down, George," said Linda. "You and I need to have a little chat. There are a lot of things you have to learn."

This confused George; after all, he had twelve years of CICS experience, including eight years with his present company. He had spent the last four years as lead analyst in charge of maintaining some of the company's most important systems. He knew all the maintenance staff and most of the system's users. What more was there to know?

Problem: Moving from a Maintenance (Static) Environment to a Development (Dynamic) Environment

As Linda describes the company to George, let us summarize their conversation.

The ABC company has hundreds of CICS application programs, running on several large mainframes. Maintaining these systems requires an experienced staff familiar with both the systems and their users. In this environment each level of the staff must have its own specific knowledge and skills.

In contrast, the Development Center staff needs an entirely different set of skills. They are responsible for developing all new applications and systems using relational databases (DB2). (For a comparison of the two environments, see Table A).

When the ABC Company created their Development Center, they staffed it with an entirely different sort of DP animal than was customary. As they soon found out, this led to some interesting management problems.

The development staff was younger, had less business and data processing experience, and was more highly specialized than the maintenance staff. Their salaries were also much lower. In addition, they were characterized by management as being (for lack of a better word) "immature."

Monday, 9:00 A.M.

"So you see, George, in the development environment the makeup of the staff is different from what you're used to. Here's your first assignment. If you have any questions, see Allen, our head analyst. His workstation is next to yours."

Directed to his new workstation, George ponders this conversation. Could such a simple difference in environments mean such an extensive change in the nature of the company? Couldn't the company have instead merged the two staffs together into a single department?

As he enters his new cubicle, George tries to put his thoughts in order. Sitting down at his ergonomically designed chair, he reviews the specifications of the programming assignment Linda has given him.

It is to be an on-line parts catalog program. Users will enter their requests for parts information using a CICS terminal. The program is to retrieve this information from several DB2 tables and display it, which sounds simple enough. George decides to speak to Allen about where he should begin.

Monday, 9:30 A.M.

As he rounds the corner, George glimpses Allen, fifteen years his junior, seated with his feet on his desk. His tie is loose, and the top button of his shirt is unfastened. "Hiya," said Allen. "You must be George. Whatcha want?"

Table A. Comparison of knowledge and skill sets of maintenance and development staff.

Maintenance Staff (CICS)	Development Staff (DB2)
Programmers	
Much CICS coding experience	Light DB2 coding experience
CICS internals knowledge	Little or no DB2 internals knowledge
Physical DB design skills	No physical DB design skills
Database Administrators	
Systems analysis/design	No analysis or design skills
Business Knowledge	Little business knowledge needed (to coordinate DB designs)
Additional CICS knowledge	Highly specialized theoretical knowledge
Analysts	
Know what works best from applications experience	Little experience to draw upon
Have heuristics (tricks of the trade)	Few heuristics
Need good communications skills	Only average communication skills needed
Typical Required Staff Training	
Company business systems	CASE tools, 4GLs, 5GLs
Intermediate CICS techniques	Relational model
Project and task management	Third-party software
Oral/written communication skills	Prototyping

Problem: Moving from Communicators to Prototypers

As George is about to find out, analysts in the Development Center are not known for their communication skills. They simply have no need for them.

In the maintenance environment, designers and analysts need to talk to users, document their needs, and translate that feedback into system specifications. In contrast, analysts in the development environment typically design a prototype application based upon preliminary sketchy information. Using this prototype as a tool, the development analyst then presents the user with a ready-made miniature system for the user to critique. Successive meetings and critiques allow the analyst to hone the prototype to fit the user's needs.

"Well, Allen, I can surely appreciate the climate here. Meanwhile, could you give me an example of another program or application similar to the one I'm designing? That would give me a head start." Allen looks back at George with a blank stare. "What examples?"

Problem: Lack of Heuristics and/or Application Examples

As George is now learning, the development of new applications using relational technology is a relatively new thing. There are few, if any, working applications, and those that do exist were designed and written by people having little or no experience. Consequently, there are no hard-and-fast rules about what works and what doesn't.

The knowledge that George has from his previous position of existing applications will still be somewhat useful. He has an excellent grasp of what the user probably requires and of the systems they are presently using. Unfortunately, George still has a lot of catching up to do.

Monday, 10:00 A.M.

"Well," says George, "I'll do my best."

"That's great," replies Allen. "Here, let me give you a quick demo of our Workbench Toolkit." Allen turns to his keyboard and begins keying furiously, explaining things at a rapid pace.

George realizes that Allen isn't using a terminal; instead, he has a micro-computer. It includes word processing, a compiler/interpreter, communications hardware and software, a connection to what Allen calls a local network, and various other development tools. George quickly becomes lost in a bewildering multitude of menus, hot keys, servers, simulators, animators, gateways, and test drivers.

Problem: New PC Products, Development Tools, CASE Tools, and 4GLs

What George is experiencing is something that has probably occurred to other applications developers, but in a more gradual fashion. First the programmer is migrated from a terminal to a PC connected to a mainframe. Then, perhaps, the PCs are connected to a local area network, allowing development to continue without degrading mainframe performance. Development center staff then slowly add software to the network, to support program compilation and unit testing. In addition, they also add some kind of automated design methodology tools and project management software.

Gradually, over a long period, the development environment evolves to the point where programmers work on self-contained systems designing and building fully developed applications. These working applications are then ported to the production environment.

The installation of these tools must be accompanied by training and documentation. Luckily for George, the Development Center's standards manual is well written, with a special introductory section for new users. Unluckily, no one seems to have a current copy. "We'll get you one," says Allen.

Monday, 11:00 A.M.

After thanking Allen for the demonstration, George heads for the cafeteria, picks up a sandwich, and sits down. Although he is lost in the complexity of the PC and its tools, he is confident that he can pick up everything quickly. After all, he reasons, if that kid can learn it, so can I!

Monday, 4:30 P.M.

George turns off his PC, cleans off his desk, and heads for home. He has sketched out a preliminary design for his program, using the structured design software on his PC. Lost at first, he eventually discovered that the F1 key provided context-sensitive help that allowed him to complete a flowchart of his design quickly. Tomorrow, he thinks to himself, I can start coding.

Tuesday, 8:00 A.M.

As George arrives at his cubicle, he notices that someone has left several thick binders on his desk, all titled, *Development Center Standards Manual*. On top is a note saying, "GP: Study this first. See me if any questions. —LL." With a feeling of foreboding, George sits down, picks up volume 1, and begins with "Chapter 1: Naming Standards and Conventions." His eyes begin to glaze over.

Problem: The Lack, or Proliferation, of Standards

In one respect, George is lucky. At least the company *has* standards. But to produce them, a lot of work was needed.

The Development Center support staff had first to cautiously and meticulously analyze the systems development life cycle (see Table B). Then, for each phase, they had to design, develop, acquire, or purchase tools to assist their programmers and analysts.

Each tool was installed on the network and appropriate instructions for it were included in the standards manual. In addition, the staff developed naming standards for databases, records, fields, files, control blocks, and many other entities. These were also included in the manual.

The resulting manual became hundreds of pages long, taking up three volumes. Changes and updates occurred frequently and had to be carefully applied to the correct volume. Such a manual is dry reading, yet it is an absolutely essential reference for every programmer and analyst.

As the Development Center grew, additional tools became necessary. Analysts, project leaders, and managers each required certain automated tools for project control and resource management. Some of these tools are listed in Table C.

Tuesday, 2:30 P.M.

"How are you doing, George?" George looks up from somewhere deep in volume 2 to see Linda grinning at him. Realizing that he has missed lunch, he gathers his thoughts.

"Huh? Oh, just fine, Linda. I'm reading the standards manual."

"Eh? Haven't you started your prototype yet? Better get cracking, George. There isn't any time in the project plan for training, and your program is due on Thursday. Don't forget, you're only allocated thirty-two hours."

"I'll get right to it." George hurriedly puts his manual down and turns to his PC. As Linda walks away, he wonders whether it was fair for her to expect him to be immediately productive. After all, he just got here!

Tuesday, 4:30 P.M.

Wearily, George leaves for home, taking the standards manual with him. He vows to study it on his own time. After all, it seems to be the only way to catch up. If he can get through it, he can begin coding his prototype first thing tomorrow.

Wednesday, 8:00 A.M.

George sleepily wends his way to his workstation and slumps into his chair. Standards manuals usually aren't the most exciting reading, and this one was

Table B. Tools for the systems development life cycle.

Phase 1: Application Planning

Accelerated Analysis
Function Diagramming
Systems Process Review
Feasibility Studies
Resource and Staff Allocation
Work Estimation

Phase 2: Systems Analysis

Functional Flow Diagramming
Data Flow Diagramming
Data Structure Modeling
Screen Design
Documentation Creation and Storage
Prototype Development

Phase 3: Coding

Source/Load Library Control
Source File Editor
Compile/Link Facility
Program Syntax Checking

Phase 4: Testing

Test Data Generator
Test Database Generator
Standard Test Harness
Program "Animator"
Regression Tester

Phase 5: Implementation and User Interface

Application Subsystems Security
Logon/Password Facility
Help Facility
Mail/Message Facility

Table C. Tools for development management.

Estimating

Work Effort Estimation
Hardware Resource Usage

Project Management

Task Assignment
Posting of Worked Hours
Project Scheduling
Reporting

Change Control

Library Management
Security

Performance Measurement

Hardware and Facility Resource Usage
CPU Performance
Software Performance
Degradation Analysis
Job and System Monitoring

---

no exception. It didn't help that someone had scrawled on the last page, "These tools are great for *presenting* solutions, but of no help in *finding* solutions. How do I do that?"

At any rate, George now feels he is up to speed on the Center's design process and tools. With a hot cup of coffee in hand, he begins to tackle his program.

Wednesday, 10:00 A.M.

"You wanted to see me?" George looks up from his program to see Donna, the database administrator. "Yes, thank you. I'm having a bit of a problem with the guidelines in our standards manual regarding coding applications using DB2. There don't seem to be any standard procedures to handle the situation I've encountered."

"What do you need to know?" Donna asks.

"I don't understand this business of handling deadlock situations. I thought the system abended your program when that happened. And I can't figure out why DB2 closes the cursors during synchpoint processing."

Problem: Deadlock Detection and Resolution

The simplest case of deadlock, or "deadly embrace," happens when each of two processes attempts to access a resource that the other has already locked. Formerly, both IMS and CICS would choose one of the processes to abend, and sometimes attempt to restart it. With the advent of DB2, however, a new possibility exists. The system now informs programs, through either an SQLCODE or an IMS status code, if a deadlock situation occurs. Optionally, the system may also roll back all of the application's database and message processing to the previous synchronization point or commit point.

There are two possibilities here. With CICS, the CICS attachment facility decides whether or not to roll back the program, based on its definition in the RCT. A -911 SQLCODE informs the program that a SYNCPOINT command with the ROLLBACK option was issued for your program. A -913 SQLCODE informs the program that a SYNCPOINT was not issued, but your program is requested either to issue a SYNCPOINT command with the ROLLBACK option or to terminate the execution of the program.

With IMS, message-driven applications (those using Fast Path) are requeued by way of a U777 pseudoabend. For non-message-driven programs the program receives an FD status code or a -911 SQLCODE, depending upon the resources that have been locked. Either of these codes indicates that all activity for the program has been rolled back.

This condition presents the application developer with an entirely different situation. The application must now be able to detect that a deadlock exists and handle the deadlock. After all, the existence of a deadlock is not a fatal error—the situation may be transient. In many cases, the program should attempt to reinitiate processing from its previous commit point, assuming that the deadlock no longer exists.

Particular attention must be paid, however, to a second, similar, deadlock that may occur. Programs must then be prepared to count the number of deadlocks encountered during processing, and perhaps only then to abend. This places the burden squarely on the shoulders of the application designer as to how to resolve these situations.

The *commit point* in DB2 is similar to the IMS Checkpoint and the CICS Synchpoint. It indicates the end of a *logical unit of work,* and indicates a point in the execution life cycle of a program at which it may be restarted. In fact, a CICS program containing SQL statements may not issue a DB2 COMMIT: to force a commit point, the CICS program issues a CICS SYNCPOINT. At that time, DB2 and CICS coordinate their respective resources, each doing the necessary logging and DASD processing, and release held resources. (For a more complete discussion of the DB2 commit, see Chapter 10.)

Problem: Cursor Processing

One interesting aspect of the DB2 commit point is that of cursor processing. CICS programs use SQL cursors so that they are able to present result tables having multiple rows to the program one row at a time. The cursor is defined in Working Storage (for COBOL programs), along with its corresponding SELECT statement. In the Procedure Division the OPEN CURSOR statement begins DB2 processing of the SELECT statement, and the FETCH statement retrieves a row of the result table.

Commit processing in DB2 requires that cursors be released, or CLOSED. This means that after doing a CICS SYNCPOINT or an IMS checkpoint the cursor must be OPENed again, thus causing repositioning and re-creation of the result table. This process may happen several times during program execution. Programmers must therefore ensure that this does not affect the performance of the program.

Wednesday, 2:00 P.M.

"Donna, could I see you for a moment?"

"Sure, George. What's wrong?"

"Remember that index you created for my Part table? DB2 isn't using it, even though I'm accessing the table randomly! It's doing a complete table space scan!"

Problem: EXPLAIN, RUNSTATS, and the DB2 Optimizer

George is learning about tuning applications in the DB2 environment. One of his latest accomplishments is learning how to use the EXPLAIN facility. This feature gives the coder an explanation of how DB2 will access tables and indexes for any given SQL statement. Since there are several ways of coding any particular query, this flexibility allows the designer to see how DB2 will attempt to satisfy the SQL statement.

To do this, DB2 EXPLAIN makes use of the DB2 system catalog. This set of tables contains information about what tables exist, what their columns are, how the columns are defined, whether they are in sequence or are clustered, what indexes exist, and so on. In addition, EXPLAIN looks at statistics regarding table size and the physical distribution of rows.

What George hasn't realized is that these statistics are not kept up to date automatically by the system; rather, they are replaced when the system administrator runs the RUNSTATS utility. This utility updates the statistics mentioned. Another thing George has forgotten is that he is in the test system. In this particular case, his test DB2 table has only a few rows. Small wonder that DB2 doesn't use the index: the entire table takes up only a single page of storage.

While Donna explains this to George, one more comment is in order. Recent versions of DB2, beginning with Version 2, Release 2, allow certain users to directly update the statistics in the system catalog, thus allowing designers to simulate production conditions, at least as far as the DB2 Optimizer is concerned.

Thursday, 8:30 A.M.

George is proud of himself. He has just moved his program to production, and users are trying it at this very moment. Before he can enjoy more than a brief flush of success, however, his phone rings. It's a user.

"George, this is Ernest. What's wrong with your new program? Only a few of us can use it at a time, and it seems to take forever to run!"

Problem: Who Is in Charge of the Resource Control Table?

The Resource Control Table (RCT) is the CICS entity controlling which CICS entities, or transactions, will be using which DB2 resources, or threads. It contains an entry for every DB2 *plan* and specifies how many threads are to be allocated as being dedicated to a plan. In this case the RCT assigned to George's program only a single dedicated thread and specified that, if threads were busy, other transactions must wait until the thread became available.

Although it seems a simple matter to change the RCT, in reality there is a question of control. The Development Center in our example consists of an applications group and a system support group. The applications group is responsible for application design and implementation, as well as the user interface. As such, this group felt they should have control of the RCT. After all, they were in the best position to know which applications were critical, how many users were using them, and what response times were allowable.

The system support group, on the other hand, felt they should have control of the RCT. It was a system function, they said, not an application function. Besides, changing the RCT meant bringing the system down to implement the change. This was clearly system support's responsibility.

This disagreement had not yet been resolved, so George found himself caught in the middle of a political battle. This wasn't all, either.

Problem: Query Management Facility "Power" Users

Query Management Facility (QMF) is an on-line facility allowing users to construct ad hoc queries using a set of menus. Users can then execute these queries against available DB2 tables. The Development Center thought that giving some of their users access to QMF training would save the developers some work. It did, but unfortunately it had an undesirable side effect.

QMF users were trained in query construction, not in query efficiency. What tended to happen was that a user would try out several forms of a query to see the result. Sometimes this created a tremendous workload for DB2, so much so that other users would be locked out from DB2 tables until a particular user's query had been processed.

In other words, QMF users had the power to bring the rest of the system to its knees. Further, after they had been trained in QMF these users couldn't simply be cut loose. Someone had to be available to answer questions and solve problems. Who should this be?

In mulling over this situation, George had a revelation. Perhaps certain often-used queries could be preprogrammed and made available to QMF users. These users would be strongly urged to use only these preprogrammed queries and to consult with the Development Center before creating their own. In addition, George had recently read about the Resource Limit Facility (the "governor") that was now available in DB2. This facility could limit a user's use of DB2 resources, particularly of CPU time.

His suggestions were accepted with general relief. For a short while, George was a hero.

THE MORAL OF THE STORY

If this story has a moral, it is that relational databases, PC technology, and recent software advances have changed the way in which we develop applications. The makeup of the development staff is changing, and the requirements for entry into the field have also changed. Moreover, the complex problems of managing both maintenance and development environments have not been solved. Further, the technical details of merging these environments have multiplied.

As managers it is our responsibility to plan, organize, direct, and control our areas of responsibility. We must address the concerns described here quickly, because they will have an immediate effect on the bottom line.

Chapter 1
Application Program Types

There are several different types of user-written IMS programs. Each type has its own distinguishing features, which will be described later. The different types are usually characterized as follows.

PROGRAM TYPES

- *Batch programs.* These programs access only off-line databases (those databases not defined to the IMS/VS control region) and are started using Job Control Language (JCL). Batch program database updates occur immediately.

- *Batch message programs (BMPs).* A BMP is a hybrid of a batch program and an MPP. It is initiated using JCL, but it accesses on-line databases. Database updates are finalized only at commit points. BMPs can interface with the message queue, but only one way at a time. A batch-oriented BMP does not access the message queue. A terminal-oriented BMP can either retrieve or send messages through the I/O PCB, but not both.

- *Message processing programs (MPPs).* These programs, which access only on-line databases, are started when IMS receives a message directed to the program's transaction code. Database updates are not finalized until a commit point is reached. MPPs communicate with user terminals and with other IMS, and perhaps CICS, systems.

■   *Fast Path programs.* These programs access Fast Path databases. They may only process single-segment messages, and cannot message-switch to another program.

IMS program types differ greatly in the following major areas:

■   *How or why they begin execution.* IMS/VS allows programs to run in batch regions, batch message regions, or message processing regions. IMS/ESA also allows for database control (DBCTL) regions. (For a discussion of IMS/ESA features, see Chapter 11.) Each of these types of region requires different resources and is scheduled using a different priority scheme.

■   *What databases the IMS program types can access.* IMS databases are divided into three categories: off-line databases, which are accessible only by batch programs; full-function on-line databases, which can be accessed by BMPs and MPPs; and Fast Path databases.

■   *How database updates are backed out upon program abend.* Most IMS database updates can be backed out dynamically by IMS. With batch programs that do not use DASD logs the submitter must back out database updates using the Batch Backout utility.

■   *How they are restarted or rerun after failure.* Batch and batch message programs are initiated using JCL and must be rerun or restarted using JCL. Message processing programs are restarted by the Master Terminal Operator (MTO).

The application environment may also determine the types of IMS programs that are allowed. The following is a short review of the various IMS program types, with their major differences and features.

Batch Programs

IMS batch programs are similar to nondatabase batch programs. They are usually longer running than on-line IMS programs and are initiated using JCL. Batch programs execute in IMS batch regions that are independent of the IMS control region. This means that they cannot access on-line databases, but they have a compensating advantage: an abending batch program will not force a control region abend, as some BMP and MPP program abends do.

   IMS batch programs do not do commits automatically. If a batch program needs to be restartable or needs to release held or enqueued resources periodically, it must do explicit commits via the checkpoint (CHKP) DL/I call. Batch program updates take effect immediately. A program abend will require that the database administrator execute the Batch Backout utility. (There is one exception: if the batch program was submitted with the BKO execution parameter and the system log used is on DASD, IMS can be requested to back out database updates dynamically to the previous commit point.)

Typical examples of batch programs are:

- *Initial database loading.* Sometimes database loading can take several hours. Such loading is best done by a dedicated load program that does not interface with the IMS control region.

- *Large report printing.* This type of processing should not be done through the control region.

- *Massive database updating.* One typical way of off-loading on-line update processing is to accumulate transactions during the day and process the updates during off-hours. To do so the database must be explicitly moved off-line.

- *Database backup, restore, or image copy operations.* Such processes are usually controlled by one or more IMS utilities. These operations are occasionally run as batch programs for speed.

Batch Message Programs

As noted, a BMP is a hybrid of a batch program and an MPP. A BMP is executed using JCL, similar to the procedure for batch programs, and runs in a batch message processing region. Since this region can access on-line databases through the IMS control region, BMPs can access on-line databases. A BMP should include checkpoint/restart logic to facilitate rerunning or restarting from a checkpoint. Because database updates are finalized only at commit points, BMPs must take checkpoints frequently enough to release held database records so that they can be used by other applications in the on-line system.

A BMP can either retrieve or send messages through the I/O PCB, but not do both in the same program. A BMP that does not interface with the message queue is known as a *batch-oriented BMP*. Examples of batch-oriented BMPs would include the following:

- *Massive database updates.* When a large amount of processing must be done against on-line databases that cannot be brought off-line, a BMP is usually executed to do this processing.

- *Database conversion and migration.* A batch-oriented BMP is an excellent vehicle for converting an IMS database to, for example, DB2 tables.

A BMP that accesses the message queue is called a *transaction-oriented BMP*. Some examples of this type of BMP would include:

■ *Background processing of queued messages.* Some systems divert low-priority on-line requests to a message queue for later processing. As these messages queue up, a BMP can be executed that will retrieve the messages and process them. This technique frees on-line applications from doing low-priority work during peak hours.

■ *A wait-for-input process.* This type of program remains in main storage until the appearance of a message in the message queue causes the program to be scheduled. To define a BMP or MPP as wait-for-input, use the WFI parameter on a TRANSACT macro for that program. The program will be scheduled and invoked normally. After this transaction processes the first input message, the program is allowed to remain in main storage once it has processed all available input messages. A QC status code is returned when the limit count is reached. Programs defined as wait-for-input must also be defined as MODE=SNGL. This causes IMS/VS to force a synchpoint whenever the program gets a new message from the queue.

Message Processing Programs

MPPs are the mainstay of the on-line IMS world. They process messages routed from terminals, access on-line databases, and respond to the originating terminals. An MPP is scheduled by IMS when a message is received whose destination is the transaction code associated with the MPP. When the MPP begins execution, it retrieves the message that caused it to be scheduled, processes it, and (optionally) sends a reply to the originator. It then typically attempts to retrieve another message, in case one came in while the first was being processed.

IMS messages are stored in IMS in one of the message queue datasets. Messages may consist of a single piece, known as a segment, or may consist of several concatenated segments.

MPPs access on-line databases and cannot access off-line databases, GSAM databases, or OS/VS files. MPPs cannot use the extended restart (XRST) facility. Instead, they must be restarted by the Master Terminal Operator. MPPs may use the basic checkpoint facility either to release held resources or to force a DB2 commit, if they access DB2 tables.

MPPs come in several varieties, depending upon their behavior. For one, MPPs can be *conversational*, meaning that in addition to receiving the input message the application receives a Scratch Pad Area (SPA). The SPA is typically used to store information too large to fit in the input message. It also allows the

MPP to save such information as user identification, security information, or database segment data from message to message.

MPPs that respond to the originating terminal are called *response* MPPs, and an MPP that does not respond to a terminal is called a *non-response* MPP. One example of a non-response MPP would be an application program that processed messages queued for later processing, similar to the transaction-oriented BMP discussed earlier.

An MPP need not respond to the originating terminal. It may instead *message-switch* to another MPP by simply passing along the (possibly updated or reformatted) message. This passing is accomplished by preceding the message with the transaction code of the succeeding MPP. An entire string of MPPs may in fact process portions of a message before the last one finally responds to the originating terminal. An MPP can also be defined as wait-for-input.

Fast Path Programs

These programs, also called message-driven fast path programs, access Fast Path databases. They are similar to MPPs but have several restrictions:

- They can process only single-segment messages.

- They bypass IMS/VS message scheduling. Instead, Fast Path programs use their own message queue.

- A Fast Path program cannot message-switch to another program. It must respond to the originating terminal.

- They must be defined in the IMS Sysgen as MODE=SNGL. A commit point is thus forced when the Fast Path program retrieves a message from the Fast Path message queue.

Fast Path programs may be defined in several ways. If FPATH=YES is specified on the APPLCTN macro for a program, all following TRANSACT macros define what are known as IMS/VS fast path exclusive transactions. These transactions will use IMS/VS Fast Path Expedited Message Handling. Specifying FPATH=YES forces the system definer to include PGMTYPE=TP and implicitly defines a wait-for-input program. Another alternative is to have FPATH=NO and PGMTYPE=TP on the APPLCTN macro. Any TRANSACT macro having the FPATH=YES parameter is then said to be fast path potential, which defines a Fast Path transaction.

CHOOSING A PROGRAM TYPE

There are obviously many program types, each with their own characteristics. These features are summarized in Table 1.1. The following descriptions refer to that figure.

Competes for IMS Resources

Batch programs do not compete with other types of programs for IMS resources. Each batch program runs in its own region, with its own log file. A batch program that abends will usually not affect other programs or the IMS control region. In contrast, BMPs, MPPs, and IFPs can bring the control region down during some kinds of abends.

Can Access On-line Databases

The term *on-line* is used in IMS to denote the IMS control region. This region is defined by a job stream (JCL) submitted during IMS start-up. All databases that are defined by DD-statements in this JCL are referred to as *on-line databases*. In reference to these databases, the IMS control region is responsible for the following:

- Dynamic backout of database updates on a program or system abend.
- Database logging and recovery.
- Checkpoint and restart processing.

Since BMPs, MPPs, and IFPs can access on-line databases, they are termed *on-line programs*. Note that nowhere have we mentioned terminals, screens, or users. Although some types of on-line programs can communicate with terminals and use message queues, doing so is not required.

Can Access Off-line Databases

Databases that are not defined to the IMS control region in the manner just described are termed *off-line databases*. These databases can be accessed only by batch programs, and then only if DD-statements for the databases are included in the batch program's execution JCL.

Can Access Message Queues

The IMS message queue is controlled by and accessed through the IMS control region. As such, the message queue is available only to on-line programs.

Table 1.1. IMS program type comparison.

	Batch	BMP	MPP	Fast Path
Competes for IMS Resources	–	Y	Y	Y
Can Access On-line Databases	–	Y	Y	Y
Can Access Off-line Databases	Y	–	–	–
Can Access Message Queues	–	Y	Y	Y
Are Database Records Enqueued?	–	Y	Y	Y
Can Access GSAM Databases	Y	Y	–	–
Can Access OS/VS Files	Y	Y	–	–
Program Invoked by Transaction	–	–	Y	Y
Program Invoked by JCL	Y	Y	–	–
Can Use Symbolic Checkpoint	Y	Y	–	–
Can Process Input Messages	–	–	Y	Y
Use of ACBLIB Required	–	Y	Y	Y
What Causes Synchpoint?	CHKP	CHKP	Auto	Auto
Who Initiates Restart?	JCL	JCL	MTO	MTO
Can Access DB2 Databases	–	Y	Y	Y
Can Access DEDB, MSDB	–	Y	Y	Y
Can Use Multisegment Messages	–	Y	Y	–
Can Be Conversational	–	–	Y	–

Are Database Records Enqueued?

A database record consists of a root segment and all its dependents. Whenever a segment in a database is accessed through DL/I calls, IMS enqueues the entire database record. By doing so IMS "holds" a lock on the record in an enqueue area until the program releases it. This can happen in one of several ways:

- By normal program termination.

- In the case of read-only access, through accessing a segment not in the current database record.

- By doing a CHKP DL/I call.

- In a single mode MPP, by getting the next message from the I/O PCB.

Because the enqueuing of database records takes up precious IMS resources, checkpointing is important.

Can Access GSAM Databases

GSAM databases are typically OS/VS files that must be accessed as databases in an IMS program. There are several reasons for doing so:

- To allow IMS to control the repositioning of an input or output file upon program restart.
- To add symbolic checkpoint processing (described in Chapter 5) to a BMP.
- To permit a BMP to produce a report without using an OS/VS file.

GSAM databases are not defined to the IMS control region, so they must be included in batch or BMP JCL.

Can Access OS/VS Files

OS/VS files are available only to programs that are scheduled using JCL, meaning batch programs and BMPs. These types of files include BSAM, QSAM, and VSAM files.

Program Invoked by Transaction

A transaction is an entity that is defined during IMS SYSGEN. Transactions correspond to programs in that a program is defined to IMS in terms of the transactions that it processes. Only MPPs and Fast Path programs are invoked by transactions, or by messages queued for transactions. Although transaction-oriented BMPs can process messages from the message queue, they are invoked with JCL.

Program Invoked by JCL

These programs are, as mentioned, batch programs and BMPs.

Can Use Symbolic Checkpoint

MPPs cannot use symbolic checkpoints, because they can be restarted only by the Master Terminal Operator. Symbolic checkpointing is described in detail in Chapter 5.

Can Process Input Messages

This point refers to accessing the message queue through the I/O PCB. Transaction-oriented BMPs can either process input messages or send output messages, but not both.

Use of ACBLIB Required

Prior to the IMS application program's execution, IMS must combine the program's PSB information with the corresponding DBD information to create an Access Control Block (ACB). This may be done either dynamically or manually ahead of time and stored in a library called the ACBLIB. There is only one of these libraries for the IMS control region, so MPPs must have their ACBs prebuilt using the ACBGEN utility. Batch programs may include the ACBLIB DD-statement in the JCL, whereas BMPs use the ACBLIB that is defined in the IMS/VS control region JCL. If an //ACBLIB DD-statement is included in BMP JCL, it will be ignored.

What Causes Synchpoint?

In IMS, a synchpoint is equivalent to a commit point. One may occur at any time during the execution life cycle of an IMS application program.

Who Initiates Restart?

Rerun refers to restarting program execution from the beginning of processing. It usually requires restoring the status of the databases to that which they had before program execution. *Restart* refers to the process of continuing program execution from the most recent checkpoint.

Can Access DB2 Databases

This description refers to whether or not IMS programs can issue SQL statements to access DB2 table data.

Can Access DEDB, MSDB

This category refers to the types of programs that can access Fast Path databases.

Can Use Multisegment Messages

Only certain kinds of programs can retrieve and issue multisegment messages. ISC and MSC links have limits on message sizes.

Can Be Conversational

Conversational programming refers to using a Scratch Pad Area (SPA), in addition to the message, to hold data.

Chapter 2
Database Alternatives

CHOOSING A DATABASE TYPE

IMS/VS is replete with different database types. Each has its restrictions, features, advantages, and disadvantages. For convenience, most of these have been tabularized in Table 2.1 and are explained below.

Multiple Segment Types

Database access methods denoted "simple" (SHSAM, SHISAM) consist of only one segment type, the root segment. Since GSAM databases are OS/VS files defined as databases only for the sake of convenience, they must be root-only. MSDBs are also root-only.

Segment Prefix

The IMS segment prefix is used to manage segments. It contains the following fields.

- *The segment code.* This one-byte code assigns a unique numeric value from 1 to 255 to every type of segment in the hierarchy, beginning with the root segment and continuing hierarchically downward, from top to bottom and left to right.

Table 2.1. Comparison of IMS databases.

	SHSAM	SHISAM	GSAM	HSAM	HISAM	HDAM	HIDAM	DEDB	MSDB
Multiple Segment Types Allowed?	-	-	-	Y	Y	Y	Y	Y	-
Segment Prefix Exists?	-	-	-	Y	Y	Y	Y	Y	-
Variable-length Segments Allowed?	-	-	Y	-	Y	Y	Y	Y	-
Checkpoint/Restart Possible?	-	Y	Y	-	Y	Y	Y	Y	Y
Can Use VSAM as Access Method?	-	Y	Y	-	Y	Y	Y	Y	-
Can Use BSAM/QSAM as Access Method?	Y	-	Y	Y	-	-	-	-	-
Can Use ISAM/OSAM as Access Method?	-	Y	-	-	Y	Y	Y	-	-
Access from Batch Region?	Y	Y	Y	Y	Y	Y	Y	-	-
Access from BMP Region?	Y	Y	Y	Y	Y	Y	Y	Y	Y
Access from MPP Region?	Y	Y	-	Y	Y	Y	Y	Y	Y
Logging Available?	-	Y	-	-	Y	Y	Y	Y	Y
REPL Calls Allowed?	Y	Y	-	Y	Y	Y	Y	Y	Y
DLET Calls Allowed?	-	Y	-	Y	Y	Y	Y	Y	-
Supported by CICS?	Y	Y	-	Y	Y	Y	Y	-	-
Multiple Dataset Groups Allowed?	-	-	-	-	Y	Y	Y	-	-
Logical Relationships Allowed?	-	Y	-	-	Y	Y	Y	-	-
Segment Edit/Compression Allowed?	-	Y	-	-	Y	Y	Y	-	-
Field-Level Sensitivity Allowed?	Y	Y	-	Y	Y	Y	Y	-	-
Primary Index Exists?	-	Y	-	-	Y	-	Y	-	-
Secondary Indexes Allowed?	-	Y	-	-	Y	Y	Y	-	-
Multiple Positioning Allowed?	-	-	-	-	Y	Y	Y	-	-
Multiple PCBs Allowed?	-	-	-	-	Y	Y	Y	-	-
Root Key Uniqueness Required?	Y	Y	-	Y	Y	-	Y	-	Y

- *The delete byte.* This byte contains several bits denoting whether a given segment has been marked for deletion from one or more of the hierarchical paths it occupies. These paths include the physical database path, the logical paths, and logical twin chains. Other bits denote whether the prefix and data portions of the segment are separated in storage, whether the database record has been marked to be deleted, and whether the segment has been processed by the IMS delete routine.

- *The pointer and counter area.* This area contains pointer information, such as the physical child, physical twin, logical parent, logical child, and so forth. It also contains some counter information used if the segment participates in logical relationships.

Variable-Length Segments

A variable-length segment in an IMS database contains a two-byte counter at the beginning of the segment. This counter contains the length of the segment, including two bytes for the counter.

Checkpoint/Restart Possible

IMS/VS controls access to and updating of on-line databases. When an IMS/VS application program performs checkpoint processing, IMS/VS must store the appropriate information about the checkpoint on the log file. Later, should the program abend IMS/VS will be responsible for repositioning databases during restart processing. Some databases cannot, however, be repositioned during restart.

Can Use VSAM

Only certain types of databases can use VSAM as the operating system access method.

An application program for initially loading a database that uses VSAM as the operating system access method cannot be restarted from a checkpoint.

Can Use BSAM/QSAM

Only certain types of databases can use BSAM or QSAM as the operating system access method.

Can Use ISAM/OSAM

Only a few types of databases can use OSAM, or a combination of ISAM/OSAM, as the operating system access method. Note that ISAM will no longer be supported in IMS/ESA Version 3.

Access from Batch Region

Because batch programs exist in isolation outside the IMS control region, they may access only off-line databases. Furthermore, some database types can be accessed only through Fast Path.

Access from BMP Region

Batch message programs (BMPs) are initiated using JCL, but they access databases through the control region. As such, they can access most database types.

Access from MPP Region

A message processing program (MPP) runs in its own region and accesses on-line IMS databases through the IMS/VS control region. Some database types cannot be accessed through the control region. For example, GSAM databases are not really databases at all and thus cannot be accessed from MPPs.

Logging Available

Changes and updates for some database types, notably GSAM, are not logged by IMS. (This situation is quite distinct from the concept of *nonrecoverable databases* possible in IMS/ESA.) With GSAM, REPL and DLET calls are not allowed, and ISRT is allowed only during GSAM database load. Hence, GSAM databases are not logged on an IMS/VS log file.

REPL/DLET Calls Allowed

GSAM databases are OS/VS files that are defined as IMS databases simply for convenience. GSAM database segments (records) may be read (with a Get call) or written (with ISRT), but they cannot be replaced or deleted. Note also that ISRT is possible only when loading a GSAM database. In other words, to create a GSAM database (i.e., to write records to a file), a PROCOPT of L (or LS) must be used.

Supported by CICS

GSAM databases and Fast Path databases are not recognized by CICS.

Multiple Dataset Groups

Having multiple dataset groups allows the IMS database designer to segregate a segment or a group of segments in a separate physical dataset. One common reason for doing so is to divide a database structure into frequently and infrequently used segments and place each group in a separate dataset. The frequently accessed segments will be more compact, thereby increasing segment access performance.

Logical Relationships

This feature allows a program to process a hierarchy of segments made up from two or more separate databases, or to process the data in a different order than the one in which it is physically defined. It is possible to do so by defining logical relationships. Using logical relationships, a pointer is stored where the segment is (logically) required, which points from there to where the segment actually exists. This technique allows the application to access data through different paths, to process hierarchies in a different order, and to invert parent-to-child relationships.

Segment Edit/Compression

The process of segment edit/compression allows a database designer both to compress segments and to encrypt segment data. Compression permits more efficient use of DASD space. Encryption provides another possible level of data security.

Although segment compression may indeed allow data to be stored more efficiently on DASD, system administrators should beware of one potential pitfall. Most compression algorithms take combinations of adjacent characters and store them as single bytes, thus achieving what is known as *data packing*. When an application retrieves data it causes the algorithm to "unpack" the data. Should the application now change the data and then attempt to replace it, the compression algorithm may not be able to pack the new data to the same degree as it could the old. The new, larger amount of data may not fit back in the location from which it was originally retrieved, thus causing IMS/VS to search for sufficient space to store it.

Field Level Sensitivity

It is the PCB that defines how an application program is able to access a database. The term *segment sensitivity* refers to whether or not a program is aware of particular segments in a database's hierarchy. *Field level sensitivity* refers to whether or not a program is aware of particular fields in a segment. The PCB may specify that a program have access only to specified fields, and in addition the fields may be reordered.

Primary Index

In the present context, the term *primary index* refers to a type of database containing an explicitly created index dataset that is part of the database type itself. HDAM databases and DEDBs, for example, have no index dataset, as root segments in them are accessed through randomizing modules.

Secondary Indexes

IMS applications process database segments in a hierarchical sequence, from top to bottom and left to right. For a particular segment the application is usually restricted to accessing segment occurrences in a key sequence. Secondary indexes allow an application to access segments in a database in some sequence other than the normal key sequence.

Multiple Positioning

Multiple positioning is an option that allows an application program to maintain several *current positions* within different database record hierarchies, using a single PCB. This method of simultaneously accessing different portions of a database consumes resources and is also difficult to understand and debug. A far better alternative would be to use more than one PCB.

Multiple PCBs

It is sometimes necessary to access two different database records in the same database simultaneously. To do this when there is only a single PCB requires obtaining positioning on the first database record, then losing it when the second database record is accessed. Thus, accessing and updating become expensive in terms of physical I/O. A more common way of handling this situation is to use two PCBs. In this scenario a different PCB is used for each of the database records. Doing so allows the application program to maintain two positions simultaneously in the same database. Because this has implications for locking and recovery, not all types of databases allow this.

Root Key Uniqueness Required

Most IMS databases are designed with root segments having unique key values. It is certainly possible, however, to define a database with no root keys, although it is not common. For example, HDAM is occasionally used to gather transaction data for later processing. Such a database is defined without keys. Only certain types of databases allow this.

DATABASE ACCESS METHOD DESCRIPTIONS

What follows is a brief overview of the available database access methods for IMS full-function and Fast Path databases. For a more complete treatment, refer to the IMS/VS Version 2 Data Base Administration Guide (SC26-4179).

Hierarchical Sequential Access Method (HSAM)

HSAM, typically used only for magnetic tape datasets, is sequential access only. An HSAM database can either be *read* or *written*, but not both, because it involves either input or output. HSAM databases can therefore not be updated in place. If an application needs to update the data on an HSAM database, two databases are required: one for input, another for output. For output, the database is treated as though it were being loaded. HSAM requires BSAM or QSAM as the operating system access method.

HSAM is extremely rare. Probably the only case in which it should be used is if sequential input or output is required to pass data to a nondatabase application but GSAM is not available.

Simple Hierarchical Sequential Access Method (SHSAM)

Simple HSAM (SHSAM) databases are a root-only version of HSAM databases. Apart from this, there are no other restrictions or features.

Hierarchical Indexed Sequential Access Method (HISAM)

HISAM is usually used for low-volatility databases, because unused space caused by segment or database record deletion is not reclaimed until the database is reorganized. HISAM exists primarily to provide sequential access to database records, with the option of having indexed access.

Simple Hierarchical Indexed Sequential Access Method (SHISAM)

Simple HISAM (SHISAM) is an interesting HISAM variant. The word *simple* indicates that it is root-only. It has a few other interesting features as well. For one, a SHISAM database must use VSAM as its operating system access method. Because SHISAM databases have no segment prefixes, they can be accessed by nondatabase applications, through VSAM macros. This characteristic makes SHISAM an interesting alternative for passing data back and forth between database and nondatabase applications.

Hierarchical Direct Access Method (HDAM)

HDAM databases are usually reserved primarily for random access to root segments. Because roots are stored in physical locations that are determined by a *randomizing module*, doing Get Next (GN) DL/I calls will retrieve the roots in physical, not key sequence. IBM supplies several prewritten randomizing modules named DFSHCDx0, where the *x* is a digit from 1 to 4. Each module uses a slightly different method to derive physical database locations, as specified by what are called the *relative block number* and the *root anchor point*, from the root segment key.

It is possible to write a customized randomizing module in assembler language that will place roots in physical locations corresponding to key sequence. Such special processing requires greate expertise, however.

It is possible to use OSAM as the operating system access method for HDAM. In this case, sequential buffering (SB) may be used. (For a more complete description of OSAM sequential buffering, see Chapter 10.)

HDAM databases are most useful for direct access to root segments. Since randomizing modules determine the physical location of segments, usually only one physical I/O is required. Contrast this with HIDAM, where an index I/O and a data I/O may both be required.

Hierarchical Indexed Direct Access Method (HIDAM)

HIDAM is a general-purpose type of database. This method allows direct access to root segments by key, as it uses an index. Sequential access is also possible.

Dependent segments are chained, using pointers. A HIDAM database must be loaded in sequence. Either VSAM or a combination of ISAM/OSAM may be used as the operating system access method. HIDAM databases require two database definitions (DBDs): one for the data portion and another for the primary index. Note that support for ISAM has been dropped in IMS/ESA.

HIDAM is best used in cases where there is a mix of sequential and direct access to segments, and for highly volatile databases.

Generalized Sequential Access Method (GSAM)

GSAM was originally conceived as a method of accessing OS/VS files from an IMS/VS application that would allow IMS/VS to handle repositioning on program restart. GSAM provides primarily sequential access and is either input or output, similar to the way HSAM operates. GSAM databases can be accessed randomly, however, using a Record Search Argument (RSA). Very few DP shops use GSAM in this way.

A GSAM database used for output is considered by IMS/VS to be in the process of being loaded. It must use either BSAM or VSAM (ESDS) as the operating system access method. GSAM databases cannot be accessed from message processing programs (MPPs). CICS/VS applications cannot access GSAM databases as IMS/VS databases, but can access them as OS/VS files.

GSAM databases are typically used to pass data from a database application to a nondatabase one. A database definition (DBD) for a GSAM database prohibits the use of SEGM and FIELD statements. There is therefore no way to specify keys for segments in a GSAM database. Consequently, specifying PROCOPT=LS is meaningless for database load.

Data Entry Database (DEDB)

A DEDB is a Fast Path database. It provides direct access to root segments by using a randomizing module. DEDBs are commonly divided into *areas,* each of which contains copies of data in other areas. This redundancy facilitates data access. A DEDB must use VSAM as its operating system access method.

DEDBs are best used for large databases that require frequent updates. DEDBs are not accessible from CICS/VS applications.

Main Storage Database (MSDB)

There are two types of Fast Path MSDBs: terminal-related and non-terminal-related. Each of these can be either fixed or dynamic. Terminal-related MSDBs are keyed by an owning LTERM in that only that LTERM can update its particular MSDB. Non-terminal-related MSDBs have no owning LTERM, and ISRT and DLET are not allowed.

Unlike all other databases, MSDBs reside in virtual storage rather than on DASD. This arrangement makes for extremely fast access. MSDBs are best for fast access and frequent updating, and for systems having very high transaction rates.

MSDBs are not accessible from CICS/VS applications.

DATABASE CONFIGURATION ALTERNATIVES

Unrelated to choosing a database type, the IMS database designer has several ways to configure the databases. Some of these are now elaborated.

Multiple Dataset Groups

A dataset group is a collection of datasets that together make up a portion of a database. A database consists most often of a single dataset group. Thus, only a few actual OS/VS datasets need be allocated for a particular database. This situation also simplifies database backout and recovery.

The database designer has the option of defining a database to consist of several database groups. The database definition will then specify which segments in the hierarchy are to be stored in each group. In this way database designers and system administrators can do basic database performance tuning. For example:

- Frequently used segments can be placed in one group, with static segments in another. Doing so would allow the volatile portion of the database to take up less DASD space and thereby reduce physical I/O.

- Segments can be assigned to dataset groups by application. In this way different application programs with unique needs can simultaneously access the database without causing contention or deadlocks.

- Very large segments or variable-length segments can be segregated from small or fixed ones. This procedure may save a lot of space, as IMS/VS needs to search for space to store large volatile segments.

Logical Relationships

Logical relationships permit a database designer to redefine the way database hierarchies are defined, rather than to duplicate databases in more than one form. They effectively change the parent-to-child relationships among segments so that hierarchies can be processed in different sequences. Logical relationships are rarely used in IMS database systems. Not only are they difficult to define, implement, and recover, but it is also difficult for analysts and systems designers to understand the advantages and disadvantages of the various alternatives. Some wonderful success stories do exist in this area, but they are the exception rather than the rule.

Logical relationships require that three segment types be defined: the physical parent, the logical parent, and the logical child. There are three ways of establishing a logical relationship: unidirectional, bidirectional physical, and bidirectional logical.

A description of these methods and all of their various pointer options is beyond the scope of this book. For a more complete description, see the IMS/VS Version 2 Data Base Administration Guide (SC26-4179).

Multiple IMS Systems

Many large IMS shops have the luxury of access to multiprocessing systems. This not only allows for running several versions of IMS/VS as, say, Test and Production but also permits several production IMS/VS systems to coexist. One common option is to distribute either the processing or the database storage across several IMS/VS systems, communicating with multiple system coupling (MSC) links.

One common configuration is to have one processor act as the terminal network front-end, processing input and output messages, queuing message traffic, and handling network data movement. A second IMS is then used to store databases and handle database backout and recovery. Either or both of the systems can handle application processing, depending upon the current workload. Such a configuration, and ones like it, is easier to tune than a single system and is much less prone to system failure.

Another common configuration is to use CICS/VS as the transaction manager. CICS controls the terminal network, uses VSAM files, TempStore, transient data queues, IMS databases, and DB2 tables to store and retrieve whatever it may be that users require. When necessary, CICS can communicate with an IMS/VS application through an intersystem coupling (ISC) link. Such a configuration requires a lot of expertise to design and maintain, but it provides maximum flexibility for future enhancements and system changes.

Chapter 3
Data Communications Alternatives

OVERVIEW OF ALTERNATIVES

IBM mainframe shops are fortunate in having two, and sometimes three, choices when it comes time to implement the on-line portion of a transaction processing system. The alternatives usually are TSO/ISPF/PDF, IMS-DC, and CICS. The first choice is expressed in this particular way because native TSO is seldom ever used. (Some programmers are even unaware that TSO has its own edit subsystem or that TSO can be executed in batch.) The customary way of using TSO with on-line systems is by using CLISTs that execute the ISPF Dialog Manager, through either a panel or a program. Many people mistake this facility for the more formal Interactive System Productivity Facility/ Program Development Facility (ISPF/PDF), for which Dialog Manager forms a basis.

At any rate, these are the three most commonly available transaction managers. What are they best suited for, and what are their various advantages and disadvantages? This chapter reviews each of these subsystems and provides advice and recommendations for their use.

TSO and Dialog Manager

Dialog Manager is capable of operating in all three of the major mainframe operating systems (MVS, DOS/VSE, and VM). Of these, the MVS operating system is the only one that also supports IMS, CICS, and DB2. Regrettably, applications operating with Dialog Manager in a TSO environment are unable to access on-line IMS databases. The usual scenario is for users to log on to MVS via the Time-Sharing Option (TSO) and invoke the ISPF Dialog Manager with the command ISPF or PDF. Once in ISPF, users have access to a variety of standard and optional features.

Dialog Manager is used in conjunction with application programs as well. Programs can be invoked from a dialog by using the ISPSTART command. Alternatively, programs can request Dialog Manager services through calling the ISPLINK service interface routine.

The basic unit of control is called a dialog. Dialogs consist of several components, as listed below.

- *File tailoring skeletons.* These template or boilerplate files are used as a basis to produce tailored output files.

- *Functions.* These specially coded commands are contained in either an application program or a command procedure.

- *Profiles.* A profile is a dataset that saves the values of certain variables across dialogs.

- *Messages.* Messages are stored in a library file for retrieval during error conditions. They are displayed as a function either of data values or of a panel execution.

- *Panels.* Panels correspond to the MFS control blocks of IMS or to the maps in CICS. A panel is a coded description of a terminal screen, complete with its attributes, literals, and the placement of message data on it.

- *Tables.* A table is a method of storing information in an array for later use during a dialog.

Each occurrence of Dialog Manager components, except for functions, is stored in a library dataset for use by one or more dialogs. Doing so allows several applications to have access to the same panels, messages, and skeletons, for example.

IMS-DC (The Transaction Manager)

With the advent of IMS/ESA, IMS-DC is now known as the Transaction Manager. This transaction-processing system handles operations relating to messages, transactions, and message queues. It manages a network of IMS terminals, routes messages between terminals and applications, queues input and output messages, schedules application programs, and provides various other system control facilities, described below.

- *Managing the terminal network.* The Transaction Manager supports the attachment of many types of terminals, including ones in remote subsystems. For on-line processing it uses the network facilities of communications managers such as BTAM and VTAM.

    During IMS system definition, the system definer describes the physical network, including the logical terminals. A logical terminal, or *lterm*, is the name of a logical device that is associated with a physical terminal. A given physical terminal may have one or more logical terminals associated with it. Messages sent and received in IMS are associated with these logical terminals' names. This feature frees the application designer from any need for knowing the physical network. Application programs therefore need not concern themselves with such factors as terminal addresses, device availability, or geographic location.

    Another advantage of this arrangement arises if a physical terminal should somehow become inoperative. In this case any logical terminals associated with the physical terminal can be dynamically reassigned, perhaps by the IMS Master Terminal Operator, to another physical terminal. Messages that might be waiting to be sent to the inoperative physical terminal can now be rerouted to another physical destination. Employing logical terminals enhances IMS security, because each such terminal can have its own unique security parameters.

- *Routing messages.* IMS processes three basic categories of input messages. The first few characters of an input message indicate its message type and identify the intended destination of the message. These categories are as follows:

    IMS commands. IMS commands begin with a slash character (/). These commands are usually requests for IMS to display the system's status or to alter a system parameter. Some commands are restricted to use by certain classes of users. Others, such as those affecting system security, are limited to use by the Master Terminal Operator.

    Message switches. If the first one to eight characters of an input message equal the name of an IMS logical terminal, the message text will be sent directly to that lterm.

    Messages. If the first one to eight characters of an input message make up a transaction code, the message text will be processed by an IMS application program.

■ *Queuing input and output messages.* When IMS receives a message, it determines the message's destination and places the message on what is known as an input queue for that destination. Such message queuing permits a terminal user to enter transactions into a system even though the application program needed to process the transaction may not be immediately available. The transactions entered while IMS is processing a previous transaction are queued for later processing.

Once an IMS application finishes processing a transaction, it places an output message on an output queue. The output message may then be routed either to the originating terminal or an alternate destination. The alternate destination may be prespecified when defining the transaction to IMS. If the output is instead being returned to the originating terminal, IMS places it in a queue for that terminal. The terminal operator may then request the message when the opportunity arises.

During IMS system generation, two message queue datasets are defined: a long message queue dataset and a short message queue dataset. Messages of up to a certain length are stored on the short message queue dataset, and the remainder go to the long message queue dataset. This division by message has implications for system performance.

■ *Message recovery.* Another feature of message definition during IMS system generation is whether a message is recoverable or not. When a message defined as recoverable is placed on a queue, it can be recovered should the IMS system shut down on either a scheduled or unscheduled basis.

IMS Fast Path (IFP) is a feature that provides its own expedited message handling. Messages to and from an IFP program bypass IMS message queue processing, thereby reducing the time that a message must wait to be processed. After IFPs finish processing, they remain in virtual storage and wait for the next message. This queuing reduces the time required by the application program to process the next message.

■ *Scheduling messages.* As a part of the process of IMS system definition, the system definer associates application programs with the transactions they will process. (This procedure is carried out using the APPLCTN and TRANSACT macros.) When a transaction is entered on an lterm, IMS uses the transaction code in the message to determine which application to associate with the transaction. IMS then schedules the application program to process the message.

Transactions can be assigned many attributes, including *normal priority, limit priority, processing limit count,* and a *class.* Based on these and various other parameters, IMS schedules application programs. IMS is able to balance its workload, if necessary, by scheduling an application that processes a single type of transaction into more than one IMS region.

- *Message Format Service (MFS).* The IMS Message Format Service facility is one of several message editors that an application can use to format IMS messages as they pass back and forth between devices and applications. MFS allows application programs to deal with logical messages instead of device-dependent data. An application program that uses MFS can interact with different devices without needing multiple versions of program logic.

  A program using MFS does not have to concern itself with the physical characteristics of the device it is to interact with unless it wants to use certain specific device features such as highlighting or form feed. Even when these features are used, the application program will request them, using logical functions through MFS. The application does not send or receive device control characters directly.

  The alternatives to MFS include Basic Edit, a generic message editor, and bypassing editing altogether. Most on-line IMS applications use MFS simply because it is so convenient.

- *Extended Recovery Facility (XRF).* The Extended Recovery Facility increases the on-line availability of an IMS system by providing an alternate IMS system to monitor the active IMS subsystem and be ready to take over when necessary. A similar facility exists in CICS.

  The XRF feature acts like a shadow IMS. In effect it waits in the wings, monitoring the IMS system. Should an outage occur, XRF takes over for the failing IMS system and becomes the active IMS.

  The XRF's effectiveness is based on the assumption that a problem creating a failure in one environment may not cause the same failure in another. Regrettably, many customers feel that anything severe enough to cause IMS to fail will probably cause the XRF also to fail soon after.

Customer Information Control System (CICS)

CICS, sometimes known as CICS/VS, is a teleprocessing monitor that also functions as an interface between an application program and the operating system. In addition to handling on-line communications, CICS accesses direct access files and databases. This allows a program to request data directly from CICS, which then handles all interfaces with the operating system.

In CICS, a single execution of an application program for a specific user is called a *task.* CICS permits a program to be executed simultaneously by a number of users. This is called *multitasking.* To do so CICS requires that the program be *reentrant.* In effect, each user running a program is given their own copy of working storage while all users share a single copy of the executable code. To execute a program a user must enter a *transaction-ID.* These unique IDs identify units of work that a terminal user can invoke.

As part of CICS system definition a systems programmer is usually responsible for defining various *tables*. The more common ones are:

- *The File Control Table (FCT)*. This table contains an entry for every file that programs will access through CICS. In addition to the file name, an entry includes the operating system access method, record format, record length, blocksize, and allowed file operations.

- *The Program Control Table (PCT)*. This table contains an entry for each transaction-ID defined in CICS and the associated program to be executed for each transaction.

- *The Processing Program Table (PPT)*. This table has entries for every program defined to CICS.

- *The Sign-on Table*. This table has entries for each authorized CICS user. These entries include the *operator-ID*, *operator name*, and an optional *password*.

Major CICS Modules

CICS consists of several subsystems called *modules*. Each of these modules has a specific function as now described.

- *The Nucleus*. The nucleus controls most of the other CICS modules.

- *The File Control module*. This module manages file processing. It interfaces directly to the operating system access methods, thus freeing the programmer from coding any file-specific or device-specific program logic. This module handles file open, close, read, write, rewrite, and end-of-file functions.

- The *Basic Mapping Support module*. This is the interface between the terminal user and CICS. Through the use of *maps* BMS issues terminal requests and data requests. BMS accomplishes most of these functions through the Terminal Control module.

- *The Terminal Control module*. This module handles communication to and from the terminal network. It is usually invoked by using BMS.

- *The Program Control module*. This module manages the flow of control from one program to the next.

There are several other modules not covered here, such as those that handle *transient data, temporary storage, dumping,* and *journaling.* These and other modules are explained more fully in the appropriate IBM manual.

Additional Features

In addition to the above, CICS/MVS 2.1 has the following special features.

- *The Extended Recovery Facility (XRF).* This facility is similar to the one mentioned previously in the IMS environment. XRF in CICS provides the following automatically:

  - Detection of system component failure.
  - Transfer to an alternate CICS/MVS 2.1 system.
  - Switching of remote VTAM SNA terminals without loss of end user sessions.
  - Recovery of non-switchable VTAM terminal sessions.
  - Support for automatic dataset and database transfers to an alternate system.
  - Operator-initiated switch to an alternate system to reduce the impact of scheduled outages.

- *Performance improvements.* These include the batching of multiregion operation (MRO) requests, the retention of DL/I database status across warm and emergency restarts, and high performance buffers.

- *Data tables.* This allows a partial or complete copy of a VSAM KSDS dataset to be held in virtual storage while the dataset is open, bypassing normal I/O processing to access data above the 16 megabyte line.

- *CICS VSAM Recovery/MVS (CICSVR/MVS).* This program assists in the recovery of lost or damaged VSAM datasets. It takes the place of a user-written forward recovery program, recovering datasets by applying the CICS/MVS journal information to recent dataset backups.

COMPARISON OF THE THREE ENVIRONMENTS

Each of the three transaction management environments described has its own advantages and disadvantages. Certain operations and features are unavailable in one or more of these environments. These restrictions, described below, refer to Table 3.1.

Table 3.1. Choice of TP monitor.

	Use TSO If	Use IMS/DC If	Use CICS If
DBMSs allowed	DB2 Only	IMS or DB2	IMS or DB2
Concurrent users	Up to 10	Many	Many
Response Time	Variable is tolerable	Short time required	Short time required
Tie-in to IMS applications	Not recommended	Possible	Not recommended
Access to IMS DB on-line	Not available	Available	Not recommended
On-line screen development	Fast	Slow	Medium
Program development	Fast	Slow	Medium
System flexibility	High	Low	Medium
Training required	Low	High	Medium

DBMSs Allowed

With the advent of DB2, access to on-line tables becomes a concern. All transaction managers can access DB2 tables. However, TSO access to DB2 requires using the Call Attachment Facility (CAF). CAF is limiting in that programs using it cannot use CICS or IMS/VS (except for IMS batch) and cannot change DB2 plan names during execution.

TSO cannot access IMS databases. IMS and CICS applications can access IMS full-function databases, but CICS cannot access GSAM or Fast Path databases.

Number of Concurrent Users

Although each subsystem is built for on-line use, the system overhead per user will vary. TSO has a reputation for requiring an enormous amount of memory per user. Many shops are familiar with the MAXUSERS parameter, which limits the number of concurrent TSO users. It is much more difficult to limit the number of concurrent IMS-DC or CICS users.

Response Time

System response time is an important factor for users. In fact, some user communities require DP shops to live up to service level agreements in which the system response time and transaction processing minimums are defined. In general, TSO response time is fastest because TSO has so much less to do.

Tie-in to IMS Applications

TSO applications are unable to send and receive messages from IMS or CICS applications. IMS and CICS applications can, however, communicate with each other, through ISC links.

Speed of On-line Screen Development

Each environment has its own product to use for screen development:

- IMS-DC uses Message Format Service (MFS).
- CICS/VS uses Basic Mapping Support (BMS).
- TSO typically uses Dialog Manager.

Of these three, Dialog Manager is far easier to learn than the others. It is not only simple to learn but can be developed and tested using ISPF/PDF. It allows, in effect, for programs to control screens or screens to invoke programs. MFS is difficult to master, and changes to production screens require corresponding IMS/VS control block changes. Shops using MFS usually buy or develop MFS-generation software tools that allow the developer to paint a screen on-line, then press a PF key to generate the associated MFS control blocks.

The great advantage of MFS is its completeness. It can handle certain options that Dialog Manager and BMS cannot, such as:

- Operator-controlled logical paging
- Multiple-device format control

- Cursor-controlled transaction routing
- Screen-dependent transaction routing

BMS falls somewhere between these two extremes. It is somewhat difficult to master but is not as mysterious as MFS, and it has more options than Dialog Manager.

Application Program Development

Sometimes the most important factor is speedy program development. In this regard, developing a TSO-based application is the quickest path, followed by CICS and IMS. Be aware that development speed does not necessarily imply *best*. Developers must weigh speed against such factors as correctness, maintainability, recovery capabilities, and the probability of future enhancements. For example, a system that will someday use IMS databases should not be developed in TSO.

System Flexibility

Flexibility in this context is used to denote the ease with which system changes and enhancements can be made. TSO and Dialog Manager applications are usually simpler, and hence easier to maintain. Equivalent applications developed in TSO, CICS, and IMS pose their own unique problems. For instance, screen changes are easiest to make in Dialog Manager, IMS database access is easiest in IMS, and deadlock detection and recovery is easiest in CICS. Each system has positive and negative qualities that affect its maintainability.

Training Required

TSO and Dialog Manager are the easiest to learn. Most programmers and analysts are acquainted with the rudiments of ISPF/PDF panels and CLISTs. However, CICS is a bit more difficult, as programmers must now learn the syntax for CICS statements. IMS has by far the most options, which makes it the most broadly usable but the most difficult to learn.

THE IMS-DC ALTERNATIVE

Connecting to IMS, CICS, or DB2

IMS programs can send and receive messages between other IMS programs by using multiple system coupling (MSC) links and intersystem communication

(ISC) links. They can also exchange data with CICS programs, using ISC links, and can access DB2 tables.

Number of Concurrent Users

As long as the terminal network can handle the workload, IMS-DC can handle an almost unlimited number of concurrent users. Response time may suffer, though, as more and more users compete for resources.

IMS-DC controls message traffic by setting priorities. In general, messages received by IMS-DC are assigned a priority, then queued for a transaction or program in order of their receipt. The higher priority messages are processed first. If a given threshold of queued messages for the same transaction is reached, a higher priority is then assigned to successive messages. This scheme allows the application designer and the system administrator to control message handling in high-volume situations.

Average Response Time

Compared to many TSO- and CICS-based systems, IMS applications seem to have only average response time. This arises primarily because of the way IMS handles message traffic.

- Many message processing programs are conversational, requiring such additional IMS resources as Scratch Pad Areas (SPAs).

- Unlike CICS programs, programs in IMS cannot directly control other IMS programs (via XCTL and LINK). Only program-to-program message switching is allowed under IMS.

Access to IMS On-line Databases

IMS applications can, of course, access on-line IMS databases.

Slow On-line Screen Development

Most on-line IMS applications exchange information with terminals by using the facilities of the IMS Message Format Service (MFS). If only the most rudimentary screen formatting is required, however, programs can bypass MFS and use basic edit. One way of doing so is to specify DFS.EDTN as the MOD-name when sending messages.

Slow Program Development

IMS programs take the longest to write. This slowness is due in part to the amount of training necessary to understand a typical IMS application. Most on-line IMS applications require knowledge of IMS database calls, MFS and message handling, a screen-generating utility, of conversational programming and SPA usage, the usage of alternate PCBs, and knowledge of such recovery considerations as rollback. Thus it also takes a long time to design IMS applications, because developers must consider backout, recovery, program restart, abend processing, and message switching.

Low System Flexibility

IMS manages to be both highly flexible and quite inflexible. It has by far a greater number of options than CICS to consider in most situations, with the exception of program-to-program communications, where CICS wins out. With so many options in IMS, there always seems to be a way to do what needs doing. As a consequence, most developers choose it, equating the number of options with flexibility.

At the same time, however, IMS remains inflexible. For one thing, it is difficult for any one designer, analyst, or programmer to learn all the ins and outs of a particular IMS tactic. And changes to IMS programs commonly require corresponding IMS control block changes, which sometimes necessitates bringing the system down. Doing so may be possible only at such specified times as 00:01-05:59 on Sunday morning, and then only if it has been previously scheduled. Luckily, most of the important control blocks can be changed while IMS/VS is up, by using the On-line Change Utility (DFSUOCU0). This utility, in conjunction with the /MODIFY command, allows changes to be made to ACBs, MFS blocks, and other system control information. This flexibility is made possible by having the changeable libraries exist in triplicate. The three versions of each of the libraries are called the inactive, staging, and active libraries. The active library is used by the system to satisfy requests for control blocks. The IMS/VS Master Terminal Operator may use the /MODIFY command to notify the database management system to make the currently inactive library the active one.

There are several restrictions regarding the use of this facility. One is that you cannot add, change, or delete MSDBs or DEDBs from any control block in the ACBLIB. You can also not make additions or changes requiring new IMS/VS modules to be added to the IMSVS.RESLIB. Furthermore, the change-over from one library to another must be coordinated very carefully. If it is not, on-line users may find themselves suddenly viewing screens they have not been prepared for.

Much Training Required

It takes several weeks to train a programmer to code basic IMS on-line programs, and even longer if special features such as conversational programming are required. In contrast, the same training takes just two to three days for TSO and Dialog Manager, and only one to two weeks for CICS and BMS.

THE CICS ALTERNATIVE

Connecting to IMS, CICS, or DB2

CICS applications can communicate easily with other CICS applications, in a variety of ways. Some techniques for such communication include using TempStore and transient data, doing a LINK or XCTL to another application, or issuing a START command. CICS applications can also communicate with IMS message queues, using Intersystem Communication (ISC) links. The program access that CICS has to DB2 resources is defined in the Resource Control Table (RCT).

Number of Concurrent Users

There are many CICS on-line systems in production today. Of all the transaction managers, CICS seems to have the lowest amount of overhead per user.

Relatively Quick Response Time

Response time in CICS/VS systems is relatively fast, compared to the response time in similar IMS-DC and TSO-based systems.

Access to IMS On-line Databases

CICS/VS applications can access IMS/VS full-function on-line databases.

Medium Speed On-line Screen Development

Screen development in CICS is usually accomplished by using a feature called Basic Mapping Support (BMS). This product assists the designer in defining *maps*, which consist of literals, fields, and data. In contrast, the ISPF Dialog

Manager is a bit easier to work with, and the IMS Message Format Service (MFS) has no component to assist in screen definition.

Average Time for Program Development

CICS programming requires some CICS technical expertise, from design to debugging. Development time in CICS is less than in IMS, where program and database changes may require that the system be shut down.

High System Flexibility

CICS was purposely designed to handle terminal network traffic. Over more than two decades it has been refined to the point where the latest system features now involve hardware advances rather than software efficiency improvements. In this regard CICS is highly flexible. (For a full discussion of IMS, CICS, and DB2 release features, see Chapter 9.)

Moderate Training Required

CICS is moderately difficult to learn to program in. The names for various things are rather cryptic, partly because transaction codes consist of only four characters, and CICS program execution is sometimes hard to follow. This is so partly because CICS contains many statements that cause portions of a program to be executed whenever a certain condition is raised, rather than through the normal flow of program logic. One example is HANDLE CONDITION. (PL/I programmers should recognize this as being similar to the ON ERROR and ON CONDITION blocks.)

THE TSO ALTERNATIVE

DB2 Only — Tie-ins to IMS Not Recommended

Applications running under TSO or optionally using Dialog Manager have no access to IMS on-line databases. They can, however, access off-line databases. Recovery and restart must be program controlled, however. This requirement usually makes designers avoid accessing IMS databases in a TSO environment.

Small Number of Concurrent Users

The maximum number of concurrent TSO users is relatively small compared to those using IMS or CICS. TSO is probably limited to three hundred concurrent users, because above this CPU and memory overhead begin to take their toll. Still, this number may be enough to support a medium-sized system with a limited user population.

Variable Response Time

TSO on-line response time is highly variable. Unlike IMS, message traffic in TSO does not operate with a variable-level priority scheme. Unlike those in CICS, TSO applications must go through a lot of trouble to transfer to other applications.

No Access to IMS On-line Databases

TSO applications cannot directly access IMS on-line databases. The only option under TSO would be for an IMS application to extract any required data to a GSAM or SHSAM database, which the TSO application could then access, through OS/VS.

Screen Development Relatively Fast

Screen development in TSO is accomplished using the ISPF Dialog Manager. Panels can be defined in ISPF Edit mode, along with the appropriate functions and messages. Although the screen options are relatively limited — there is no operator logical paging, for example — screens can be defined quickly and implemented almost immediately.

Fast Program Development

Applications that access Dialog Manager services need only invoke the services routine ISPLINK with a CALL statement. There are no difficult database calls or terminal device handling routines required. The ISPF Dialog Manager handles the messages, screen painting, error control, data editing, and more.

High System Flexibility

Despite its limited number of screen options and its lack of access to CICS and IMS/VS resources, ISPF Dialog Manager is highly flexible. Applications are easy to maintain, they contain no complicated access path selection logic, and they rarely require much expertise to code or debug them.

Average Training Required

Learning to use ISPF Dialog Manager may take a few days of training. By far the best way to do so is by hands-on experience.

SUMMARY

Each of the transaction managers surveyed here has its own advantages and disadvantages, which make them suitable for particular kinds of applications.

■ TSO, using Dialog Manager, is best suited for small applications that access VSAM files and perhaps DB2 tables. Access also to DB2 can be accomplished by using the Query Management Facility (QMF). TSO is easy to learn and simple to operate. Programmers can develop applications in it quickly. The TSO environment has poor backup and recovery capabilities, however. It is therefore unsuitable for mission-critical applications.

■ CICS is probably the best balanced transaction manager. It has been around the longest—over twenty-two years—can execute on a variety of platforms—both mainframe and minicomputer—and is probably the most reliable system. Programs in CICS can access DB2 tables, IMS databases, VSAM files, and a host of CICS-specific resources.

■ Of the three transaction managers, IMS has the most options. This makes it the most flexible, but in name only, for its application and system changes take the longest to test and install. IMS also requires more training than the others, and it takes a long time to design, code, test, debug, and implement applications in it. IMS requires a lot of training—for database administrators, designers, analysts, and programmers, among others. There are so many options in IMS that staff often tend to specialize just in their favorite areas.

      The positive side of this situation is that there are probably more data stored in IMS databases worldwide than in all other mainframe database management systems combined. IMS is everywhere and will no doubt stay that way for quite a while. Even though there is currently a move afoot to migrate applications from IMS to DB2, doing so will take decades. A parallel might be drawn here to the history of COBOL. COBOL was declared a dead language in the early 1970s. Many pundits proclaimed that it would fade away as shops migrated to PL/I or other high level or fourth generation languages. Yet COBOL still exists, as strong as ever. The same will happen to IMS.

Chapter 4
Database Loading

Loading a production database is something that usually happens to it just once in its lifetime. (After the first time, this process is called a *reload*.) However, even though loading takes place only once, it may nonetheless be the cause of later processing inefficiency, DASD overallocation, and too-frequent database reorganization. This chapter explores various loading scenarios and methods and describes cures for some of the most common problems.

THE LOADING STRATEGY

System designers and database administrators are the ones responsible for putting new IMS database systems into production. Part of this process involves the definition, allocation, and population of production databases. There are two different initial states for a production database: the empty state and the equilibrium state. Each state requires a different loading strategy. (There is, incidentally, a third state, called the transient state, not covered here. Examples of this type include GSAM databases that exist only during the lifetime of a particular job.)

The Empty State

Databases that begin life with no segments in them are called empty ones. (Sometimes this description includes databases initially containing only a control segment.) Examples of empty databases include those used for data entry or transaction accumulation, ones used to hold data that is to be deleted after use, and some databases used for auditing and security information. In all these cases, the production database starts off with little or no information and amasses data as time goes by.

A typical loading strategy for an empty database is to load or insert a single segment, then immediately delete it. Doing so accomplishes two things:

■ All production applications that access the database with a PROCOPT other than L or LS are hereby prohibited from accessing it until it is loaded. After loading a single segment, then deleting it, IMS considers the database loaded, even though there may be nothing in it. Normal production processing can now proceed.

■ For databases using VSAM as the operating system access method, loading the first segment causes VSAM to format all the necessary control intervals (CIs) and control areas (CAs) with the appropriate free space bit maps. For a potentially large database this process may take some time, so it is best done just once for the entire database, in a nonproduction environment. After this process has been completed, the database will be completely formatted for future use. Production applications inserting new data will not now encounter the slowdowns caused by formatting.

Loading an empty database is usually accomplished with the DFSDDLT0 utility. This utility, commonly called DLT0 (dee-ell-tee-zero), allows one to execute DL/I calls against databases, to retrieve, insert, and delete data, and to monitor the results. This utility is simple to use. Its most common usage is during program testing, at which point it is used to print small portions of databases before and after program execution.

Using DLT0 or a user-written program to load an empty database requires having a PSB containing a PCB for the database that has a PROCOPT of L or LS. PROCOPT=L indicates that the PCB is used for the database's initial loading. PROCOPT=LS indicates that, in addition to the initial loading, the program will present segments to be loaded, in ascending key sequence. These options are discussed in more detail below.

The Equilibrium State

Databases that begin life with valid production data already loaded are said to be in equilibrium. This condition indicates that although the database may grow in size as time goes on, its initial state is normal. Examples of this type of database include those that have been converted from one DBMS to another, or converted from a nondatabase application to an IMS one. In such cases, production data already exist in the source system and the target production IMS system must be brought up to the correct data level. Other examples include control databases containing pointer or indexing information.

The typical loading strategy for an equilibrium database is either to use an existing or write a new application load program. This program gathers input data for the database from the source (OS/VS files, calculations, DB2 tables, other IMS databases, and so on) and loads or inserts it on the new database. Some IMS database access methods require special loading procedures. (HIDAM, for example, requires that root segments be loaded in key sequence.) These restrictions are now explained.

LOAD PROGRAM OPTIONS

IBM supplies a sample load program called DFS0ADBL. A description of it may be found in Appendix C of the IMS/VS Version 2 Data Base Administration Guide (SC26-4179). It is a general-purpose load program, but it is not used frequently. For one thing, it has several restrictions:

- It can read only a single input file, which must be processable by QSAM.
- Each input record must be in the required format and contain data for only one database segment.
- Variable-length segments are not supported.

Apart from these reasons, most developers require particular reporting from the initial load program, including control information, counts of records processed and segments inserted, and other information to be used to ensure that loading was successful.

There are two kinds of load programs: *basic*, or *rerunable*, and *restartable*. The normal situation is for a load program not to be restartable. There is an interesting reason for this. As noted, a load program must use PROCOPT=L or LS to load a database. But if the load program abends, what state is the database in? Is it loaded, though incomplete, or not? If the program has done no checkpointing, a program abend will cause IMS/VS to back out all database changes dynamically. In other words, the database must then be reloaded from the beginning. Suppose now that checkpointing has been done. Again, a program abend will cause IMS/VS to back out the database changes to the previous checkpoint. In this case, however, IMS/VS will consider the database to be loaded. Further processing must now be done using a PROCOPT other than L or LS.

At this point one might be tempted simply to restart the load program. Unfortunately, because the load program was using a PROCOPT of L or LS to load the database, that particular PCB can no longer be used. How about changing the PCB to have a PROCOPT of, say, A or I? Regrettably, IMS/VS will not allow a program to be restarted if the PSB has been changed or a different PCB is used for loading.

Basic Load Programs

The restrictions just described are not that important for load programs that insert only a small amount of data or run just for short periods of time. In these cases, user-written load programs should be rerun from the start if they abend. (This assumes, of course, that the state of the database at the time of the program's abend is not to your satisfaction.) On the other hand, either a large-sized database or a short "load window" may preclude you from writing a basic load program. For example, a ten-hour basic load program that abends after nine hours must be rerun from the beginning. Apart from the waste of time and resources, this type of program can sometimes be run only during the evening or on a weekend. Some developers would consider a one-week delay in a project that was caused by a load program failure to be unacceptable.

Restartable Load Programs

It is possible to write a database load program that is restartable. To do this there are certain requirements:

- The load program must be run under the supervision of the IMS/VS Utility Control Facility (UCF). This is a program (DFSUCF00) that can control the execution of the IMS reorganization and recovery utilities. It can be used to generate JCL statements for the utilities and to stop, then later restart a job.

- The database being loaded must use VSAM as the access method.

- The load program must be able to recognize certain control information and events upon restart. Some of these are:

  The database PCB status code will be set to UR. At this point the key feedback area will contain the fully concatenated key of the last segment inserted prior to the last UCF checkpoint taken. If no UCF checkpoints have been taken, this area is set to binary zeroes.

  The program must be responsible for the repositioning of any OS/VS files.

  The first DL/I call must be an insert (ISRT) of a root segment.

- The program must be able to recognize the UC, US, and UX status codes in the database PCB.

For further information about the Utility Control Facility, see the IMS/VS Utilities Reference (SC26-4173).

SPECIAL DATABASE CONSIDERATIONS

Loading some database types requires special steps in processing, some of which are listed below.

HISAM and SHISAM Databases

Segments loaded to a HISAM or SHISAM database will be stored in the order they are presented, with root segments required to be inserted in ascending key sequence. If dependent segments are allowed, they must be inserted in hierarchic sequence. The PROCOPT must be L.

GSAM Databases

As we have seen, GSAM databases are not really databases at all, but OS/VS files defined to IMS/VS as databases, for the sake of convenience. Still, the only way to insert a segment (record) into a GSAM database is to use an ISRT DL/I call with a PROCOPT of L or LS. Segments are inserted in the order they are presented. This procedure is typical write processing for GSAM.

HDAM Databases

HDAM databases use a randomizing module to establish the placement of root segments. Dependents must, however, still be inserted in hierarchic sequence. In most situations the sequence of root segment inserts does not matter, though it may in one case. Some IS shops implement HDAM databases with highly customized randomizing modules that place root segments nonrandomly. Some, in fact, attempt to place root segments in physical order in the VSAM or OSAM dataset. This is usually done so that sequential access to root segments, via GN DL/I calls, will retrieve the roots in key sequence, thus eliminating the need for a secondary index. With such a customized randomizing module, if roots are inserted in key sequence, IMS/VS will attempt to place them in physical sequence. However, if there is not enough room in a block for all the roots that randomize to it, IMS/VS will use pointers and overflow areas. Then, as more and more roots are inserted, more and more overhead is required and load time thus gets longer and longer. In this situation, IS shops should analyze the effects that customized randomizing modules may have on database load.

One additional scenario is common. Because "true" randomizers attempt to distribute root segments evenly across the root addressable area, typical HDAM databases are allocated to be somewhat larger than actually required. This extra size tends to shorten synonym chains and assists the randomizer. Upon database loading, however, each root segment insert must correspond to one physical block I/O. Inserting 10,000 roots and their dependents may then mean having 100,000 physical I/Os, if an average of ten roots randomize to the same block.

This unfortunate side effect can be eliminated by sorting roots in physical order before they are inserted. This sorting can be accomplished by writing a load program that invokes the randomizing module for each root segment to be processed. The returned values of the relative block number (RBN) and root anchor point (RAP) are first stored in a record consisting of these two values followed by the root segment. These records are then sorted by RBN and RAP. The sorted records are next read by the load program and inserted in that sorted order. This procedure causes IMS/VS to insert the roots in their physical order, thus minimizing the number of physical I/Os.

HIDAM Databases

HIDAM roots must be loaded in key sequence, with dependents loaded in hierarchic order. A PROCOPT of LS is required. HIDAM database load information is typically sorted in root key sequence order prior to being loaded.

Data Entry Databases

Use the DEDB Initialization Utility to initialize a Data Entry Database. Then load the database, using a Fast Path program.

Main Storage Databases

A Main Storage Database (MSDB) is not loaded by an application program. It is instead loaded automatically by IMS/VS when the IMS/VS control region is initialized. Record descriptors for MSDBs must exist in member DBFMSDBx of IMSVS.PROCLIB, with database records themselves stored in IMSVS.MSDBINIT(0).

LOGICAL RELATIONSHIPS AND SECONDARY INDEXES

If the DBA defines logical relationships or secondary indexes for a database, additional IMS/VS utilities must be run before and after the load process (see Figure 4.1).

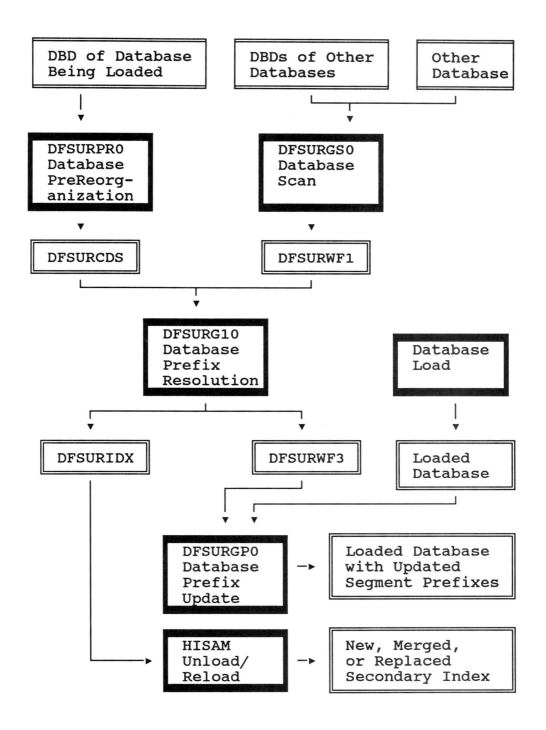

Figure 4.1. Job sequence for a database load involving logical relationships or secondary indexes.

The Database Prereorganization Utility (DFSURPR0)

This utility reads the DBD of the database being loaded and produces a dataset (DFSURCDS) containing pointer information. This information will be used to resolve pointers later, if logical relationships or secondary indexes exist. This utility must be run before the database load is run.

The Database Scan Utility (DFSURGS0)

This utility scans other databases and their DBDs that participate in logical relationships with the database being loaded. It reads the DFSURCDS file and produces a work file (DFSURWF1) that contains prefix and pointer information from these other databases. This utility must also be run before the database load is run.

The Database Prefix Resolution Utility (DFSURG10)

This utility reads the DFSURCDS and DFSURWF1 work files, then produces two output work files. The first, DFSURWF3, contains sorted and consolidated prefix information regarding logical relationships. The second, DFSURIDX, contains secondary index information. This utility must be run after the database load is run.

The Database Prefix Update Utility (DFSURGP0)

This utility reads the DFSURWF3 work file and updates segment prefixes on the loaded database. Naturally, it must be run after the database load.

The HISAM Unload and Reload Utilities (DFSURUL0, DFSURRL0)

These two utilities together read the DFSURIDX work file, create intermediate work files, and then create, replace, or merge, the resultant secondary index datasets.

AFTER DATABASE LOAD

After completing the database loading process, the database administrator should periodically monitor database performance. There are several tools available to do this, some of which are now described.

DB Monitor

The DB Monitor program (DFSMNTB0) and its associated DB Monitor Report program (DFSUTR30) collect data from IMS/VS control blocks during DL/I calls. They can be turned on and off using the MON= parameter in the JCL. They report the status of such items as VSAM buffer pool and database buffer pool statistics, program I/O, and DL/I call statistics.

Reorganization Utilities

In addition to being used for loading, unloading, reorganizing, and reloading databases, the various reorganization utilities are used to collect a variety of statistics about databases. Each utility produces its own report describing each database in question.

Database Surveyor

The Database Surveyor Utility (DFSPRSUR) produces statistics about the blocks and records accessed for specified databases. It is typically used to scan all or part of HDAM or HIDAM databases to determine if reorganizing them is required. It produces a report describing the physical organization of the database, including a breakdown on the size and location of free space.

IMS Monitor Summary

The full name of this utility is the IMS Monitor Summary and System Analysis Program II (IMSASAP II). It is a performance analysis and tuning aid for databases and data communications.

Space Management Utility

The Space Management Utility (SMU-II) has several features. It can be used to validate the accuracy of pointers in HD databases. And it can also be used to tune HDAM databases.

Summary

System designers must take all of these database load options into account, from both a performance and a project viewpoint. Database reorganization is usually done for performance reasons, either to clean up unused free space, to reallocate DASD space, or to make usually just minor modifications in database structure or features. Such reorganization must be done on a periodic basis, in a procedure similar to that of the initial database load. Developers should keep the following points in mind:

- Database reorganization load time will be approximately equivalent to the original database load time. Thus, keep track of database load performance and related statistics so that reorganization can be scheduled productively.

- Because different database access methods have different load characteristics, the choice of access method may be affected by load performance. Loading an HDAM database, for example, may require presorting records by their relative block numbers and root anchor points. Doing so requires invoking the randomizing module from an application program. This must be done in assembler language, as the randomizing module's calling sequence is nonstandard. (It cannot be CALLed from a COBOL or PL/I program, for instance.)

- The database load may affect system testing. For systems that require parallel or pilot system testing, this restriction may mean having multiple databases to load and back up.

Part 2

IMS Application Systems Considerations

Chapter 5

Checkpoint/Restart

REVIEW OF BASIC CONCEPTS

In order for IMS/VS to control access to on-line data, it must know which users are accessing the data and when. To do so, IMS/VS requires that all on-line programs run under the control of the control region. The control region is responsible for the protection of on-line data and for allowing programs to access those data. It utilizes the techniques of enqueuing and commit points to accomplish these goals. These terms, and others important to the process, are now discussed.

Recovery Considerations

Part of the systems design process for a batch or on-line system must involve planning for abnormal termination of programs and for recovery after a disaster. Part of this planning should involve consideration of the following procedures:

- Automatic, program-controlled, or manual backout of database changes in case of abnormal termination of a program.

- The provision of database recovery procedures in case of hardware error or a massive software failure.

- Automatic or program-controlled notification to the on-line system that database changes made at a certain point should now be made permanent.

■ Checkpointing of long batch runs or involved on-line runs to allow for program restart at other than the beginning of processing.

The I/O PCB

Database recovery sometimes requires that the program participate in the process. This is usually handled with certain DL/I calls, to be described later. Such calls require the program to reference the I/O PCB. For batch programs the I/O PCB is usually not included in the PSB. This exclusion can be overridden by using the CMPAT=YES PSB option. This option gives the program a dummy PCB that acts like an actual I/O PCB.

Database PCB Fields

The database PCB mask in an application program contains several fields that are important to the recovery process.

■ *The Key Feedback Area Length.* This field specifies the length in bytes of the concatenated keys found in the Key Feedback Area. This length may vary, depending upon that of the last segments processed.

■ *The Key Feedback Area.* This area contains the concatenated keys of the last segments in the data structure that is to be processed. It is typically used during program restart to reposition a PCB to the proper place in the database, if necessary.

The IMS Log File and Log Records

The IMS Log File contains certain records written by IMS/VS that are used to produce statistics about IMS usage. It also holds records used by IMS/VS to effect the recovery or backout procedures on databases. In general, these log records contain information that allows IMS/VS to reconstruct changes made to a database by an application program. By applying these changes, in reverse order, IMS is able to back out a database to its status as of a certain time. This point is called a synchronization point or synch point.

Database Records and Enqueuing

When an on-line program accesses a database segment, IMS/VS puts a hold on the entire database record. The database record then becomes unavailable to other programs. The record is held until the program using it releases it. Releasing occurs in one of two ways:

■ If there is read-only access to the record, the record will be released when the program moves to another database record in the same data structure (PCB) that contains the first record.

■ In the case of update access, the record will be released when the program reaches a synchronization point.

Obviously, if the resources just mentioned are not released, after a time the IMS/VS control region will run out of memory in which to hold them. At that point the control region itself may abnormally terminate with a U775 abend, resulting in the abnormal termination of all on-line application programs active at that time.

The design of application programs must include provisions for automatic or program-controlled release of these resources. The release can be accomplished successfully only at a synchpoint.

The Logical Unit of Work

A logical unit of work, which is usually equated with a transaction, was at one time used in IMS/VS systems to define synchronization points. These were simply points during the execution life cycle of an application program when all database updates were in synch, meaning mutually consistent.

CHECKPOINT PROCESSING

Whether or not to use a checkpoint call revolves around the decision to force a synchpoint during application program processing. The biggest considerations are:

■ *Concurrency.* An application that locks a database record or records can hold up production processing, including that of on-line transactions.

■ *Abend processing.* If the application abnormally terminates, we must ask whether the error can be fixed and whether the program can take up processing where it left off.

These and various other considerations are discussed below. Because batch program checkpoint considerations differ substantially from those for on-line programs, they are discussed first.

Batch Program Checkpoint Considerations

There are two main reasons that batch programs may be designed to issue checkpoint calls:

- Sometimes, during system evolution, batch programs evolve to a state where they must be able to access on-line databases. This process is usually handled by running them as *batch-oriented BMPs*. Doing so may require checkpoint processing.

- If the batch program is especially long running, the program may issue checkpoint calls to establish points at which it may be conveniently restarted.

Upon abnormal termination, it may be necessary to undo any changes that might have been made to databases. IMS/VS does not do this automatically. Undoing database changes may be accomplished using the Database Backout utility, which will back out changes to the database record on the IMS/VS log file. Alternatively, a copy of the database may be used to restore it.

After restoring the affected databases, the program can sometimes be restarted from the most recent checkpoint. This restarting will depend upon the type of checkpoint calls issued. The matter of program restarting, which is common to all types of programs, is discussed separately later.

On-line Program Checkpoint Considerations

On-line programs typically use checkpoint calls to force the occurrence of synchpoints, thereby releasing enqueued resources. Upon abnormal termination, IMS/VS automatically

- Backs out all database changes made since the last synchpoint.

- Throws away all messages held at temporary destinations.

- Throws away any input message that the program might have been processing at the time of the abnormal termination.

Commit Points

Before the advent of DB2, the point in the execution life cycle of a program where locked data and held resources were freed and database changes made permanent was called a synchronization point, or synchpoint. This stage is now more commonly referred to as a commit point. When a commit point occurs in an IMS application program, the following steps usually take place:

- Database changes are made permanent.
- Updated or enqueued database records are made available to other applications.
- Held resources, such as output messages held at temporary destinations, are released.
- The Master Terminal Operator (MTO) is informed that a commit has taken place.
- IMS/VS logs the commit onto the IMS log file.

If a program abends, IMS/VS does the following:

- If the program was at the time of abend accessing DB2 resources, DB2 and IMS/VS coordinate the backing out of all database and table changes to the previous commit point.
- IMS/VS discards any output messages that the program has produced, except those sent using an Express Alternate PCB.
- It discards the input message in process.
- It notifies the MTO that the program has abended.
- IMS/VS and DB2, if applicable, release any held or enqueued resources.

A commit may be explicitly requested if the program does a CHKP call. But a commit may also be implicit, as when a new message is retrieved from the I/O PCB, except for message processing programs that are defined to IMS as MODE=MULT.

The notification to the IMS/VS control region that an application program has reached a commit point may be accomplished in several ways, depending on the program type.

Batch and Batch-oriented BMPs. The only time the control region can know that a commit point has occurred is when the program issues a checkpoint call. Remember that in batch programs database updates occur immediately, messages cannot be sent, and log records are written immediately.

Single-mode MPP. Here a commit point is reached automatically each time the MPP issues a call for a new message. In addition, a commit point can be forced by issuing a checkpoint call. Note that only basic checkpointing is available to MPPs.

Multiple-mode MPP, Transaction-oriented BMP. With this situation a commit point is reached either by issuing a checkpoint call or at a program's normal termination.

Checkpoints

An IMS/VS application program uses the CHKP checkpoint call to inform IMS/VS that it wishes to force a commit point. If the program is also accessing DB2 resources, this condition then forces a DB2 commit also. Observe that the SQL statement COMMIT is prohibited in IMS/VS programs. There are two types of checkpoints: basic and symbolic. The two differ mainly in their relationship to restart procedures. With basic checkpoint the following occur:

■ It is up to the program to handle restarts, including program reinitialization.

■ It is up to the program to back out any changes made to OS/VS files.

■ Program coding changes are prohibited between a program's abnormal termination and program restart.

Message processing programs (MPPs) and message-driven fast path programs must use basic checkpoints. This checkpoint allows the program to release resources and finalize database updates. However, it cannot be used as the basis for a program restart, because the XRST (extended restart) DL/I call is not allowed. In addition, no save areas of Working-Storage can be specified as parameters on the CHKP call when using basic checkpointing. The use of the save areas is reserved for symbolic checkpointing. When using basic checkpointing in a message processing program or a transaction-oriented BMP that reads messages from the message queue, the CHKP call returns the next input message.

In addition to releasing resources and finalizing database updates, symbolic checkpointing allows the program to save portions of its Working-Storage on the IMS log file. This, along with a checkpoint-ID, permits IMS/VS to restore the program to the state it was in immediately after any checkpoint that might have been taken. This procedure permits an application to be restarted from a specified checkpoint. Batch and batch message programs (BMPs) may use either basic or symbolic checkpointing, depending upon the reasons for forcing a commit point.

There are a few items worth highlighting about certain aspects of checkpoints.

■ With a transaction-oriented batch message program that uses checkpointing, the CHKP call retrieves the next input message. If you use this technique, do not use the Get Unique (GU) DL/I call to retrieve messages — doing so forces an IMS commit point. If the program must be restarted, it can be restarted only from a checkpoint, not the point at which the GU call was issued.

■ A batch-oriented BMP that accesses fast path databases must issue a CHKP DL/I call prior to normal termination or else the program will abnormally terminate with a U1008.

■ An interesting kind of pseudo-checkpointing called *rescheduling* can be done in an MPP. Using this technique, the MPP periodically gathers status information about the current state of processing, collects it into a message, and sends the message to itself. After this the program typically acquires the next message out of the message queue. If the program was defined as MODE=SNGL, retrieving a new message thereby defines a synchpoint. Resources are then released, and the program continues processing the message received. It may be either a new message or the rescheduled message.

Since the symbolic checkpoint is more flexible and far more common than the basic checkpoint, the symbolic checkpoint is recommended.

Using the Symbolic Checkpoint

To use the symbolic checkpoint in a program that accesses OS/VS files, these files should be accessed as GSAM databases. This procedure allows the GSAM databases to be repositioned during program restart. At the time the program issues the CHKP call, it must pass information to IMS/VS. This information includes:

■ An 8-byte checkpoint-ID. This *ID* should be unique, both within the specific application program and among other application programs. It is possible to use blanks (spaces) for a checkpoint-ID, but this will prevent restarting the program from specific checkpoints.

■ The addresses of all areas within the application program that should have their values reset upon program restart.

The checkpoint-ID is used by the system to identify a checkpoint. This ID is given to the master terminal operator and printed on the system log. It should thus consist of EBCDIC characters. Upon program restart, the system reads the log file forward until it encounters records that have an ID matching the checkpoint-ID that was supplied. These log records contain the areas of the application program that were passed on to the system at the time of the CHKP call. To restart the program IMS/VS loads a new copy of the program, then replaces and/or restores the areas of the program that were saved on the log file during the checkpointing process. This process effects most of the program reinitialization required.

The areas within the application program that are passed in the CHKP call should be those areas of static storage that are necessary for a program restart. These areas will probably include counters, totals, and control information. Any areas not specified will have their values set to what they were at the time the program was originally invoked.

The first DL/I call that the program must issue is the XRST call. This instance is the only time this call is issued. Issuing this call signals IMS/VS that the program is using symbolic checkpoint. The program should issue the call by using a blank I/O area twelve bytes long. Upon its return, the program should look at the I/O area. If it is nonblank, this means that the program has been restarted.

Upon program restart it is the responsibility of the program to reestablish positioning in all non-GSAM, non-IMS, and non-DB2 databases. If the restarted program now abends it may be restarted, again using the same procedures.

Issuing a CHKP call in an MPP or a transaction-oriented BMP will also retrieve a message segment from the message queue, if available.

Checkpoint Frequency

Checkpointing, recovery, and restarts are probably the most important issues in BMP design. When choosing a checkpoint frequency, steer carefully between two extremes:

- An application that checkpoints too rarely, or not at all, will enqueue resources, thereby locking out other applications. And there is a further danger. Because IMS/VS stores enqueuing information for all executing applications, it will eventually run out of space. If this happens, the control region may abnormally terminate, along with any applications running at that time.

- An application that checkpoints too frequently wastes IMS/VS and DB2 resources through unnecessary commit processing. Also, since program checkpoints are displayed on the IMS/VS master terminal, extremely frequent checkpointing can generate screen after screen of messages. This inconvenience may be frowned on by the Master Terminal Operator. In addition, a large number of checkpoint messages in a short period of time can fill the buffer used for the master terminal, causing a control region abend.

There are no hard-and-fast rules on how to pick a good checkpoint frequency. As a general rule, some manuals recommend doing so "every ten or fifteen minutes." Doing so is extremely difficult to implement, however. Most

IS shops have standards regarding the way programs are to measure resource consumption. This procedure usually involves counting DL/I calls and weighting them, based upon their functions. For instance, a Get call (GU, GN, GNP) for a database that is read-only would have a much lower weight than a REPL call. In addition, some mechanism is set up to have the program acquire its checkpoint threshold externally, usually by reading an OS/VS file or a control database segment. This approach allows system administrators, database administrators, and application designers to tune application systems.

These rules are normally modified depending upon the production environment and the quantity and type of the resources used by the application. Only experience will help in choosing a reliable frequency.

RERUN AND RESTART PROCEDURES

Rerun versus Restart

Upon a program's abnormal termination, IMS/VS will initiate recovery procedures. For on-line programs it will back out database changes, delete messages held at temporary destinations, and delete log records that are being held. At this point the programmer must analyze the problem to determine what steps to take next. Information may be required from

- The program dump
- Any program output
- A region dump
- The Master Terminal Operator
- The system log.

The steps the programmer might take may include

- If it is a batch program, using the IMS/VS Database Recover utility to restore all databases affected
- Changes to input data
- Changes to the application program
- Flushing a message processing region
- Changes to PSBs and DBDs
- Program rerun or restart.

To make application program changes the programmer must consider that the only information available to the program at restart will be the values of data saved in areas passed to IMS/VS through the CHKP call. Upon restart the program will issue an XRST call to restore these areas.

To restart a batch or batch message program, JCL is submitted specifying

- The checkpoint-ID of the checkpoint from which to start. Optionally, the operator may specify the string LAST. Doing so will cause IMS/VS to restart the program from the most recent checkpoint on the log file.
- The log file containing checkpoint log records.

Message processing programs are restarted by the MTO.

Database Backout and Backup

The term *database backout* refers to the process of undoing prior changes to a database. It occurs in various situations.

- When an on-line BMP or MPP program terminates abnormally, IMS/VS flushes all database records that had been enqueued since the last synchpoint. This procedure has the effect of never applying changes that had been made.

- When a batch program terminates abnormally, the programmer may execute the Database Backout utility. This program will use the IMS/VS log file and the current database to undo any changes that had been made.

Chapter 6
IMS System Design Considerations

GENERAL CONCERNS

System design usually follows a plan called the systems development life cycle (SDLC). (See the Introduction for a more complete treatment of the SDLC.) Each IS shop does design differently, but most take the traditional approach, which looks something like this:

- Develop user requirements
- Analyze requirements
- Logical Data Design
- Physical Data Design
- Programming
- Testing
- Implementation and maintenance.

A more contemporary approach, favored by progressive shops, resembles a program loop, and usually looks like this:

- Develop user requirements
- Analyze requirements
- Develop prototype application
- Review prototype with user
- Make adjustments to prototype
- Test prototype adjustments
- System test
- Implementation
- Maintenance.

In this case, the maintenance step is baked in to the review prototype with user step.

As a part of these and other methodologies designers, users, and analysts routinely meet to discuss user requirements, hardware and software alternatives, service level requirements, and business data modeling. During these discussions five main concerns usually manifest themselves: auditability, recovery, data integrity, performance, and maintainability. These issues are now described in more detail, in the context of IMS-based systems.

Auditability

General Principles

Auditing is said to be the responsibility of the auditor. The auditing process has been with us since the time of the pharaohs, but the auditing of data processing systems is a relatively recent phenomenon. It could be said that the advent of data processing created the jobs of information systems auditor and chief information officer (CIO).

In general, the IS auditor's job is to verify the accuracy, timeliness, and correctness of the whole IS process. To do so the auditor must have the participation and cooperation of the data processing staff. Because part of the auditing process will include testing programs and verifying their output, audit controls and auditlike procedures must be incorporated into systems as part of the systems design. Some systems, including the following, will require more stringent auditing than others:

- Financial systems, such as deposit accounting, general ledger, accounts payable, and the like.

- Systems in such regulated industries as chemical manufacturing, pharmaceuticals, and electric utilities.

- Systems designated mission critical, which is to say those systems whose failure would mean the failure of a business. Some examples might include airline reservations systems, electronic data interchange, and electronic funds transfer.

Auditability in IMS Systems

IMS systems pose no new problems to auditors that have not already been solved for more traditional batch environments. The only real concern here is that some of the standard auditing techniques may cause system performance problems.

Consider the case of an IMS message processing system where data are exchanged between programs by using message switching. All messages accepted by IMS/VS are logged on the system log, so the auditor can capture this information by processing archived log files. This is easier said than done, however. IMS/VS log files contain a great deal of information, including before and after images of segments, messages, checkpoint and recovery records, and a host of statistical information. It was not too long ago that shops using magnetic tapes for log files went through over 300 log tapes per day, at the rate of one 2,400-foot reel every five minutes! That's a lot of data to search through.

To assist the auditor in such a case, the system designer and the auditor should meet during the process of system definition and identify specific control points. These points should be programs that participate in the auditable data flow and can be modified to capture data during processing. This capturing facility is then designed to be turned on and off by the auditor, allowing them to gather and analyze specific data flows through particular segments of a system.

Another case involves on-line database updates that must be audited. Again the IMS/VS log file contains before and after images of database segments, along with all the other items mentioned earlier. To monitor changes in these areas the auditor must be able to capture and analyze them. How could this process best be audited?

One alternative would be to have a capturing facility that stored copies of the before and after segment images on an audit database. For a small system this provision might suffice. For an active on-line system, however, this approach has several disadvantages. First, two or more on-line applications attempting to store information on the audit database simultaneously may run into contention or locking problems. Second, since inserting information on the audit database involves physical I/O, duplicating the before and after segment images onto this database effectively doubles the amount of physical I/O needed for the application. Third, if an on-line program abends, IMS/VS must dynamically back out changes to the audit database and do the same for other databases. This step slows down the recovery process. Finally, the additional physical I/O involved in storing copies on an audit database might affect on-line system performance.

A better way of auditing involves using the IMS/VS message queue. Any programs that make auditable database changes construct messages containing the before and after images of changed segments, along with needed control information. These messages are then sent to a special nonresponse MPP. Should an on-line program abend during this process, the messages will be thrown away by IMS/VS and not routed. In this arrangement the special nonresponse MPP would run at a low priority. Its job would be to collect these audit-related messages and store them, perhaps on a database. This facility would allow the auditor to select particular programs or databases for auditing and analysis.

Finally, IMS/VS log files already contain a complete summary of all database and data communication activity throughout a system. Why design complicated facilities that add programs, databases, and so forth, and must themselves be tested and verified? The IMS/VS log files provide a comprehensive history of the system and can be used with a minimum of bother.

Auditing IMS systems is no more difficult than auditing traditional DP systems. The audit procedures must, however, be built into the system during the analysis and design phases. If not, the imposition of or changes in audit requirements will adversely affect system development or performance.

Recovery

The IS system designer must plan for disasters. The meaning of the word *disaster* in this context ranges from a program bug to hardware failure to an operations error to acts of God. The effects of each type of disaster can be minimized, though in different ways.

Program Bugs

It is said that testing shows the presence, not the absence of bugs. System developers can never hope to find all the bugs in a system or application. As systems mature, enhancements and additional features add their own additional bugs. Fixes for bugs even sometimes contain their own bugs.

In this environment the best that can be done is to try to anticipate the most common bugs and act to prevent them from causing further problems. Some typical tactics include the following:

- *Control totals.* These totals would include record and segment counts, column and field summations, cross-footing, batch totals, and other schemes that attempt to minimize program processing errors: invalid loops, invalid or incomplete file processing, incorrect transaction processing sequences, and so forth.

- *Data editing.* These steps include all manner of parity checking, redundancy checking, check digits, range checking, edit tables, reasonableness checks, and other checks that try to reduce the number of data errors, such as digit interchange, nonnumeric characters, out-of-range conditions, and the like.

- *Interception of error conditions.* Most programming languages have features that allow the program to determine whether certain types of fatal errors are about to happen. For example, COBOL programs can test fields for NOT NUMERIC, thus avoiding data exceptions.

- *Formal test planning.* Developing test plans seems to be honored more in the breach than in the observance. Test plans should be developed as part of system design, not after program coding. Program test plans should include strategies for testing all program logic paths, forcing the program to edit every input field, producing all possible error messages, and verifying all possible output states. While all of these tests are seldom possible to have, planning to install tests is simply a matter of good design.

Hardware Failure

A decade ago, hardware was the whipping boy of programmers and analysts. Crashing disk drives, stuttering printers, and faulty terminals were blamed for all kinds of errors. Modern hardware is, by contrast, extremely durable. Actual hardware problems are rare today, but they still happen.

System developers cannot plan for every eventuality, but they can minimize any adverse effects of hardware failures. Some common approaches include frequent and regular backups of databases and important files, preventive maintenance, and a shotgun approach to dataset allocation. This strategy involves spreading files and databases among several DASD volumes so that the failure of one spindle or of a control unit will not affect an entire system.

Operations Error

In the past the typical operator error might have involved mounting the wrong tape, dropping a disk pack, or tripping over a power cord. Modern DP operations are nothing like this. In fact, the most common operations error has nothing to do with operations at all. Here are a few examples.

- In one DP shop, test jobs submitted by programmers had job names consisting of their initials followed by a single digit. This led to having job names like MEF1, RDC9, and the like. One day an operator called up John Edward Smith, an applications analyst, and said, "John, one of your test jobs has been running for eight hours. Should I cancel it?" When John asked what the job name was, the operator replied, "It's JES3." "Cancel it," said John, and the operator did. Unfortunately, this wasn't John's test job: it was the Job Entry Subsystem of MVS.

■ In another DP shop, the manager for the Securities Insurance and Real Estate System (SISRES) noticed that their disk pack containing financial tracking information was getting full. The manager immediately called operations and asked that the SISRES pack be removed and an empty one put in its place. A bewildered operator did so. Unfortunately, the pack removed was the SYSRES, or operating system residence pack.

■ In a third DP shop, a new applications manager attempted to bring his system "into the nineties." System input in the past had consisted of large magnetic tapes. An analysis of the tapes showed that only a small portion of each tape contained data, with the remainder being empty. This manager specified that henceforward all input should be on 5¼-inch diskettes. Wishing to be helpful and frugal, the data entry facility that provided this company's data purchased some used single-density diskettes. Their hardware then wrote data on only one side of the diskette. DP operations was told that the data were "on Side 1" of the diskettes, so they inserted the diskettes in the appropriate manner. Unfortunately, the data entry company considered the diskettes to have sides 0 and 1, whereas DP operations thought they had sides 1 and 2. The application therefore processed the wrong side of the diskettes. This problem was not noticed for several weeks.

One can't help but laugh at these scenarios, yet they bring out an important point. DP operations is responsible for processing data — not for understanding, analyzing, or designing systems. It is the system developers who are responsible for giving operations the appropriate instructions. In addition, they are also responsible for formulating contingency plans to deal with possible miscommunication or mistakes. Typical strategies to do so include having written system run procedures, twenty-four-hour help lines, automated or at least well-documented backup and restore procedures, and clear, concise instructions. The "Keep it simple, stupid (KISS)" maxim also applies to job operations.

Acts of God

Acts of God include earthquakes, tornadoes, floods, and all other types of natural disasters. In such cases the system designer is almost helpless. There are very few alternatives in systems design that can cater to recovery in the event of a building collapsing.

The strategies for dealing with these types of disasters should involve the entire data center. One common method is to store database and dataset backups in an off-site vault. Another is called either the cold site or hot site method. The cold site is another DP location where a business's applications can be run in case of a disaster at the primary site. The usual criteria for a cold site is that it be available within forty-eight hours of the primary site's failure and that no more than three days' business be lost in the process. A hot site takes this concept one step further by making a hot site available almost immediately after the primary site's failure. Many companies have mutual cold site arrangements so that the failure of one company's site will still allow it to move applications to one or more other sites.

Recovery of IMS Systems

Planning for the recovery of IMS systems is relatively simple. IMS has two types of utilities for database backup: image copy and reorg/unload. The Image Copy utility does just that: it makes a duplicate copy of an IMS database, including any dead data. (Remember that segments deleted from most databases are marked as logically deleted in the Delete Byte, although the physical segments remain.)

The unload utilities scan databases, then store segment information as records in a sequential file. This technique allows the database administrator to save DASD databases on tape.

Good backup procedures, like good joke telling, depend on timing for their effectiveness. Typical DP shops make image copies of important databases and unloads of others on weekends. More volatile databases may be backed up nightly. Another alternative is to use the On-line Image Copy utility. This utility makes a backup copy of a database while the on-line system is up and allows concurrent access to the database. If there is any updating activity on the database during the execution of the On-line Image Copy utility, reference to the log files will be required if the database must be restored.

Restoring IMS databases is also simple. IMS has a utility called Change Accumulation, which takes a database and applies all changes to it that are logged on the IMS log file provided. Doing so allows a database administrator to take a weekend database image copy and, say, Monday's and Tuesday's log files and run Change Accumulation. The utility will use the log files provided to update the database as of its status after all the Tuesday transactions had been completed. Change Accumulation consolidates all log records pertinent to recovery from many logs into a single file, known as an accumulation of change. This single file is then input with an image copy of the database to the Recovery utility. Variations on this theme are common.

Unload backups of databases can be reloaded, restoring them as of a specific point in time. A database backout utility also exists that will undo changes to a database, in the reverse order of their application. This technique allows a DBA to take today's database and back out all changes made during the day. This capability may be especially useful in those cases where programs already put into production are found to contain processing errors. In a shop where on-line systems must be kept up twenty-four hours a day, the backup and recovery procedure is nontrivial.

Nightly unloads and weekend image copies are typically made of critical or volatile databases. These unloads or copies are then usually stored on site in a protected vault. Sometimes copies of highly critical data are stored in off-site vaults or at either cold or hot sites.

Data Integrity

In the context of a database the term *data integrity* is usually used to mean that the data in the database are both correct and complete at a specific point in time. While the ideas of correctness and completeness seem rather simple, a concise definition of data integrity is rather elusive. In *Relational Database Writings: 1985-1989* (Addison-Wesley, 1990), author C. J. Date reviews some basic integrity issues and proposes a language in which to formulate integrity rules. The topics in this paper are beyond the scope of this book. Interested readers are urged to refer to it for more complete coverage of this topic.

In the context of IMS databases, data integrity is usually controlled by the database management system. To the user IMS presents a view of the data to the user. This view is in the form of segments and messages that the user obtains and issues through the DL/I language interface. The DBMS guarantees that the data are correct and complete through some or all of the following:

- *Program isolation.* Generally speaking, this feature assures that one application program cannot affect data accessed by another.

- *Database recovery control (DBRC).* This software subsystem functions as a lock manager. For any application that accesses database segments or messages (resource), this feature locks the resource for use by that application. Other applications are thus prevented from changing that data.

- *IMS Resource Lock Manager (IRLM).* This software product also functions as a lock manager. Indeed, an IRLM is required for DB2's use. Sometimes the same IRLM is used for locking both IMS and DB2 resources accessed by the same application.

- *Checkpoint recovery.* IMS uses checkpoint processing to assure that a database is complete and correct at a point in time. This point is called a synchronization point, or commit point. The concept of checkpoints is covered in detail in Chapter 5.

In general, data integrity is a property of the data. Database administrators sometimes confuse data integrity with *security*. Security is a system that protects data against unauthorized users. Data integrity protects data against authorized users.

Performance

Everyone is concerned about performance. Users wish their on-line transactions to execute quickly. Analysts and programmers wish their programs and systems to be maintenance-free. Database administrators concern themselves with total system performance.

During system design the application analyst and database administrator often find themselves on opposing sides. Tuning a particular application or database for fast access or quick user response may adversely affect other systems. The analyst is naturally eager to please the user for which the system has been developed. The DBA must balance the needs of many users across, potentially, several systems and hardware platforms. How can these two views be reconciled?

Service Level Agreements

One method of balancing these conflicting needs is through the use of a service level agreement. This is an agreement arrived at during the logical system design phase of the SDLC. The parties to it include the user, the design analyst, and the database administrator. These participants meet to establish both the measurement criteria for system performance and the methods for deciding whether overall performance objectives have been met.

Maintainability

One of the principles of structured programming methodologies over the last two decades was that program modularization and top-down design would make programs more maintainable. Lamentably, this has not happened. That it has not is not the fault of the methodologies but rather of how it was they were used.

How Programs Actually Used to Be Designed

The methodologies for structured design and programming are more than just coding rules: they are rules for organization, formality, standardization, and completeness. There is little redundancy in these rules —it is all or nothing. In other words, you cannot apply each rule or procedure as you see fit, simply ignoring the rest.

Many DP shops bought in to a given methodology and then proceeded to compel their staff to use it. This heavy-handedness was akin to buying a hammer and using it to pound nails, tighten screws, paint walls, and sand boards. Somehow DP management forgot the maxim of the right tool for the right job. Forced to use a new methodology they did not fully understand, DP staff used the portions they did understand and ignored those they did not, such as coupling and cohesion. Rules that required more work but seemed foolish, such as comments in source code, using program flow charts, and so on, were skimped on or simply not followed. The systems that resulted could at best be called quasi-structured.

What They Did Wrong

These historical designers and managers had not considered one of the most basic rules affecting software: maintenance happens. Even in shops where over 80 percent of the staff hours were devoted to fixing program bugs and enhancing existing software, this major fact of DP life was forgotten. Today we recognize this situation and plan for it.

Planning for Maintenance

Most methodologies used today incorporate the maintenance step in their SDLC. Designing and implementing a system is now seen as also including its ongoing maintenance. During the feasibility study and cost/benefit stages of the systems analysis, developers and designers take into account the costs of maintenance. This process usually includes the following steps:

■ *Baking application test procedures into the system.* Test plans are developed as part of the system and application design. As testing proceeds, test programs, test data, and results are kept. This set of procedures forms part of the delivered system. Future changes and fixes will almost certainly require testing and retesting. Why reinvent the wheel? Having old test results along with later ones may also form a basis for system auditability.

■ *Estimating system life and forecasting maintenance costs over that life.* Logical systems design almost always includes selecting among several alternatives. Some of these include:

Hardware: Mainframe versus minicomputer versus microcomputer; hard-wired terminals, PCs with dial-up lines, or a local area network (LAN);

DASD storage, tape storage, or mass storage, and managing the interaction of these.

Software: Choice of a programming language, a database management system, and of a teleprocessing monitor; use of utilities or user-written applications; whether or not to use CASE tools.

Staff: Number of analysts and of programmers; their skill levels and experience levels; project scheduling, workload balancing.

As part of this process the designer must consider the costs of maintenance over the life of the system for each of these alternatives. Maintenance costs per se will be different, depending upon the choices made.

■ *Standardizing programming practices*. This procedure minimizes the need for special staff training, as most programs will be coded at the same level. The staff transferred to maintain a new system will thus already be familiar with existing standards. And development staff will already have experience in how applications are coded.

■ *Budgeting for maintenance staff*. This procedure is a relatively new phenomenon. Designers now include as part of their systems budget a staffing plan for systems maintenance, either over the life of the system or for a certain period following implementation. Although these monies seldom come from a development budget, estimating these costs forces the developer and the department that is to maintain the systems to understand the future commitments that must be made. This evaluation sometimes leads to not developing a system if its maintenance costs will be too high.

■ *Minimizing the need for human intervention*. Some DP departments have staff devoted to fixing production problems. Some of these problems are simple to fix, such as data entry errors that cause program abends. However, such errors are very costly to fix in this fashion. It would be far better to have some error checking built in to the application instead. Data checking, control totals, and the like are relatively easy to include in a program and help to minimize a system's downtime. More complex scenarios, such as having a program resolve a deadlock situation, must be handled on a case-by-case basis.

All these factors should be considered to be part of the system design. The systems of the future will almost certainly include relational database management systems, distributed processing, and micro-to-mainframe links. We must routinely build maintenance into these systems if we are not to be swamped with maintenance problems soon after system implementation.

Maintaining an IMS System

IMS systems pose few special maintenance problems, at least as far as program fixes are concerned. There is more work involved in maintaining IMS programs, however, than in others. Consider the following IMS-specific conditions:

- *Program abend*. This condition will involve several things:

  An IMS program abend usually causes IMS/VS to mark the program internally as being STOP-ed. It then requires operator intervention to START the program again. Also, depending upon the type of abend, one or more databases may be STOP-ed.

  A batch or BMP abend may require rerunning or restarting the program from a previous checkpoint. JCL must be available to do this, but first someone has to fix the program error, if any, and test the program. Major program problems, or JCL problems, may preclude a restart. This impasse may force the database administrator to back out database changes.

- *Incorrect program or PSB definition*. This problem usually involves using incorrect processing options, having missing PCBs for databases, misordered PCBs either in the PSB or in the program ENTRY statement, or an invalid SPA length. (For a description of how programs are defined to IMS/VS, see the APPLCATN and TRANSACT macro definitions in the IMS System Definition manual.) These problems require some rethinking of requirements, along with perhaps some IMS/VS control block changes. Most PSB changes can usually be done within twenty-four hours for most IMS/VS installations, using the On-line Change utility.

- *Incorrect database definition*. This problem is a major one that may require restructuring a database. If this is done, what will happen to the current data? Sometimes a database can be unloaded, deleted, redefined with a new structure, and then reloaded. But doing this may be quite difficult, depending upon the actual changes required. Another option would be to delete and redefine the database, then write an application to read the IMS log file to capture all the changes made to the previous database. The program would then make the appropriate changes to the newly structured database. This process is not as easy as it sounds.

- *Invalid program processing*. This problem may be the toughest of all to find, let alone fix. The maintenance staff must first determine the point in the life of the system at which the program error was introduced. Then someone must decide how to recover the system's databases. Should an image copy that is perhaps several weeks old be used as a base? If so, this may involve running the Change Accumulation utility with several hundred archived log files. Should the current database be backed out, perhaps back to several weeks ago? Should the programmer write an application to survey the database and fix it? How about deleting it and starting over?

As can be seen, none if these choices are very palatable. This problem points up the need for accurate systems design in the IMS environment.

Typical IMS Maintenance Tasks

There are several customary maintenance tasks that crop up in IMS systems. Here is a sampling.

- *Adding checkpointing.* This task is probably the most common IMS maintenance one. It is also the way that most beginning programmers first learn how to do checkpointing. Every IMS batch and batch message program should be designed with checkpointing included in it. Even if it isn't implemented, the structure should still exist. *There is no reason not to always have checkpoint logic in a program's design.*

- *Converting batch processing to BMP.* This, too, is common. The usual reasons are as follows:

  The databases used by the program will now be part of the on-line system. The databases will now be the responsibility of the IMS control region and can be accessed only through it. Doing so requires having a BMP or MPP.

  Making the program restartable involves adding checkpointing as described above, and sometimes changing references to OS/VS files to GSAM databases.

- *Adding DB2.* This activity is becoming more and more common every day. In fact, many shops are now converting from IMS-DB to DB2, or else adding DB2 to IMS applications. This process involves much more than simply converting DL/I calls to SQL statements, although some shops are proceeding along these lines. This interaction is covered in much more detail in Chapter 9.

The bottom line is that an IMS system should not be cause for worry. If developers can anticipate the needs of the IMS maintenance staff during the stage of systems design, cheaper and more easily maintained systems will result.

IMS DESIGN CONSIDERATIONS AND GUIDELINES

Presenting a complete guide to IMS systems design is outside the scope of this book. There are, however, many related and important topics that should be considered during design, some basic, some advanced. More importantly, these considerations are the ones that IMS system developers seem to skimp on or even forget entirely.

Use Available Design Aids

There are many system design aids that the IMS system developer should consider using.

Structured Design Methodologies

IMS systems —in fact, all hierarchic and network/plex database systems—lend themselves to design using structured methodologies. With their emphasis on data flow and process flow these methodologies allow the developer to break down processes into simpler ones while keeping a grasp of the overall system. Many of these methodologies contain within them structured programming guidelines.

CASE Tools

Computer-assisted software engineering (CASE) tools are not new; the term *software engineering* itself dates from the late sixties. Today we enjoy a wide variety of available third-party software tools to assist in the various phases of the SDLC. Some of these are:

- *System design aids.* These tools, which are frequently PC based, help the analyst by coordinating the data and process flows visually. This usually occurs with the aid of diagrams representing program logic, files, reports, data flows, edit processes, and the like.

- *Code generators.* These tools take the results of the system design and turn it into code. Probably the earliest code generator was a product in the mid-1960s that read decision tables and created COBOL programs to implement these tables.

- *On-line debuggers.* With this tool the programmer could step through program execution logic and monitor the program flow and data values.

Most of these products allowed the user to specify or change data values, set breakpoints, change the order of statement's execution, and halt when the value of a variable in storage changed.

- *Test data generators.* This process, which is more than just file creation, involves analyzing program code and variable storage to generate data to test program logic. Some products allow the tester to specify the type of test data to generate, such as reasonableness tests, invalid data tests, range tests, and the like.

- *Abend aids.* Being able to read a dump used to be the hallmark of the guru. This task is no longer the domain of the expert, however, as formatted dumps are now the norm. Some products go beyond simple dump formatting, to explain the error code, some common reasons for the error, display the instruction that caused the error, and give the values of any data fields referenced by the instruction. This advanced state of abend aids dramatically speeds up maintenance, for programmers no longer need dump-reading skills to determine what if anything went wrong and if so where.

In the late 1980s several companies began to integrate CASE tools into packages. The term *integrated CASE tools* has by now become somewhat abused, as companies have attempted to market their packages as complete solutions to systems design. As of this writing, *no* package currently available represents a completely integrated set of CASE tools for the systems development life cycle. Some may come close, but none do it all.

Develop Unit-of-Work Standards

Part of every application system that uses a DBMS involves units of work, sometimes called transactions. The word *transaction* is used in this context to mean any collection of data, along with its correct processing, that must be completed as a whole for it to be valid. This phenomenon is rather common in data processing, because transaction processing systems comprise most of today's applications. It becomes very important to pin down this definition during IMS system design. The transaction will be the unit of work that is the basis for backout and recovery, as well as the determinant of how resources are to be load-balanced. Here are some of the considerations.

Standard Work Units

Most DP shops have developed their own definition of a standard work unit. This unit is usually defined as a range or amount of physical I/O, memory usage, and CPU usage performed by a given task. Checkpoint or commit processing may be done only between work units, never in the middle of one.

The main advantage of having a standard work unit is that programs and databases can thus be more easily tuned. Programs can now be measured for efficiency and compared on the same basis. Databases can be tuned regardless of the processes used to update them. Another big advantage is that defining a unit of work within an application allows tuning to be based on that unit. Because programs should be required to checkpoint after every so many work units, say, this count or threshold can be input to the program from some external source. Program resource usage can then be monitored and tuned without making program changes.

The main disadvantage of using a standard work unit is the difficulty of measuring it within an application program. For one thing, units based on physical I/O are difficult for a program to gauge. Those based on CPU usage require programs to query the operating system constantly for the current time. This may affect program performance. Programs may also need to obtain some measure of elapsed time for concurrency or deadlock considerations.

Recovery Plan

Standard work units also assist the designer with capacity and recovery planning. Developing a work unit plan allows one to estimate the amount of work the system will do—the amount of resources it will consume. These numbers then become part of the estimating process as the developer and database designer forecast hardware requirements, system load-balancing, and backup and recovery requirements. Some of the questions to be answered are:

- Will this system provide the correct service level? Will turnaround time and response time meet the user's needs?

- How much storage will be required for log files, image copies, and unloads? How often must databases be backed up?

- How will this particular volume of units of work affect the terminal network?

- How long will it take to recover from a system problem or from a disaster? How much work will this involve?

These considerations are important from both a budgetary and system service viewpoint. In short, developers are responsible for delivering a system that meets the user's requirements, and this includes providing the ability to recover from most errors.

Standardize Error Handling

Some IMS shops have coding conventions for program error handling. These standards usually involve displaying or storing an error message containing the error's location, the type of error, the values of important variables, status codes, and other information. This error reporting should be standard across all IMS systems. Some items tend to be forgotten, however, such as a few that are listed here.

- Where are these error messages to be printed? Some shops direct their error messages to a printer defined to IMS as an LTERM. Unfortunately, this printer may be hidden in a corner of the computer room floor and thus rarely be monitored. The point is that program fatal error messages requiring human intervention should be directed to a place where they will receive immediate attention. This location may be a terminal staffed on a twenty-four-hour basis or a hardcopy printer in a room staffed by help desk personnel.

- Who will see and process these error messages? A clerk/typist may not be the best person to judge which messages are of immediate concern and which can be given a lower priority. On the other hand, hiring an experienced IMS systems designer to handle program error messages seems to be an inferior alternative.

- How are these error messages to be interpreted? This process should be reserved for program fatal error conditions requiring quick attention or human intervention. If programs persist in sending warning messages or merely informational notices to this printer, real problems may not receive attention, reminiscent of the story about the boy who cried "Wolf!" too often.

- Once received and acted upon, what will happen to the error messages? Are they to be kept, logged, and stored? Will they be analyzed later? Consider the case of a system that regularly abended on Friday night, because of a data exception. It was several months before someone finally noticed the regularity of the problem and addressed it. As it turned out, the abend occurred in each case in a different program. Strangely, each time the abending program was one farther along in the job flow. Someone finally realized that the remaining programs in the system probably had this error as well, as in fact they did.

Perhaps what we need to do is charge program maintenance costs back to the department that developed the programs. We should at least inform them of problems that arise.

Hybrid IMS-DB2 System Concerns

Many shops are hopping on the DB2 bandwagon, as IBM continues to improve and enhance their relational DBMS. Some shops are even taking this one step further by planning to convert all their applications to DB2. Although this topic is covered fully in Chapter 9, we will here consider some design implications. The present emphasis will be on design. Many of the recommendations will involve choices to make that will affect system performance.

Prohibit Needless On-line Database Alteration

Some systems designers pride themselves on developing an on-line system. Regrettably, this process sometimes turns out to be a blatant waste of data processing resources. The point is that noncritical systems should not be allowed to affect the performance of critical ones. In any case, take a good look at your system during the design process and determine whether on-line database updating is really required. Some alternatives to it are to:

■ Migrate noncritical applications to another hardware platform. This process may involve employing another mainframe, a minicomputer, micro-computers, or perhaps a network.

■ Handle updating on an "as possible" basis. Collect the requested database updates for later processing, either at night or during periods of a light system workload.

■ Segregate volatile systems. This step would involve having a separate DASD allocation and limited on-line access. Also consider limiting the number of concurrent users.

■ Charge back users for their updating privileges. If their application will affect other critical applications, make users pay for this privilege.

Measure Performance Options

As a well-known DB2 systems pundit once said, "One measurement is worth a thousand expert opinions." In other words, do not follow performance advice blindly. Upcoming Program Temporary Fixes (PTFs), new releases and versions of software, and new techniques may make your "high performance application" a dog. Such advice as the following should be tested, measured, and analyzed on your own system under actual "battle" conditions.

■ "Denormalize for Performance." This may be popular advice for DB2 users, but it also applies to some IMS systems as well. In general, this phrase refers to living with some data redundancy while diminishing the amount of physical I/O. This sounds commendable, but you should still measure the actual savings. The price you pay for denormalization includes difficulty in maintaining referential integrity, limited flexibility for system enhancement, and more complex design and performance tuning.

■ "Always use HDAM (or HIDAM, or something else)." Such specific advice is almost never completely right. Although a particular access method may be just right for someone else's environment, it might not be right for yours. In the case of HDAM versus HIDAM, for example, there are several considerations:

Are you using ISAM/OSAM? If so, are you using sequential buffering? If so, what is the size of the SB buffer pool? Are you aware that support for ISAM will be dropped in IMS/ESA?

Are you using VSAM? If so, what control interval size are you using? Will performance be affected if this is changed? What is the size of the shared resource pool, and what allocations are used for VSAM buffers?

What randomizing module are you using for HDAM? Is it customized? Why or why not? If not, would customizing affect its performance?

What is your level of CPU utilization? Will decreasing (or even increasing!) it affect performance?

How do you handle database backout, reload, and recovery? Are there additional requirements such as logical relationships or secondary indexes? What if these should arise as future enhancements?

As you can see, there are many considerations. The only way to determine what is best for your environment is to try it.

Chapter 7
Abends and Debugging

COMMON IMS CODING MISTAKES

Even now, almost two decades after the advent of IMS, after billions of lines of IMS code have been written, IMS programmers seem to make certain mistakes over and over again. The following seem to be the most common.

Confusing Parentage and Positioning

Any IMS database defined with several types of segments has what are called parent segments and child segments. One common database processing scenario involves reading, and perhaps updating, all of the child segments for a specific parent. There are several ways to accomplish this in an IMS program. Most programs begin by doing a Get Unique (GU) call with a qualified SSA for the parent segment. After this they usually do one of the following:

1. Do Get Next (GN or GHN) calls with unqualified SSAs for the child segments. Stop processing when the next occurrence of a parent segment type is reached.

2. Do Get Next within Parent (GNP or GHNP) calls with unqualified SSAs for the child segments. Stop processing when a GE status code is returned.

Neither method has any great advantages over the other. There are, however, a few pitfalls for the unwary, some of which are now described.

Initial Child Processing

Programs must be able to handle the situation where no child segments exist under the specified parent. In Case 1, the first Get Next call will return a GE status code, meaning segment not found. In Case 2, however, IMS will return a GP status code, meaning no parentage established. To use the GNP and GHNP calls correctly, application logic must first make sure that the parentage has been set. This technique occurs through successfully retrieving a child segment.

This logic is not as "dirty" as it seems; in fact, it conforms to most structured design principles. A typical logic diagram for processing zero or more input entities for records, children, and the like is shown in Figure 7.1. In this figure there is a separate logic "box" (a module of program code) that handles the first logical occurrence of the entities being processed. This module corresponds to the initial read of a file or to the first retrieval of a child segment. Following this step is logic that tests for end-of-file or its equivalent. If this condition is false, the main body of logic processes the current entity and then retrieves the next.

In our particular IMS situation we need a section of code devoted to retrieving the first child segment and then testing for a not found condition. In our Case 2 this need corresponds to doing a Get Next (GN) call and testing for a GE status code, meaning segment not found. If we get a GE status code we know there are no child segments to process. If we get a Blank (Spaces) status code, we then enter our main body of logic.

Multiple Positioning

Sometimes the database structure is a bit more complicated than a simple parent-child relationship. Additional child segments may exist at several levels, and some segments may perhaps participate in logical relationships with other segments in other databases. Also, program processing may be a bit more complicated than our examples. Consider the simplified version of a customer database shown in Figure 7.2. It contains customer segments, sales order segments, and line item segments.

Suppose that a program needs to process the entire database. Doing so might involve processing all the sales orders for each customer, which implies also processing all the line items for each sales order. One way of coding this logic would be to process the database segment by segment, as in our original Case 1. Another way would be to code it using a nested loop. The outer loop would process sales order segments, while the inner one would process line item segments, corresponding to Case 2. In either case the program may encounter a situation where no line item segment exists for a sales order. This condition may be an awkward one to handle, especially if the program must

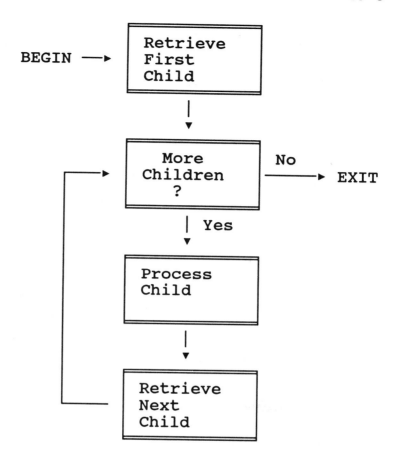

Figure 7.1. Logic diagram for child processing.

keep track of parentage or updating parent segments based upon its children. Here multiple positioning may help.

Lazy Error Processing

Debugging Statements

Many programmers find out the hard way, usually by making coding errors, that coding errors always occur. Error checking and debugging statements are usually added only after the fact, in a "minimalist" style. (No doubt programmers figure that their debugging statements are useless since errors happen so rarely.)

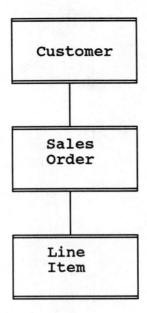

Figure 7.2. A multilevel database.

This issue is an important one in the IMS and DB2 environments. Analysts should build into the design any standard debugging logic that can be foreseen. Such logic often includes

- Echoing input
- Keeping record and segment counts
- Providing trace output
- Printing program statistics
- Input and output of control or audit information
- Passing condition information to succeeding steps.

Programmers should build debugging statements into their programs with the thought that they are to be there permanently. The easiest way to accomplish this is to make the execution of debugging statements conditional, based on the value of a specified switch. This switch could be set to DEBUG to allow statement execution, or Spaces otherwise. Multiple switches, or multiple values of the same switch, could also be used that correspond to various levels of debugging or severity.

This procedure has several advantages. First, the so-called "removal" of debugging statements can be accomplished by a simple switch value setting. This step is much easier than commenting and uncommenting code. Second, program debugging, enhancement, and documentation become easier because maintenance programmers have the debugging code already available. Third, specific debugging statements are now easier to find, for they must occur in company with the debug switch. Searching for this switch is much easier than trying to find, for example, all occurrences of DISPLAY and EXHIBIT, especially if the program listing has a cross-reference or one has access to an on-line editor.

In IMS programs, debugging is complicated by certain restrictions. MPPs, for example, may not use DISPLAY statements or, in general, any statement that sends its output to SYSOUT or SYSPRINT. Some considerations are that

- Batch programs and BMPs may contain statements that produce output on SYSOUT or SYSPRINT. This procedure is the most common way of checking these programs.

- All types of IMS programs, including ones using DB2, can be tested using the Batch Terminal Simulator II (BTS-II) program product from IBM. This product allows the programmer to execute an IMS program while at the same time displaying the values of I/O areas, status codes, SSAs, and other items of interest. Regrettably, BTS's DB2 status displays are woefully inadequate and sometimes even unreadable. Note that in the BTS environment DISPLAY statements are allowed and may be routed to the terminal or a file.

- Debugging an MPP can be simplified by defining additional fields on the screen as debugging fields. These fields may display debugging or status information or their information may be used as input to select specific debugging logic. Warning: Such a feature may prove so useful that users may want it installed in all their systems.

Production Error Processing

Many sophisticated systems, especially on-line ones, generally require that programs edit input information and inform the operator or controller of errors. This error checking is usually accomplished with standard validation procedures and use of a set of standard error messages. Some systems go even further by requiring all programs to contain skeleton logic for standard program functions. Some of these functions include

- Validation of numeric fields
- Translation of error message codes to standard error message text
- Processing of interprogram and intertransaction data transfers, such as IMS conversational programming

- Interrogating and setting terminal attributes, as, for example, highlighting errors in fields
- Fatal error message routing.

The last item is especially important. All the applications in a particular system should follow the same set of error checking and reporting standards. In an IMS environment doing so may involve reserving one printer or set of printers as error printers and routing all program error messages to them. This setup is usually arranged by defining a standard error message format, then creating the appropriate Working Storage and Procedure Division code. When an error occurs, the program sets the values of the required variables, such as the error message number, the message text, control information, the database in use, and so on, and invokes the error paragraph. This paragraph then formats the error message and routes it to the correct LTERM.

Too often, programmers neglect to fill in this error logic completely. This makes finding program errors difficult. I recommend that complete error processing be required before a program can pass its design, coding, and test walkthroughs.

Let us make one last comment before leaving the subject of error processing. Establishing standard error and abend processing logic for on-line programs (MPPs) often requires a lot of work. This thoroughness is required because on-line programs should never be allowed to abend, especially in a production environment. At worst, an MPP encountering a fatal error should prevent users from being able to do further processing, while notifying the application developer of the problem that caused the condition.

Checkpoint Frequency and Restart

The most common problems in IMS are associated with checkpointing. Checkpointing and program restart were covered in much more detail in Chapter 5. For now let us concentrate on the most common mistakes made with checkpointing.

Checkpoint Frequency

The IMS/VS Version 2 Application Programming manual says that "a general recommendation [for batch programs] is one checkpoint call every 10 or 15 minutes." This is easier said than done, however. Some shops have taken this guideline literally and code time-of-day calculations into programs. After an elapsed time of, say, ten minutes, the program does a checkpoint. Apart from its wasting of operating system resources by this accessing of the time of day, this method ignores the enormous effects that physical I/O and database record enqueuing have on overall system and application performance.

Another common method of measuring program resource consumption is to count DL/I calls. Typical call numbers per checkpoint range from 35 to 200. Again, this method ignores physical I/O, although it is a bit closer to it than the previous method.

By far the most common method of measuring resources is to take a weighted sum of all the DL/I calls performed during the course of the program's execution. With this technique each call is given a different value. One typical system uses the following:

Weight	DL/I Calls
1	GU, GN, GNP (for PROCOPT other than GO)
2	ISRT (GSAM only)
3	GHU, GHN, GHNP (for PROCOPT other than GO)
5	DLET, ISRT (non-GSAM)
8	REPL

After the sum of weighted calls reaches a predetermined value, say 200, the program does a checkpoint. This system is usually coupled with a method of tuning the checkpoint frequency externally. Batch programs read a single input record from an OS/VS file containing the checkpoint frequency. BMPs can read the same file, using GSAM. System administrators can thus monitor actual resource usage for programs and adjust their frequencies upward or downward as necessary.

Batch Program Restart

Checkpoints in batch programs are not done to finalize database updates; those are done immediately when a DL/I call is issued. The usual reason for having checkpoint calls in batch programs is to release enqueued database records. These records are unavailable to other IMS programs but, more importantly, they consume resources in IMS while being held. A program that enqueues database records without releasing them via CHKP calls risks terminating the IMS control region with a U775. This problem is in fact a common occurrence in some IMS shops. If your program abends with a U775, it may be because some other program caused IMS to exceed its enqueue space.

Many IMS analysts are unaware that IMS can dynamically back out database changes made by a batch program after a program's abnormal termination. Historically, this was the job of the programmer using the Batch Backout utility. With later versions of IMS, however, this procedure may be accomplished automatically, by specifying the BKO execution parameter in the JCL and using a DASD log file.

BMP Restart

BMP restart is by far the most common occurrence. Many IMS shops have converted batch programs to BMPs. In the process they installed checkpointing, GSAM databases, and sometimes program-controlled rollback (ROLL and ROLB). This arrangement is even more common in BMPs that access DB2 resources. In IMS a deadlock usually causes a program abend. For IMS programs that can access DB2, a deadlock can be resolved in IMS/VS and DB2 by rolling back a program's database and table updates to the previous commit point, then returning control to the program. The BMP must now be able to handle situations where it has been reset to the end of the previous transaction, either explicitly, through ROLL or ROLB DL/I calls, or implicitly, by a system-resolved deadlock.

Restart is usually accomplished by submitting JCL similar to that of the original, using the value LAST as the checkpoint-ID. IMS then uses the most recent checkpoint on the system log for the program. Of course, this would be done only after the problem that had caused the program to abend had been fixed. Some problems may, however, preclude program restart:

- Incorrect database structure. In this case the database, as defined in the DBD, is bad.

- Invalid or incorrect PSB. Here processing options, sensitive segments, or index specifications were either incorrect or omitted.

- Insufficient data stored in checkpoint save areas. These areas are specified in the XRST and CHKP call and point to areas of Working Storage that are to be saved by IMS. If you forget to save a data item needed for restart, it will not be there.

The problems that involve changing a DBD, PSB, or ACB will not allow IMS to restart the program. Those involving checkpoint save areas will allow restart, but they may prevent the program from acquiring sufficient information to reposition itself or continue processing successfully.

Ignoring PCB Information

Apart from checking the status code, most programmers never refer to the other fields in the PCB mask. Most of them have dull-sounding names, but they sometimes contain a wealth of information (see Table 7.1). A summary of their contents follows. Too often the programmer is insulated from the PSBGEN process. At the very least, the programmer and analyst should have a listing of what is in the PSB.

Table 7.1. The PCB masks.

```
     The I/O PCB

  01   I-O-PCB-MASK.

       05   LTERM-NAME          PIC X(8).
       05   RESERVED-FOR-DLI    PIC XX.
       05   STATUS-CODE         PIC XX.
       05   CURRENT-DATE        PIC S9(7) COMP-3.
       05   CURRENT-TIME        PIC S9(7) COMP-3.
       05   MSG-SEQUENCE-NUM    PIC S9(8) COMP.
       05   MODNAME             PIC X(8).
       05   USER-IDENT          PIC X(8).


     The Alternate PCB

  01   ALT-PCB-MASK.

       05   DESTINATION-NAME    PIC X(8).
       05   RESERVED-FOR-DLI    PIC XX.
       05   STATUS-CODE         PIC XX.


     The Database PCB

  01   DB-PCB-MASK.

       05   DATABASE-NAME       PIC X(8).
       05   SEGMENT-LEVEL       PIC 99.
       05   STATUS-CODE         PIC XX.
       05   PROCESSING-OPTIONS  PIC X(4).
       05   RESERVED-FOR-DLI    PIC X(4).
       05   SEGMENT-NAME        PIC X(8).
       05   KEY-FEEDBACK-LEN    PIC S9(8) COMP.
       05   NUM-SENSITIVE-SEGS  PIC S9(8) COMP.
       05   KEY-FEEDBACK-AREA   PIC X(n).
       05   UNDEFINED-REC-LEN   PIC S9(8) COMP.*

       * UNDEFINED-REC-LEN used for GSAM only.
```

The I/O PCB

LTERM-NAME. When a message is received, the LTERM-NAME contains the name of the logical terminal that sent the message. With ROUTING=YES it is set to the MSC Link name for remote transactions.

RESERVED-FOR-DLI. These two bytes are reserved for DL/I. If bit 1 is on (the bits are numbered from 0 to 15), this designates a remote transaction.

STATUS-CODE. This field gives a description of the results of the DC call.

CURRENT-DATE. This field gives the Julian date that IMS/VS received the entire message and enqueued it as input for the program. The format is 00YYDDD. CURRENT-DATE is not present for a message originating from a non-message-driven BMP.

CURRENT-TIME. This field gives the time of day at which IMS/VS received the entire message and enqueued it as input for the program. The format is HHMMSST. It is not present for a message originating from a non-message-driven BMP.

MSG-SEQUENCE-NUM. This field is the sequence number that IMS assigned to the message. It is not present for a message originating from a non-message-driven BMP.

MODNAME. This field is used only with MFS. When a GU is issued, IMS/VS places the MOD used in this area. If you wish to send a reply using a different MOD, replace this field with the appropriate MOD name and issue an ISRT.

USER-IDENT. 1. If sign-on (RACF) is not active in the system, this field is SPACES. 2. If sign-on is active and the message retrieved was sent by a BMP, this field is the PSB name of the BMP. 3. If sign-on is active and the message was sent by a terminal, this field is either the user's identification or the LTERM name of the terminal.

The Alternate PCB

DESTINATION-NAME. This is the LTERM or the transaction code to which you wish the message sent.

RESERVED-FOR-DLI. These two bytes are reserved for DL/I.

STATUS-CODE. This field provides a description of the results of the DC call.

The Database PCB (Including GSAM)

DATABASE-NAME. This field is the DBD name of the database. It is not used by GSAM.

SEGMENT-LEVEL. This field is the level number of the lowest segment on the last path encountered while searching for the segment requested. It will always be set to 1 for root-only databases.

STATUS-CODE. This field gives the results of the DL/I call. On initial program scheduling this field is set to one of the data availability status codes (NA, NU, Spaces). See the INIT DL/I call in the IMS Application Programming manual for further information.

PROCESSING-OPTIONS. This field specifies the processing options given on the PROCOPT parameter of the PCB statement. Note that this field tells you nothing about processing options that were explicitly specified for segments on any SENSEG statements for that PCB.

RESERVED-FOR-DLI. These two bytes are reserved for DL/I.

SEGMENT-NAME. If a retrieval has been successful, this field contains the name of the segment. If it was unsuccessful, this contains the name of the last segment encountered along the path to the segment requested. On program initial scheduling this field contains the database type: DEDB, GSAM, HDAM, HIDAM, HISAM, HSAM, INDEX, MSDB, or SHISAM. The segment name is not returned if the database type is GSAM because GSAM databases do not have segment names.

KEY-FEEDBACK-LEN. This field gives the current length of the Key Feedback Area (see below). For GSAM this is always 12.

NUM-SENSITIVE-SEGS. This field is the number of segment types in the database to which the program is sensitive. It is not used by GSAM and is always set to 1 for root-only databases.

KEY-FEEDBACK-AREA. After a successful retrieval call this field contains the concatenated key of the retrieved segment. If the call was unsuccessful, it contains the concatenated key of the lowest segment encountered during the search. If it was unable to find a root segment, this area is set to binary zeroes. For GSAM this field is 8 bytes long.

UNDEFINED-REC-LEN. In GSAM only, if RECFM=U is specified, this is the record length retrieved. It must be set by the program for ISRT calls.

Efficiency Considerations

Although programs and programmers are both supposed to be removed from considerations of physical design, in practice this is seldom the case. Many programs take advantage of such features as

- The database access method (HDAM, HIDAM, HISAM)
- The existence of pointer types such as physical child, physical twin, and the like
- The existence of secondary indexes
- The presence of search fields for a segment.

These features allow analysts and programmers to determine specific access paths and accessing methods for target data. Although such sophistication may be commendable, there are several factors that application designers and system administrators must take into account:

- Designing and coding programs by using special accessing methods locks programs into their present database design, preventing DBAs from making otherwise transparent changes to database structures. A program that uses a secondary index, for example, may have to be rewritten if the secondary index is redefined or deleted. Another common example would be a program that accesses root segments using Get Next (GN) calls with an unqualified SSA and does so assuming that the roots will be in ascending order by segment key. This assumption is valid if the database access method is HIDAM. Unfortunately, if the access method is changed to HDAM the assumption no longer holds true, assuming that a special randomizing module is not used.

- Program efficiency is difficult to define and even more difficult to measure. The most expensive system resource is I/O; thus programs today are usually written with physical I/O minimization in mind. Sadly, the programmer — and, of course, the program — have little or no data available to them about the physical environment. For example, in the early 1980s it was popular to code IMS programs to fit a standard work unit. This unit was set up to control the wide variance in the amount of IMS resources that transactions then used. Each transaction was to keep track of the quantity of resources it consumed and either terminate or reschedule itself or become quiescent after using its "standard" share. Unfortunately, the standard was sometimes defined in units that programs could not measure easily, such as 35 physical I/Os, or one CPU second.

    The situation is even more complex today. Most modern database management systems coexist with transaction managers, other DBMSs, communications subsystems, and operating systems. The performance tuning of such conglomerations of software and hardware products is a complicated job precisely because there is so much interaction between subsystems. It is for this reason that coding an IMS program or application system for maximum internal efficiency may actually decrease overall system performance.

In summary, considerations of program efficiency, sometimes called *micro-efficiency*, are probably not as important as meeting a system's specifications and its maintainability needs and producing the right output. Programs that have special features should document them clearly. Some of the more common features that should cause no special problems are

- Using multiple PCBs
- Using multiple positioning
- Assuming that there will be certain processing options
- Assuming the existence of a special-purpose HDAM randomizing module.

DEBUGGING AN IMS PROGRAM

Debugging is a means to many ends. It is used variously to test newly written code, fix production problems, test system enhancements, and validate the proper functionality of a system. Including a database management system within the testing equation forces analysts to weigh yet one more factor. This factor will affect program coding and testing estimates and thus affect program completion dates and project delivery dates. It is essential that all IS personnel understand and apply standard testing methods.

Testing Methods

There are only a few major differences between debugging an IMS program and a non-IMS program. Their similarities are many, though:

- Creation of test data
- Use of a standard test plan and test cases
- Inclusion of DISPLAY statements or their equivalent to display intermediate results, switches, and so on
- Using an on-line debugging aid to step the program through various sections of code
- A testing strategy for unit tests, string tests, and subsystem tests.

The actual testing of IMS programs, however, involves a little more effort on everyone's part to help achieve a correct, maintainable application system.

Some of these methods are described here, according to their place in the systems development life cycle.

Application Analysis and Design

There are several things the application analyst and database designer can do to assist in future program and subsystem testing from the outset.

■   *Design for program modularity.* Applications that are modularized can be tested module by module. Then the modules can be united, during integration testing. This process is particularly important in IMS programs, where database access logic may be spread widely throughout the code.

　　　　As part of this process, programmers should separate database accesses into separate modules (e.g., COBOL paragraphs). Doing so will not only allow modular testing but permit code sections having similar functions to be grouped physically. (COBOL paragraph names could be prefixed with a two- or three-character function identifier, for example.)

■   *Consider using skeleton or boilerplate code.* This practice is common in large on-line systems where programs must perform such standard functions as setting the screen attributes (highlight, protect, color, etc.), validating numeric fields, accessing control files, and sending error messages to the terminal operator. By requiring all applications to be written within the standard boilerplate, system designers can be assured that all programs are performing their tasks correctly. In addition, program problems can be more easily isolated.

　　　　Some shops have taken this advice to an extreme by attempting to include all possible standard services in such skeletons. Some such services of these might include electronic mail message routing, interfaces to system tutorials and user training subsystems, elaborate help systems, complex security and audit packages, off-line dispatching of resource-consuming tasks, and carrying over extensive user information from one application to another. This certainly makes the analyst's and programmer's job somewhat easier, but it creates a situation where several weeks of training may be necessary to train employees in the basics of just the skeleton. Further, having a large average program size translates to requiring additional memory and thus possibly creating performance implications.

■   *Create common error processing procedures.* Include in every program a section of code that informs the system or an operator about fatal program errors. Design programs so that error recovery and reporting are an integral part of the process.

Application Programming

Application programming should

- Include debugging statements at the coding stage. Don't wait until test time to add them—and don't assume that your code will always work. Insert these statements so that they will be executed conditionally, depending upon the value of a switch.

- Learn to use third-party products. Many IS shops are now using personal computers to design, code, and test programs before transferring them to a mainframe. Such products include structured design packages, code generators, test data generators, program animators, and even micro-to-mainframe links. Using a PC to do some of the necessary programming will be much cheaper than using the mainframe, especially during peak hours.

Application Testing

The application testing process should

- Use the DFSDDLT0 utility to test the results of DL/I calls. This utility is useful for simple tasks such as printing database segments, displaying position in a database, and testing certain sequences of DL/I calls.

- Again, learn to use available third-party products. Almost every IMS shop has one or more software products they use in testing and debugging. These utilities include test data generators, program test case analyzers, and dump interpreters. IMS dumps can be difficult to read, so a dump-reading utility can save hours of tracing through EBCDIC and hex code.

- Keep track of errors for later reference. It is rare that someone encounters a genuinely new error. Most often, the ones you face will have been solved before by someone else. Keep a log of any program problems you hear about and their solutions. If convenient, cross-reference these problems by their error type. In this way you are better prepared to cope with errors or similar situations you may encounter in the future.

Part 3
Distributed and Relational Considerations

Chapter 8

Linking to Other Systems

THE DISTRIBUTED ENVIRONMENT

A distributed environment is a set of related data processing systems wherein each system has its own capacity to operate autonomously but has some applications that execute at multiple sites. This flexibility is accomplished by moving application processes around among sites. Some of the systems may be connected with teleprocessing links into a network in which each system is a node. The separate systems may operate on different architectures or have their own operating systems.

In short, a distributed environment means that, for whatever reasons, a company's or enterprise's important data are located in different sites on a computer network. In this context, *site* refers to each instance of a database management system that participates in a distributed environment. Two distinct database management systems on the same processor would then be considered two sites.

To make the implementation and portability of functions through different systems easier, IBM has introduced Systems Application Architecture (SAA). SAA is an application interface architecture consisting of a set of software interfaces, conventions, and protocols. SAA serves as the framework for developing consistent applications across the current and projected future offerings of the three major IBM computing environments: System/370, AS/400, and PS/2. These interfaces, conventions, and protocols are designed to provide enhanced consistency in the following areas:

Material in this chapter is adapted from *Introduction to Distributed Relational Data* (GG24-3200) (pages 1-8, 34-48, 73-76) © 1988 by International Business Machines Corporation. Reprinted by permission.

- *Application Programming Interface (API).* Languages and services that application developers use in building software.
- *User access.* Design and use of screen panels and user interaction techniques.
- *Communications support.* Connectivity of systems and programs.
- *Applications.* Customer applications and software built and supplied both by IBM and other vendors.

TERMS AND DEFINITIONS

This section defines some of the most common terms used to discuss systems in a distributed environment. It is important to distinguish always between systems that merely provide some kind of remote access to data and systems that have a true capability managing distributed data.

Distributed Processing

Distributed processing means that the location of the data determines where the application processing will be done. The application function must be *moved* to the place where the data are located. IMS/VS Multiple System Coupling (MSC) is one product supporting this type of distributed processing. Through Intersystem Communication (ISC) protocols, CICS also allows two or more CICS subsystems to be interconnected.

A logical process needing data located at different sites therefore has to be split into two processes, with each one implemented by a separate application program at each site. The data at one site may have to be moved to the other to be able to process the whole transaction in one site. One of the basic characteristics of a transaction, that it is an atomic unit of execution, thus becomes more difficult to honor. Therefore, in such an environment the application may carry the responsibility for maintaining data integrity within the logical transaction.

Remote Access

Remote access defines an environment in which data are copied from another (remote) source and made available to a local receiving site. The data received are then processed on the local site. The data are thus moved to the location where the processing takes place.

The data at the remote site are usually maintained by a database management system (DBMS). To obtain the data, a user at the local site sends a request to the DBMS at the remote site. To provide access to the remote site, a program at the local site (the requester) has to communicate with a program at the remote site (the server) to process the request for data. Consequently, the requester, through its own application or some other means, has to know where the data are located. The application usually takes care of the data integrity.

This kind of environment is often restricted to read-only access. There is thus no need for integrity control by the remote DBMS with these kinds of requests. They are typically initiated by programs on intelligent workstations or query products running on the host computer. IBM's Enhanced Connectivity Facility (ECF) and Host Database View (HDBV) provide this kind of remote access support.

Distributed Data

Distributed data concerns the distribution of and access to both flat files and relational databases. Data distribution across systems can be supported at various levels and implemented through a number of design choices. Different implementations will lead to different results in terms of data availability, portability, storage requirements, and performance.

Distributed Files

Some support for distributed files already exists. For instance, manually transferring files from one system to another has been supported since the earliest days of the computer industry. File distribution plays an important role in supporting distributed data processing. There is an architecture already defined to manage and control current and potential future implementations, which is known as Data Distribution Manager Architecture, or DDM Architecture.

Distributed Databases

As mentioned, a distributed environment is characterized by data of interest to a particular enterprise being located in different sites on a computer network. A distributed database exists when a logically integrated database is distributed over several physically distinct but linked sites. In spite of data being located at different sites, each will have similar properties that will tie them together. Users may then need to correlate data from different locations to satisfy their own requirements. This property makes a distributed database quite different from a set of local databases that reside at separate sites on the same computer network.

An important characteristic of systems supporting distributed databases is that the system itself—not the application—manages the data at multiple locations. From the user's point of view, a set of distributed databases should look like a single database. The user should be able to think absolutely in terms of logical data objects and not be concerned with where or how many times those objects may physically be stored.

The integrity of databases distributed over multiple sites is controlled by the system, without the application's having to be aware of where the data are located. To support this function in general implies that there has to be a DBMS on each site that is involved in this type of distributed data.

Distributed Database Management Systems

A distributed database management system (D-DBMS) is a system that performs all the traditional functions of a DBMS at each local site for local databases. Furthermore, it should provide all functions that might be required to manage the distributed databases, as well as the functions to access and control the distributed data. Some of the capabilities of such a DBMS are

- *Remote database access.* Providing control and transaction access to remote databases is one of the most important features of a distributed DBMS. It should be present in all systems that claim to have a distributed database component.

- *Location transparency.* This feature can be provided in different amounts. The D-DBMS itself, not the program, should know where the data are physically located. In a D-DBMS the user should be able to issue requests as if the data were all stored locally.

- *Coordinated integrity control.* Another important function of a D-DBMS is to guarantee the integrity of distributed databases. All sites involved in program updates should communicate with each other and check the agreement to commit updates.

- *Site autonomy.* Each site in a D-DBMS has autonomous processing capabilities and can execute local applications. There should be no centralized critical resource shared by the sites that would become unavailable with a local DBMS function's failure.

- *Database administration and control.*

- *Transaction integrity.*

- *Concurrency control.* This feature deals with the synchronization of different transactions. Synchronization means the sequence of transactions that change the databases. There are different approaches available to institute concurrency control. Resource locking is one of the most frequently used techniques.

- *Recovery of distributed transactions.*

LEVELS OF DISTRIBUTED RELATIONAL DATA PROCESSING

Remote Requests

Remote request data accessing occurs when the request for access to the data is made by an application that consists of a single SQL statement. Typically, the site at which the application is developed does not contain a local relational DBMS. The application sends the source SQL statement to the remote site, where the optimization and access are done.

To support the remote request, either the application or some front-end process must have the capability of routing the statement to the remote site.

Since the entire SQL statement is being sent to the remote site, there must exist at that site a function capable of passing what is called the shipped SQL statement to the DBMS. This application program interface (API) processor function acts as a server to process SQL statements, then passes them to the local DBMS, which supports the SQL language. The server implicitly invokes commit processing at the completion of the SQL statement and returns the results and status to the requesting application.

The characteristics of the remote request are that it has

- One request per unit of work.
- One DBMS per request.
- One DBMS per unit of work.
- One unit-of-work manager.
- Commit requested by the remote DBMS, not by the local application.

Remote Unit of Work

Having the remote unit of work relaxes the restriction of requiring at most one SQL statement within a given unit of work. Within a transaction or unit of work the application may perform multiple SQL statements on distributed data. To support remote unit-of-work access a requester process independent of the application is required. This process identifies the remote site for a target object, makes the connection to the remote site, maintains this connection across the unit of work, and maintains state information on the progress of the transaction across multiple SQL statements within the same unit of work.

A counterpart server process is also required at the remote site. This server receives the SQL statements, passes them to the DBMS, maintains state information across all SQL statements within a unit of work, and maintains the connection to the requester until COMMIT or ABORT.

The characteristics of the remote unit of work are that it has

- Multiple requests per unit of work
- One DBMS per request
- One DBMS per unit of work
- One unit-of-work manager
- Commit requested by the local application, not by the remote DBMS.

Distributed Unit of Work

Having distributed unit-of-work support permits access to multiple sites. Within a single transaction or unit of work, objects that are targets of SQL statements are allowed to span multiple sites. However, all objects of a single SQL statement are still constrained to exist at a single site.

Because multiple sites are involved, the unit-of-work management functions at all sites must support a protocol that synchronizes commit processing at each site, such as the two-phase commit protocol (see Chapter 9). Commit coordination must be performed by the unit-of-work manager functions at the requesting site.

It is also necessary to have a server processor at each remote site, connected to the requester process for the duration of the unit of work. With multiple sites, one coordinator process is required at the requesting site and multiple participant processes needed at each of the remote sites. At commit, the unit-of-work manager at the requesting site, which acts as the coordinator of the two-phase commit process, must communicate with the remote unit-of-work managers.

The characteristics of the distributed unit of work are that it has

- Multiple requests per unit of work
- One DBMS per request
- Several DBMSs per unit of work
- Several unit-of-work managers
- Commit coordinated at the local application site.

At this level of access, there are four forms of accesses within an application program:

- *Multisite read.* This process can perform multiple SELECT statements, each referring to a different site. Each SELECT is constrained to a single site.

- *Local site update.* This process can perform multiple SELECT statements referring to different sites. In addition, it can perform update statements referring to the local site. Each request is constrained to a single site.

- *Single site update.* This process can perform multiple SELECT statements referring to different sites. It can also perform update statements referring to one site, whether local or remote. Each request is constrained to a single site.

- *Multisite update.* This process can perform multiple SELECT statements referring to different sites. It can likewise perform update statements referring to different sites. Each request is constrained to a single site.

Distributed Requests

The distributed request function offers the greatest flexibility in terms of distributed data access, as well as the fewest application constraints. Each SQL statement can access several distinct objects, stored at multiple separated remote sites.

An application within a unit of work may perform several SQL statements that span multiple unique remote sites. Therefore, both database and unit-of-work management facilities are required at each site. The unit-of-work manager at the requesting site is the coordinator of commit processing.

The characteristics of the distributed request are that it has

- Multiple requests per unit of work
- More than one DBMS per request
- Several DBMSs per unit of work
- Several unit-of-work managers
- Commit coordinated at the local application site.

In a distributed request there are three types of accesses within an application program:

- *Multisite read.* Each request can read objects at multiple sites.

- *Multisite read, single site update.* Each request can read objects at multiple sites but update only a single site.

- *Multisite update.* Each request can read and update objects at multiple sites.

DISTRIBUTED SYSTEM CONNECTIONS

Typical IMS Interfaces

Distributed systems connecting multiple IMS subsystems generally implement MSC links between the communicating subsystems. This linkage allows message traffic to flow through the network but also allows conversational processing. Linking into a CICS subsystem almost always requires having an ISC link. Conversational processing with a CICS transaction will thus not be supported.

Typical CICS Interfaces

In CICS several kinds of distributed processing are supported. ISC allows CICS transactions to be interconnected in several ways, as described below.

■ *Distributed transaction processing.* In the context of CICS, distributed transaction processing allows the entire application to be divided into a distributed set of programs, each accessing its own local data. (For example, a CICS application program executing at one site can invoke another CICS program at another site, without having to cease execution itself.) The data may be of any type supported by CICS. The end user initiates the overall transaction by invoking the first of these programs at their local site. As it executes, that program can invoke programs at other sites, which can in turn invoke other programs, and so on. The whole set of programs is considered to be a unit of work for recovery purposes.

   Because CICS does not maintain any kind of directory giving the location of each program, knowledge of how the data are distributed has to be built into the application logic.

■ *Function shipping.* Function shipping provides complete location transparency at the application program level. Application programs can in turn provide such transparency to the end user. Programs can issue DL/I database calls or VSAM access against remote data exactly as if those data were at the local site. CICS/ISC will then intercept that call and ship it to the appropriate remote site by referencing a directory that gives the location of each database or file. A mirror transaction is established at the remote site to issue DL/I calls to the database on behalf of the original transaction and to return the result to that program. Function shipping is restricted to DL/I databases and VSAM files.

■ *Function routing.* CICS/VS transactions can be routed from one region to another under the control of specifications in the Program Control Table

(PCT), or as directed by the user terminal. Messages are routed automatically to the appropriate site where they are to be executed. The associated programs are executed and responses returned. Transactions that are initiated in one site may route their output to terminals located in another.

MULTIPLE SYSTEMS COUPLING (MSC)

Terminology

The connection between two systems is called a *link*. All links must be defined during the process of IMS/VS system definition for each IMS/VS system. There are two types of links: physical and logical. A physical link is simply the actual hardware connection. A logical link is the mechanism through which a physical link is related to the transactions and terminals that make use of that link. The assignment of a logical link to a physical link can be specified during the stage of system definition or made dynamically by the Master Terminal Operator during system execution.

Physical Links

MSC supports four types of physical links:

- A binary synchronous communication (BSC) line using BTAM
- A channel-to-channel (CTC) adapter (for OS/VS2 MVS only)
- Main storage to main storage (MTM)
- Synchronous Data Link Control (SDLC) using VTAM.

Only the BSC line, VTAM, and the CTC adapter represent actual hardware links. The MTM link is a software link between IMS/VS systems running in the same processor that is intended primarily for backup and testing. If the CTC link is used, both ends of the connection would have to be operating under OS/VS2 MVS. The physical links' buffer sizes must be equal between the two systems. If BSC is chosen for the physical link, one side must be the master and the other the slave.

Several IMS/VS systems coexisting in a single processor may be linked to each other by one or more links of each physical type. The MTM link is recommended when two or more IMS/VS systems reside in one processor.

Logical Links

A logical link relates a physical link to the transactions and terminals that can use that physical link. Each system in a multisystem configuration has one or more defined logical links. For instance, two IMS/VS systems defined to communicate with each other, each through a specific logical link, are called *partner systems*. To establish a connection between two IMS/VS systems, each partner must have a logical link definition. These two definitions must specify the same partner identifications and be assigned to the same physical link. IMS/VS system definition assigns a number to each defined logical link. These numbers are assigned sequentially, beginning with 1, in the order in which the links are defined. A logical link can be reassigned to a different physical link, but the two systems must always communicate through a logical link partnership.

The SDLC link that uses VTAM has the capability of allowing multiple sessions to use the link. In IMS/VS system definition you can specify how many sessions are to share the SDLC link. Each session that is activated becomes a logical link between partner systems.

IMS/VS system definition does not require that a physical link be specified for each logical link. The assignment of a physical link to a logical link can alternatively be made on-line, using the IMS/VS /MSASSIGN command. There can be no communication between partners until the assignment has been made.

Data Partitioning

Multiple System Coupling provides the ability to connect geographically dispersed IMS/VS systems so as to allow programs and operators in one system access to the programs and operators in connected systems. Communication is permitted between as many as 255 IMS/VS systems running on any supported combination of OS/VS1 and OS/VS2 MVS systems in one or more supported processors.

MSC also provides a way to extend the throughput of an IMS/VS system beyond the capacity of a single processor. This extended capacity is possible if the IMS/VS applications can be partitioned among systems so that either

- Applications execute in more than one system with the databases' contents split between systems in what is called horizontal partitioning.

- Applications execute in one system, with the complete database that they reference being attached to that system through vertical partitioning. The transactions can originate in any system.

In a multisystem environment the term *local system* is used to identify a specific system within the multiple configuration. All other systems are considered to be *remote systems*. A transaction that is processed in the same system in which it is entered is thus called a *local transaction*. Correspondingly, a transaction entered into a system from a terminal or link that is not processed in that system is known as a *remote transaction*. Remote transactions and output messages from processing programs both form part of the message queues. Their transfer to a remote system is controlled by MSC support. Output messages are queued under the logical terminal's name. If they are destined for a remote system, their destinations are called *remote LTERMs*.

Data Flow within Multiple Systems

The flow of a transaction in a multisystem environment through processing requires a few steps in addition to those needed in a single system environment. In an input terminal system MSC support is responsible for the transfer of queued remote transactions to the processing system, where the transactions are again queued. An application program reply will be queued by its destination. Subsequently, transferring of the reply causes it to be queued for output in the input terminal system.

Message Routing

The message routing function of MSC supports transaction processing by more than one system, by more than one application program either in the same or in different systems (by program-to-program message switches), and message switches between terminals whether in the same or different systems. Conversational processing is available to any system in a multisystem configuration.

The path through which IMS/VS passes a message from its point of origination through processing is called a routing path. One or more systems may be included in a routing path. The routing path that comes to be defined depends on the configuration of the multisystem and the functions assigned to each system.

Message routing is accomplished in a multisystem configuration by logical destinations, as in a single system environment. A destination is considered either a logical terminal or a transaction code. It is considered a local destination if it resides in the local system and a remote destination if it resides in a remote one. In a multisystem environment each system knows by way of system definition all local destinations and all remote destinations that may potentially be referenced by that system. IMS/VS system definition requires that all local and referenced remote destinations be defined with unique names, except for MSC directed routing.

Message routing occurs automatically according to the defined scheme unless either the routing exit routines or MSC directed routing is employed for dynamic routing control.

MSC directed routing is a function of MSC that allows an application program to specify the system name (MSNAME) and the destination within that system for a message to an LTERM or an application program. The receiving application program can determine the MSNAME of the system that originally scheduled it. With directed routing, the specified remote destination, a transaction or an LTERM in another system, does not have to be declared explicitly in the IMS/VS system definition for the sending system. This flexibility enables different IMS/VS systems in the MSC network to use the same logical names for terminals and use transaction codes for applications programs. Names must still be unique within a system, however. The Multiple System Verification utility cannot detect errors associated with MSC directed routing.

The path between any two systems is called a logical link path. One or more logical link paths must be defined for each logical link. A logical link path, which is defined in the MSNAME macro, specifies a system identification (SYSID) for the system in which messages using this path are to be processed and a system identification for the system is defined.

Each system in a multisystem configuration has one or more unique system identifications, ranging from 1 to 255. SYSID assignments are implicit, based on the logical link paths defined by MSNAME macros. Each system maintains a SYSID table containing all logical link paths defined in that system.

Transactions are assigned to logical link paths in the APPLCTN macro definition. If any logical terminals in a remote system are referred to by messages originating in the local system, the logical link definition must also include NAME macros to identify those remote logical terminals, unless directed routing is to be used.

Use CTC links, if possible, rather than BSC or SDLC links. The processor requirements to support a CTC link are lower for each message than for BSC or SDLC links.

Conversational Processing

Conversational processing is available to terminals attached to any system in a multisystem configuration to the same extent as it is available in a single system. The first requirement is that all transactions used in a conversation must be defined as conversational in each system of a multisystem environment. The input system is the one that controls the conversational resources for the duration of the conversation. When this system receives a conversational transaction, it inserts the SPA as the first message segment, then routes the message to the destination application program.

Each step in a conversation can be processed by any system in a multisystem configuration. Program-to-program switches can, for instance, be routed from system to system. SPAs used in multisystem conversations must be defined as being fixed length. The SPA size specified must be the same for all transactions that are to participate in the conversation.

Generally, multisystem conversations are transparent to terminal operators and application programs. One exception occurs if a conversational program inserts a message to a response alternate PCB in a remote system. By implication, this destination is in the input system and will thus be verified by that input system. In this instance destination verification includes ensuring that the specified logical terminal is still assigned to the input terminal. If the logical terminal has been reassigned, the input system will invoke the conversation abnormal termination exit routine and terminate the conversation. Under these circumstances no status code is returned to the application program.

The other exception occurs if an application program that does not execute in the input system uses the SPA to specify a transaction code and thereby to pass control of a conversation to another program. If the transaction code specified is invalid, the input system will invoke the conversation abnormal termination exit routine and terminate the conversation. Again, no status code is returned to the application program in such a case.

Recovery Considerations

Each system in a multisystem configuration uses the full recovery capabilities of IMS/VS.

Message Recovery

MSC ensures that messages are not lost or duplicated across a multisystem link, as long as no system in the configuration is cold started and no log records are lost. Preserving log records is accomplished by logging information about a given transmission in both the sending and receiving systems. This information is restored during restart and exchanged between systems once the link is activated. The sending system can then dequeue a message received by the receiving system but for which the acknowledgment was lost because of a link or system failure. The sending system can also resend a message that was sent but not enqueued by the receiving system because of a failure in that system. If a system in a multisystem configuration fails to recover, the messages for which it has recovery responsibility will be lost.

Application Programming

For the most part, communicating with a remote terminal or program has no effect on how you code your program, because MSC handles the message routing between systems. For example, if you receive an input message from a remote terminal and want to reply to that terminal, issue an ISRT call against the I/O PCB, just as you would to reply to a terminal in your system. There are situations, however, in which MSC will affect your programming:

■ When your program needs to know if an input message is from a remote terminal or a local one. For example, if two terminals in separate IMS/VS systems had the same logical terminal name your program's processing might be affected by knowing which system sent the message.

■ When you send a message to an alternate destination in another system.

Directed routing makes it possible for your program to find out whether an input message is from your system or a remote one and to set the destination of an output message to an alternate destination in another IMS/VS system. With directed routing you can send a message to an alternate destination in another system, even if that destination is not defined as being remote.

MSC directed routing does not support a program-to-program switch between conversational transactions.

Receiving Messages from Other IMS/VS Systems

When an application program retrieves an input message, the program can determine whether the input message is from a terminal or program in its own IMS/VS system or from a terminal or program in another such system. There may be situations in which an application program's processing is changed if the input message is from a remote terminal rather than from a local one.

If you have specified ROUTING=YES on the TRANSACT macro during IMS/VS system definition, IMS/VS does two things to indicate to the program that the message is from a terminal in another IMS/VS system.

First, instead of placing the logical terminal's name in the first field of the I/O PCB, IMS/VS places the name of the MSC logical link in this field. This is the logical link name that was specified on the MSNAME macro at system definition. However, if the message is subsequently sent back to the originating system, the originating LTERM name will be reinstated in the first field of the I/O PCB.

Second, IMS/VS turns on a bit in the field of the I/O PCB that is reserved for IMS/VS. This bit is the second one in the first byte of the two-byte field.

Sending Messages to Alternate Destinations in Other IMS/VS Systems

To send an output message to an alternate terminal in another IMS/VS system your system must have an MSC link with the system to which you want to send the message. To establish one you issue a CHNG call against an alternate PCB and supply the name of the MSC link that connects the two IMS/VS systems. If there is a security violation in your message, MSC will detect it in the receiving system and report it to the person at the originating terminal.

INTERSYSTEM COMMUNICATION (ISC)

Intersystem Communication is a part of the IMS-DC feature that allows an IMS subsystem to take part in an SNA subsystem connection called an application-to-application session, which uses LU6 protocols. An ISC link can connect an IMS application either to other IMS subsystems or to a CICS subsystem. Communication is between application programs in the two subsystems. The subsystems themselves, which are called *session partners*, support logical flows of data between applications. Message routing sometimes requires involving an application to determine a given message's destination. ISC also permits Fast Path and Message Format Service (MFS). Specific routing parameters may be overridden or modified by using MFS.

Both MSC and ISC permit a user to route transactions and distribute transaction processing. MSC is used primarily to distribute conversations among two or more IMS subsystems, allowing resource sharing. ISC is typically used to connect IMS to CICS or to allow an application in one subsystem to use the services in another, such as a message queue or a database.

In general, IMS-to-IMS transaction communications using either of these features are transparent to their applications. Each IMS system defines transactions as either local or remote. When an application sends a message, IMS checks the transaction code against its tables. If the transaction specified is local, IMS schedules it; if remote, IMS uses a link to route the transaction.

This arrangement is satisfactory for remote requests or remote units of work, but higher levels of distributed processing are not supported. That is, unit-of-work commits, rollbacks, or synchpoint processing must all be application driven. Doing so involves a high degree of cooperation between applications among what might become potentially many IMS systems, an arrangement that is difficult to design and tune.

Chapter 9

DB2 Coding Considerations in IMS Programs

DB2 AND IMS COEXISTENCE

How do IMS and DB2 coexist, and which is in control? As more and more sites come to employ them simultaneously, data integrity and timely response become paramount concerns.

Peaceful Coexistence

DB2 is IBM's relational DBMS for the MVS operating system. With DB2, users perceive the data as being stored in a collection of tables. Applications then manipulate these tables, using Structured Query Language (SQL) to make inquiries, produce reports, and derive further tables. The strength of DB2, as well as other relational DBMSs, lies in its ability to handle ad hoc queries. Some other DBMSs, such as IBM's IMS/VS and Computer Associates' IDMS, have generally proven superior for transaction processing applications.

Many new systems are being developed to combine DB2 tables and IMS/VS databases, using IMS/DC as the data communications subsystem. IMS/DC users communicate interactively with IMS/VS applications, which then access IMS/DB databases, DB2 tables, or both. An inventory control application, might, for example, access an IMS/DB inventory database, update a vendor DB2 table, then produce a report on-line.

How do IMS/VS and DB2 coexist? Do application programs exist within both environments at once? This chapter addresses these questions and presents solutions to some common problems.

First we will see how the IMS/VS and DB2 subsystems communicate with each another.

Connections and Threads

The DB2 subsystem allows other subsystems, such as TSO, CICS, and IMS/VS, to access its DB2 resources. IMS/VS does so by establishing a communication path to DB2 called a connection by using the DB2-IMS/VS Attachment facility, other facilities being used for TSO and CICS. IMS/VS may then create one or more of what are called threads on that connection. A connection is analogous to a railroad right-of-way between two cities, in that it establishes a two-directional pathway between subsystems. Using this analogy, the threads correspond to the railroad tracks. They connect specific subsystem users (origins) with specific DB2 resources, or destinations. One or more threads may be present on a given connection.

The Attachment facility creates two kinds of threads upon connecting IMS/VS to DB2. It first creates a command thread from the control region to DB2 once the first DB2 command is entered from an IMS/VS terminal. Terminal operators use these command threads to issue DB2 commands such as −DISPLAY THREAD. The Attachment facility then creates a transaction thread once an application has issued its first SQL statement. The transaction thread connects a single IMS/VS application to DB2.

During IMS/VS start-up, the control region attempts to connect to DB2. The IMSVS.PROCLIB dataset contains a member that informs the control region of the necessary DB2 connections. It is possible to have several connections simultaneously between IMS/VS and DB2, each to a different DB2 subsystem. At region start-up time a connection is established to all the DB2 subsystems that have been defined in the dependent region's subsystem member (SSM) of IMSVS.PROCLIB. Dependent region connections require that a connection already exist between the control region and DB2.

Before completing the connection, the Resource Access Control Facility (RACF) or its equivalent checks the DB2 subsystem's name to authorize the connection. If RACF does authorize the connection, a connection is completed between IMS/VS and the particular DB2 subsystem. Connections for Message Processing Programs (MPPs) are therefore created before the execution of application programs.

Alternatively, a Batch Message Processing (BMP) region will establish its connection to DB2 when the application executes its first SQL statement. This procedure may result in having a BMP begin execution without having an active DB2 subsystem. BMPs must consider this possibility by checking the SQLCODE after the execution of their first SQL statement. (Note that "first SQL statement" refers to an *executable* statement, such as SELECT or OPEN

CURSOR.) Some of the possible SQLCODE values are −922 (Connection Authorization Failure), −923 (Connection Not Established), and −924 (DB2 Connection Internal Error). BMPs and MPPs both create transaction threads when issuing their first SQL statement.

Should either DB2 or IMS/VS fail, the connection will also fail. The failing subsystem must then be restarted and the connection reestablished. If just the connection fails, however, then only it will need to be reestablished. An abnormal termination of an IMS/VS transaction will cause both DB2 and IMS/VS to back out any changes made to their respective resources.

Two-Phase Commit

IMS/VS does not finalize database updates immediately when it is in an on-line environment. Instead it holds them until a synchronization point (synchpoint) occurs. At that time all database updates are committed, and any IMS/VS resources held by the application are released. The application may at this time explicitly generate synchpoints by using the CHKP call, for example. Synch-points may even occur naturally, at program termination, or upon receiving the next message from the message queue.

For DB2 the corresponding term for synchpoint is the *commit point*. In a TSO environment, for example, DB2 holds table updates until they are committed, using a COMMIT SQL statement.

Application programs in IMS/VS cannot issue a COMMIT statement. How then can DB2 resources be committed and locks released? How do IMS/VS and DB2 coordinate what are referred to as their points of consistency; that is, their synchpoints and commit points?

DB2 table changes are committed during IMS/VS synchpoint processing. This commit process consists of two distinct phases, with IMS/VS acting as their coordinator. Table 9.1 summarizes the sequence of events during this so-called two-phase commit process, described below.

IMS/VS Commit: Phase 1

IMS/VS first writes a *Begin Commit* record to its log. It then informs DB2, and other subsystems, such as Fast Path, that they are to *Prepare to Commit*. Each subsystem informs IMS/VS whether or not it can continue with the commit process by returning a *Ready to Commit* response. If a subsystem is unable to continue, IMS/VS informs all the subsystems that the current Units of Recovery (URs) are to be rolled back. If DB2 fails, upon restart it will back out any changes made to DB2 resources, without needing to connect to IMS/VS.

Table 9.1. The two-phase commit process.

IMS/VS Commit: Phase 1

IMS/VS writes a BEGIN COMMIT record to its log.
IMS/VS begins Commit protocol.
IMS/VS issues PREPARE TO COMMIT to DB2.

DB2 Commit: Phase 1

DB2 logs all table updates.
DB2 writes an END PHASE 1 record to its log.
DB2 ensures that log buffers are written to the logs.
DB2 retains all locks and returns a READY TO COMMIT response to
    IMS/VS.

IMS/VS Commit: Phase 2

IMS/VS commits all its resources.
IMS/VS writes a CROSS OVER SYNCHPOINT record to its log.
IMS/VS ensures that the log buffer is written to the log.
IMS/VS issues a COMMIT to DB2.

DB2 Commit: Phase 2

DB2 writes a BEGIN PHASE 2 record to its log.
DB2 ensures that the log buffers are written to the logs.
DB2 commits its resources and releases locks.
DB2 writes an END PHASE 2 record to its log.

IMS/VS End of Two-Phase Commit

IMS/VS writes an END OF COMMIT record to its log.

DB2 Commit: Phase 1

Next, DB2 logs table updates, writes an *End Phase 1* record to its log, and ensures that this record is externalized. DB2 thus assures itself that the log is complete. It then returns a *Ready To Commit* response to IMS/VS. For a brief period beginning at this point, the DB2 Unit of Recovery is referred to as indoubt. Should either IMS/VS or DB2 fail now, the failing system must be restarted and the connection be reestablished. IMS/VS will then inform DB2 whether or not to commit or roll back resource changes found to be associated with the in-doubt unit of recovery.

IMS/VS Commit: Phase 2

If all subsystems have responded as being ready to commit, IMS/VS logs a *Cross Over Synchpoint* record. It then ensures that this record has been written to the log and issues a *Commit* message to the other subsystems.

DB2 Commit: Phase 2

Just prior to this point, the DB2 unit of recovery was classified as in-doubt. Now, DB2 writes a *Begin Phase 2* record to its log and ensures that the record becomes externalized. Should DB2 fail after this event, upon restart it will commit changes without needing to connect to IMS/VS. After committing its resources, DB2 next logs an *End Phase 2* record. IMS/VS then logs an *End Of Commit* record. This step ends the two-phase commit process.

In-Doubt Units of Recovery

Either IMS/VS or DB2 or both may fail during a two-phase commit process. If so, each builds a recovery list for DB2 units of recovery that have not been committed. The list built by DB2 is called an in-doubt list. The list built by IMS/VS is called the Residual Recovery Entry (RRE) list. IMS/VS logs these entries during checkpoint processing. During the resolution process the IMS/VS Attachment facility compares the lists built by IMS/VS with those from DB2 and deletes those it can resolve. Both systems then either back out or commit the unit of recovery.

At the end of the process some URs may remain in-doubt. If so, IMS/VS informs the Master Terminal. The database administrator must now resolve these URs manually by listing the appropriate IMS/VS and DB2 log entries. In DB2 the command "−DISPLAY THREAD TYPE(INDOUBT)" identifies these URs. The DBA then uses the DB2 command "−RECOVER INDOUBT" to either back out or commit the resource.

MPP Programming

Let's explore some specific problems and situations associated with the IMS/VS-DB2 environment. First we will consider message processing program concerns.

Deadlock (The "Deadly Embrace")

IMS/VS resolves a deadlock in an MPP environment by selecting one of the contending programs as the offender (sometimes called the victim). This will usually be the program that has, according to IMS, done the least amount of work. IMS halts the offender by generating a U777 pseudoabend. This step allows the other contender to have access to the locked resource. The IMS/VS database management system dynamically rolls back the offender to its most recent point of consistency and requeues it there. This process is completely transparent to the application program.

Nonresponse MPP Usage

An MPP need not communicate with a terminal but may be invoked from another MPP by using a *message switch*. These MPPs are called nonresponse ones because they cannot respond to a terminal. These MPPs should not be used to update DB2 tables used by on-line processes. Should either DB2 or IMS/VS fail, the table updates may become part of an in-doubt unit of recovery. Until DB2 and IMS/VS then resolve the unit of recovery problem, the data in the table will not be consistent and may adversely affect on-line processes.

DB2 Resource Allocation

Thread creation and application plan allocation occur in DB2 when the MPP executes its first SQL statement. Until then, the MPP has no way of obtaining information about the status of DB2. All that the program can assume is that a connection does exist. If the application plan does not in fact exist or is somehow invalid, the SQLCODE returned for the first SQL statement will probably be -923 (Connection Not Established: DB2 Allocation Error).

Inquiry-Only MPPs

MPPs can be defined in IMS/VS as "inquiry only" by specifying INQUIRY=YES on the TRANSACT macro in the IMS/VS Sysgen. This means that the program is therefore not able to update any IMS databases. One side effect is that in the DB2 environment an MPP defined as being inquiry only cannot issue any of the following SQL statements: INSERT, UPDATE, DELETE, CREATE, ALTER, DROP, GRANT, or REVOKE. Any attempt to do so will result in an error return code (SQLCODE) of -817. In other words, the MPP is also inquiry only in DB2! (For more information on this topic, see the DATABASE 2 Messages and Codes manual.)

Batch Message Programming

We can now look at the second IMS/VS-DB2 environment, batch message processing (BMP). As with MPP programming, certain specific concerns crop up.

DB2 Resource Allocation

DB2 connection, thread creation, and application plan allocation occur when the BMP executes its first SQL statement. Until then the BMP has no way of obtaining information about the status of DB2. Should a BMP begin to execute without there being an active DB2 subsystem, the SQLCODE returned after the execution of the first SQL statement will be nonzero. Some of the possible codes are −922 (Connection Authorization Failure), −923 (Connection Not Established), and −924 (DB2 Connection Internal Error). If the application plan does not exist or is invalid, the SQLCODE returned will probably be −923.

Use of OS/VS Datasets

IMS/VS and DB2 do not log the changes made to OS/VS files. Therefore, BMPs that access OS/VS files may not be restartable. This limitation is particularly important if the BMP contains a long-running internal sort. Such programs may have to be rerun from their beginning. To be restartable, however, the checkpointing must not interfere with the creation or sorting of the Sort file.

When IMS/VS restarts the application, the program becomes responsible for repositioning any OS/VS datasets. This step is usually accomplished by retaining a counter or key that indicates the last record processed, then using this information to skip forward through the input file until the correct record is found.

DB2 Cursor Processing during Checkpoint

During checkpoint processing, DB2 closes any open cursors. To simplify program logic, all applications should explicitly close all cursors before doing a checkpoint and also explicitly open them afterward. It is thus necessary for SELECT statements contained within cursor definitions to provide for this. In most cases the program can use one or more host variables to keep track of the last row returned by the FETCH statement for the cursor. The host variables are then included in the WHERE clause in the SELECT SQL statement for the cursor. Figure 9.1 shows one example of such cursor control.

```
EXEC SQL
  DECLARE PART_CURSOR
     CURSOR FOR
          SELECT PART_NUMBER, PART_QTY, PART_COST
            FROM PART_TABLE
            WHERE    PART_NUMBER > :LAST-PART-NO
            ORDER BY   PART_NUMBER
END-EXEC.


EXEC SQL
  FETCH   PART_CURSOR
      INTO  :IN-PART-NO, :IN-PART-QTY, :IN-PART-COST
END-EXEC.

IF   SQLCODE   EQUALS   ZERO
     MOVE   IN-PART-NO   TO   LAST-PART-NO.
```

Figure 9.1. Sample SQL showing cursor control.

Choice of Output Media

BMPs are frequently used to print reports. Thus, application designers should design applications that are restartable but do not adversely affect report generation. In particular, using an OS/VS file or a standard output file (SYSOUT=x) may preclude restart. Neither IMS/VS nor DB2 log changes to these media, so if the BMP fails it must be rerun from the beginning to produce a complete report.

Several alternatives for report output are available to allow the application to be restartable. Applications may use either GSAM or SHISAM databases, Fast Path databases, or DB2 tables to hold report records for later processing and/or printing. Each of these methods involves special — sometimes bizarre — considerations.

GSAM databases provide a convenient way of importing and exporting OS/VS files to and from IMS/VS. Although GSAM database changes are not written on the IMS/VS log, IMS/VS still keeps track of the relative record being processed and stores this information during the checkpoint or synchpoint process. Upon program restart, IMS/VS uses this relative record information to position the GSAM database at the proper record. GSAM databases defined with VSAM as their access method cannot, however, be repositioned by IMS/VS during restart; BSAM must therefore be used instead of VSAM.

SHISAM databases provide an even more secure form of report output media, because IMS/VS writes SHISAM database changes to the IMS/VS log. SHISAM allows the application designer to use the database's indexing capability to route or otherwise separate reports by type, depending on the value of the index. SHISAM databases can also be used for small reports produced by MPPs.

Fast Path databases may be a speedy method of storing large quantities of data, but not many technicians are familiar with it, and few applications exist as examples. Therefore, unless enough supporting technical expertise exists, I would recommend not using Fast Path.

Applications may be designed to store report records in a DB2 table for later printing or access. Users could then access portions of the report on-line. Employing a DB2 table allows the application designer great freedom in designing report delivery criteria, as well as in designing security considerations.

It is probably not wise to store large reports in DB2 tables. If doing so becomes necessary nonetheless, a fast way of doing it is to preload the table with empty rows, using the DB2 LOAD utility. Records can then be placed in the table using UPDATE rather than INSERT SQL statements. UPDATE is significantly faster in this situation because VSAM would not have to format control intervals and control areas. In addition, index maintenance will not be necessary. Such formatting and maintenance is done during the insertion of records during LOAD execution.

Deadlock Detection and Resolution

We now come to the most interesting feature of BMPs in the IMS/VS-DB2 environment.

In a BMP environment IMS/VS resolves a deadlock situation by rolling back IMS/VS and DB2 resources and returning control to the application. If the application was trying to access an IMS/VS resource, the call will return an *FD* in the status code for the Program Control Block (PCB) used in the call. If a DB2 resource was instead being accessed, the application would receive an SQLCODE of -911. In both cases, IMS/VS and DB2 would roll back database updates to the previous point of consistency, the synchpoint, before returning control to the application.

In a CICS/VS-DB2 environment the deadlock situation is even more interesting. CICS applications that access DB2 are defined in the Resource Control Table (RCT) with a parameter specifying whether or not CICS and DB2 should roll back resource updates to the previous synchpoint before returning to the application. If so, an SQLCODE of -911 is returned. If not, the SQLCODE is -913. CICS application designers therefore have more options available for handling deadlock situations.

Application designers must take these particular deadlock situations into account. They signify not fatal errors but simply that the application has encountered a deadlock, which may no longer even exist. If not, the program may be able to retry processing and continue with execution with no further problems. However, the lock causing the deadlock may be a long-term one. In this case, the program will enter an infinite deadlock and rollback loop. To avoid looping in this fashion, application programs should keep track of the number of times they encounter a deadlock situation, indicated by an IMS/VS FD status code or a DB2 SQLCODE of −911. After a suitable number of occurrences, the application should terminate with an error condition.

It is not clear from IMS/VS and DB2 reference manuals whether GSAM databases are in fact repositioned when execution resumes after a deadlock. In general, GSAM databases are repositioned only after a restart due to program abend. The program may then issue an XRST call, which will explicitly reposition the GSAM database as of the previous checkpoint. Unfortunately, trying a subsequent XRST call, to force repositioning, will result in a U102 abend.

When continuing an execution after a deadlock, IMS/VS restores the values of variables stored in the checkpoint work areas. The program may, however, be knee deep in logic. In other words the program must explicitly check for deadlocks in any program section that attempts to access an IMS/VS or DB2 resource. The very same check is likewise required in sections at higher levels that also invoke such sections. Being able to perform this check requires that application designers anticipate the logic needed to monitor the situation.

Summary

We have here covered some of the most important aspects of the IMS/VS-DB2 environment. Here are the three that seem most significant:

- Resolution of any in-doubt URs
- Alternatives for storing report data
- Necessity for batch message application programs to handle deadlock situations.

In-doubt URs are created by IMS/VS or DB2 failure, or the failure of both, during commit processing. Application programs can be made less vulnerable to this problem by judicious selection of checkpoint procedures and resource allocation. Although no hard-and-fast rules exist, programs should get their checkpoint frequency from an external source. This practice will make program testing and tuning easier. The impact may also be lessened if you design resource access to minimize table and tablespace locks and database record enqueuing.

Several alternatives for report media can be found in the IMS/VS-DB2 environment. In general, small reports should be produced by nonresponse MPPs and stored in DB2 tables. Doing so allows for maximum flexibility. Use BMPs for somewhat larger reports, and place them on GSAM databases. Reports with multiple routing or their own breakdown requirements can be stored on a SHISAM database, with an application program using the index to perform subsetting.

Deadlock is usually the exception rather than the rule. However, in a large on-line system the possibility of deadlock may be significant. BMP application designers must consider deadlock resolution as part of necessary program overhead. The need for it will change estimated programming and testing times and may require some creative testing procedures. The maintenance of such programs may be especially difficult, because adding a single IMS/VS database call or SQL statement may require massive coding changes. Program and design documentation must take this difficulty into account.

Finally, the implementation of recovery coding for deadlock situations may be difficult to test. Consider the problems involved in creating a situation where two applications are forced into a deadlock. One—brute force—method of testing an update application is first to go into the Query Management Facility (QMF) and issue a query that retrieves all the rows in a given table. Assuming that the table contains more than about twenty-five rows, this query will require several screens in QMF. Until the last screen has been reached, or until the QMF user issues a RELEASE QUERY command, QMF holds a "share" lock on the table. The update application will now be locked out of updating the table, and it should encounter either a deadlock or a "resource not available" condition.

Application design in the IMS/VS-DB2 environment is more complicated than in either environment alone. Designers must therefore keep their wits about them and be cautious and thorough.

SQL TECHNIQUES IN IMS PROGRAMS

This section deals with using SQL in IMS programs. Although most of the information herein deals directly with DB2, IMS application designers also should take it into account, because future business applications may be converted from IMS to DB2. Worse still, potential systems may even require concurrent access to both IMS and DB2 databases.

Checkpoint Logic

Many IMS programs include checkpoint logic, either to release held resources or to handle recovery or restart after the abnormal termination of a program.

An IMS program that contains DB2 statements must deal with an additional complication, the allocating and releasing of DB2 resources. Such resources are usually acquired through the use of locks, which are released when DB2 does a commit. In an IMS-DB2 program, the DB2 commit happens during an IMS checkpoint. This step takes place as part of a two-phase commit (discussed earlier in this chapter). The major concern for the application analyst is that commit processing forces all open cursors to be closed.

The DB2 cursor is the method used in application programs to access single rows of a result table. Remember that DB2 processes such queries using set logic, under which all results passed back to applications are in the form of tables. Rather than requiring some kind of variable-length mechanism for a program to secure the results of a query, DB2 permits the following process:

1. As part of static storage, the program defines a SELECT statement, using a DECLARE CURSOR statement.

2. During program execution the cursor is OPEN-ed. This stage then causes DB2 to begin evaluating the original statement defined by the cursor. At this time DB2 may or may not create the complete result table.

3. The program next issues a FETCH command against the opened cursor. This procedure causes DB2 to return the first row of the result table to the program.

4. Succeeding rows of the result table are now obtained, using a FETCH command.

5. After the last row is fetched, DB2 informs the program through the value of the SQLCODE that the end of the result table has been reached. The program now CLOSEs the cursor.

This process becomes much more complicated if a checkpoint must be taken after cursor OPEN and before cursor CLOSE. Because the cursor must be closed for the checkpoint (commit) to take place, it must then be reopened after the checkpoint. If the cursor is simply OPEN-ed, however, the entire result table is recreated. This function is, after all, what the program is requesting by opening the cursor.

Imagine an SQL SELECT statement that returns a result table of 10,000 rows. If a checkpoint is taken every 1,000 rows, the 10,000-row result table will be recreated ten times. This practice is noticeably wasteful of resources.

To avoid this scenario, the original DECLARE CURSOR statement must be expanded. Typical applications for this purpose define the query by giving it an additional predicate in the WHERE clause specifying that it create an ordered result table having key values greater than the value in some host variable. This variable is then set to the value found in the last row FETCH-ed. Thus, in our imaginary example, result tables of 10,000, then 9,000, and so on, to 1,000 rows will be created. This result is somewhat better, but not much. Another alternative would be to save the entire result table in either an IMS database or a permanent DB2 table before going ahead with processing. In this case, however, a program abend at any point could create recovery and restart problems.

There is no completely satisfactory answer to this problem, but application designers can still avoid most of its attendant problems by being careful in their query formulation.

Locking and Data Contention

There are several options regarding the way locking is implemented in IMS and DB2. The usual arrangement seems to be to use the required IMS Resource Lock Manager (IRLM) for DB2 and Database Recovery Control (DBRC) for IMS/VS. If IMS resources need to be shared among applications and other subsystems, however, IMS usually uses IRLM. In this case DB2 and IMS can share the same IRLM, though doing so is sometimes not recommended, "for performance reasons." Although these reasons are not explicitly stated, they include considerations of lock duration and timeouts. (A detailed discussion of lock managers and how they work is beyond the scope of this book. For a more complete treatment, refer to the appropriate IBM manuals.) System administrators wanting different parameters used for IMS/VS and DB2 resources will use two IRLMs. Note that defining an IRLM takes lots of tedious grunt-work. I personally don't recommend doing it twice.

Adding DB2 to the equation changes the way that locking and contention are handled. Now programs can be informed through a status code or SQLCODE that a deadlock has been resolved and the program's database updates have been rolled back to the previous commit point. This situation, discussed earlier in this chapter, must be handled by additional program logic or database and table structuring.

One way of reducing the threat of deadlock is to use collision fields. A collision field is a special field in an IMS segment, or a column in a DB2 table, whose value indicates whether the remainder of the data in the segment or row are available for use. An application requiring one or more segments or rows first accesses and changes the values of the collision fields to some value indicating that it is in use. Once this has been done successfully the application can continue, knowing that all the necessary data will be available. The collision fields would be reset back to "available" after processing has been completed.

The disadvantages of collision fields include the following:

- They take up additional space, which can be prohibitive in large segments or tables.
- Using them may almost double the amount of I/O done by the DBMS, because segments are retrieved more than once.
- Program size increases because programs are required to hold segments or rows in memory for simultaneous updating.
- Collision fields may create deadlocking on the collision fields themselves.

Another solution to the contention problem is that of using control tables. A control table implemented in DB2 would contain one row for every requested resource in the system. Programs wishing to access these resources would proceed as follows:

- By accessing rows of the control table corresponding to required resources for update purposes.
- Setting each row to indicate "resource in use."
- Storing the rows back in the control table.
- Releasing locks on the control table, perhaps by doing a checkpoint.

At this point the control table is now available to other users, and it is indicating that some resources are in use. Regrettably, there are many disadvantages to this method:

- A program abend during resource processing leaves the control table indicating "resource(s) in use" when in reality they are not.
- The control table becomes highly volatile, making performance and recovery a problem.
- These tables can cause contention problems.

Despite these disadvantages, having a control table appears to be a popular method for reducing or avoiding resource locking problems. I strongly recommend against using them, however. Instead, use good application design.

Ad Hoc Processing in an On-line Environment

In general, IMS systems are designed with transaction processing in mind. Most of the common structured design methodologies consider work both in terms of process flow and data flow. Relational modeling and ad hoc processing are concepts foreign to most IMS professionals.

The best advice concerning whether or not to do ad hoc processing in an on-line environment is simply, do not. Although DB2 is admittedly still in its infancy, on-line performance suffers because there is such a profusion of interfacing subsystems and such a lack of well-optimized access path selection. There are several alternatives to developing on-line ad hoc systems, which are described below.

- Take production data, offload it to a separate system, and use ad hoc queries in this system. In this manner, any query performance problems will not adversely affect other on-line systems. IBM's Query Management Facility (QMF) can be used in this regard.

- Use the Resource Limit Facility to limit the hogging of resources by ad hoc queries.

- Prohibit on-line updating. This is not as terrible as it sounds. Allow updates to be entered on-line, but batch them for processing at a later time, presumably when the system is less fully loaded. This option may be unacceptable in a twenty-four-hour on-line environment.

- Give users distributed processing capabilities. IBM's Enhanced Connectivity Facility (ECF) and Host Database View (HDBV) program products allow, say, PC users to download production DB2 tables to a microcomputer, select the required data for processing, update the tables locally on the PC and, finally, upload the result tables to the mainframe. The point is that offloading CPU and DASD consumption from mainframe to PC isolates other on-line systems from the process, allowing them to perform better.

Time and Date

The addition of DB2 and its associated built-in SQL functions to a program permits it to access time-of-day and date information from DB2. Using this feature should be avoided if at all possible. Not only is it inefficient to use a powerful database management system to get today's date, but DB2 must return it as the response to a query. Since the FROM clause is required in the DB2 SELECT statement, getting the time of day or date requires accessing a DB2 table, despite the fact that the table is never referenced. (Some shops that still insist on getting the date in this fashion have defined for themselves a special table called the STUPID_TIME table to use for this purpose.)

There are several alternatives available for accessing the time and date. Most programming languages have their own facilities or reserved words for accessing these. The I/O-PCB in an IMS program will return the date and time when a message was queued for a given transaction. Perhaps the best solution would be having an in-house assembler subroutine that would invoke the appropriate operating system routine.

Variable-Length Data

Although IMS allows databases to have variable-length segments, they are not common. Shops using DB2, however, always seem to define some columns with the VARCHAR attribute. This means that table rows are implicitly understood to be of variable length. This characteristic has a great impact on the way DB2 does its logging.

A general rule for DB2 logging of table updates is that DB2 logs the first changed byte through the last changed byte in the row. Because a row containing a VARCHAR column has a Row Length Prefix field at the beginning of the row, we thus conclude that changing the length of a VARCHAR column causes DB2 to log from the beginning of the row (remember that the Row Length Prefix has changed) through the last changed byte (the end of the row, since the length change has shifted succeeding columns one way or the other).

Referential Integrity

Referential Integrity (RI) usually is not a problem in IMS. By default, deleting a segment automatically means also deleting its physical children. However, in DB2 this is not always the case. DB2 tables can be defined using primary key and foreign key relationships having *delete rules* so that some new options become possible:

- Deletion of a parent row in one table may be prohibited if any related child rows exist in another table.
- Deletion of a parent row in one table may cause a related child row in another table to have its key value set to NULL.
- Deletion of a parent row in one table may cause one or more related child rows in another table to be deleted. This effect may be cascaded, causing further rows in other tables to be deleted, and so forth.

These options are discussed more fully in the appropriate IBM DB2 manuals. The important thing to remember here is that IMS-based applications are usually written with the built-in assumption that the DBMS will handle RI issues. The addition of DB2 tables and associated logic may then mean that applications must hard-code this logic. This requirement is especially true in hybrid applications with related IMS and DB2 structures.

Using the EXPLAIN Facility

The EXPLAIN facility of DB2 gives the designer and programmer a look at the access path that DB2 has chosen for a selected SQL statement. The EXPLAIN statement is commonly used in the SPUFI environment for single SQL statements. Alternatively, one can specify EXPLAIN(YES) during plan binding to explain all SQL statements for a particular plan.

Before using EXPLAIN it is necessary to create a table into which DB2 will put the results of the process. After execution, this plan table will contain a row for every query or subquery in the original SQL statement. The meanings of the columns in the EXPLAIN table are interpreted in the IBM DB2 manuals, as well as in various DB2 books on the market. Here, let us concentrate on the things EXPLAIN will *not* tell you.

Indexes and Foreign Keys

EXPLAIN will not inform you if a plan will use a particular index to access a foreign key. (For definitions of primary and foreign keys, see the discussions of Referential Integrity in the DB2 Application Programming manual.)

Use of Sequential Prefetch

Sequential prefetch is a performance feature of DB2. Generally speaking, if the optimizer determines that a tablespace scan will take place that will span over forty pages, it will turn on the sequential prefetch bit for that plan. During query execution if DB2 determines that sequential prefetch is permitted, based on the availability of system resources, it will use it for that plan. During execution, after sixteen pages have been synchronously read, DB2 will initiate a prefetch of pages 32–47. The assumption is that by the time the program gets up to reading page 32, it will already be in the buffer pool. (For more information on this feature, see the appropriate IBM DB2 manual.) EXPLAIN will not tell you if the query in question can in fact use sequential prefetch.

Predicate Evaluation Sequence

Some SQL queries have multiple predicates in the WHERE clause in the SELECT statement. EXPLAIN will not tell you the order in which it evaluates the predicates to determine the access path chosen.

Statistics and Assumptions

The DB2 catalog contains statistical information about all the tables in the system. In particular, it keeps data regarding key cardinality, or the number of unique values in a column, the number of rows in a table, and other measurements. These statistics are not updated automatically; to create them you must run the RUNSTATS utility. Until you do, DB2 will continue to use certain assumptions regarding the range and distribution of values of certain columns.

These statistics are then used by the optimizer at bind time to determine the chosen access path to be used by queries. Invalid or out of date statistics, or none at all, may cause the optimizer to select an inefficient or costly access path. EXPLAIN does not inform you which statistics or assumptions were used by the optimizer.

IMPLEMENTING A RELATIONAL DBMS: WHAT COULD GO WRONG?

During the last several years I have been involved with many clients who have implemented or were considering implementing a relational DBMS (RDBMS), usually DB2, for their mainframe applications. In almost every case, these customers made one or more mistakes during this process. They later described these mistakes as learning experiences to make the memory of them less painful.

This first section explores the various problems these people encountered during the process of implementing a relational DBMS, and how many of the mistakes could easily have been avoided. The first set of problems involves the reasons behind the decision to purchase a RDBMS. The second set describes what sometimes happened afterward.

Common Pre-Implementation Mistakes

Suppose that your installation is considering installing a relational DBMS, say, IBM's DB2. What could go wrong?

Choosing a Relational DBMS for the Wrong Reasons

Many clients choose a relational DBMS because it just seems the thing to do. Simply because a DBMS is relational, or at least claims to be relational, does not necessarily mean that it is the correct choice.

To choose DB2 as a DBMS simply because it is relational is like buying a hammer and then looking for nails to pound with it. Purchasers should first define the job they want to accomplish, then, after thorough analysis, determine which products to buy.

An analogy can be drawn here to the difference between people who buy cars and those who buy transportation. Some people would consider choosing only between a Chevrolet and a Cadillac; they are purchasing cars. Others might choose among riding the bus, buying a Chevrolet, or acquiring a Chevrolet with a chauffeur. These people are purchasing transportation.

Failing to Perceive the Coming Staff Evolution

Computer-assisted software engineering (CASE) is now coming of age. Soon integrated tools will be available that will be capable of automating every phase of the systems development life cycle. Developers will be using these tools on personal computers along with fourth- and fifth-generation languages, local area networks (LANs), and distributed systems.

Programmers and analysts will eventually require less skill in such traditional areas as procedural programming (COBOL), applications expertise, human-to-human communications, and business systems. More emphasis will be placed on prototyping, knowing PC-based software, data modeling, and third-party software. This observation applies to present as well as future staff.

This disruption in the knowledge and skill profiles of DP staff will require revolutionary new ways of dealing with this situation. How will managers structure salaries if two-year people come to have more valuable skills than ten-year people? Which staff members will be trained, and in what? Should staff be separated into maintenance and development departments, or be commingled?

Managers must plan now for ways to adapt to these changes before implementing a relational system. The entire way that applications development is being done will change, which will affect staff skills, training, and performance.

Necessary Training Not Available

Although it is generally recognized that it is easier to learn SQL coding than, say, IMS coding, to agree on this is still a far cry from saying that less total training will be required after implementing DB2. Organizations using DB2 for new applications will now have to change the way they develop systems.

The relational model is not new. Unfortunately, few shops have really bought in to this nonhierarchical way of looking at data and processes. The result may be the development of hierarchical systems using DB2 as the DBMS. In this way any potential benefits of the relational model will be negated.

Before implementing a relational DBMS, organizations must first acknowledge the usefulness of the relational model. In addition, since little training is available in this area organizations must be prepared to make a commitment to developing internal education or searching out whatever is available in the marketplace.

Insufficient DASD Space

In any type of conversion, developers must make allowances for extra DASD requirements. These needs include having space for copies of production files, sort work space, database reallocation, and the like. The implementation of DB2 requires just a bit more thought, however.

One of the biggest differences DBAs notice between IMS and DB2 is the relative sizes of their buffer pools. In IMS a two or three megabyte buffer pool is considered average. In DB2, however, buffer pools of twenty-five to thirty megabytes are not uncommon. This order of magnitude difference in buffer pool size really comes into play when implementers come to allocate DASD space for paging.

Another common occurrence when implementing DB2 is that organizations typically want to convert databases from IMS-DB to DB2 tables. This process may not be as simple as that of running DXT. Because several systems may interface with the databases in question, it may be necessary to have versions of both the IMS and the DB2 databases coexist until the conversion has been completed. Such coexistence will require having both DBMSs, each with its own logs, catalogs, database image copies, backups, and so on.

In other words, if you plan on implementing DB2 and converting IMS databases, your long-term DASD requirements may need some looking into. Plan on adding plenty of cushion in your DASD space estimates.

Outdated Systems Design Practices

Most analysts are familiar by now with traditional structured design and programming methodologies and their attendant diagramming techniques: Warnier-Orr, Yourdon, Jackson, HIPO, DeMarco, and the like. Most of these methods share the following features: 1. They assumed that the system being designed or modeled had files that could be accessed sequentially or randomly, with keys; and 2. they assumed that the logic processes acting on data files were essentially hierarchical.

With the appearance of the relational data model and relational DBMSs these assumptions are no longer universally valid. Thus, systems based on relational models cannot be designed efficiently using older methodologies, because the fundamental assumptions underlying them are no longer true. What is needed is newer methodologies to define relational systems.

Such methodologies do exist today, but organizations are only slowly beginning to use them. This situation is due partly to a resistance to change but partly also because these new systems have not yet displayed track records to speak of. By far the biggest reason, though, is that most organizations' budgets preclude making the necessary investments in hardware, software, and personnel training.

Before implementing a relational DBMS, look long and hard at the way you intend to develop the relational systems. If you plan on using a set of standard systems development tools, determine if they will be able to handle relational systems.

Failing to Take Advantage of the PC Environment

This oversight is not really a mistake. It is, however, an opportunity that most organizations could take more advantage of. Today more and more systems operate on-line in real time and require twenty-four-hour availability. Familiar examples are automated bank teller machines, airline reservation systems, and industrial process control systems.

In such environments application developers may threaten the performance of a production system by their very existence on the mainframe. This problem may occur either because developers consume valuable CPU cycles, allocate or lock the necessary DASD, or cause other system bottlenecks. These situations can easily be remedied, though, by providing developers with PC-based tools for designing, coding, and testing.

Many PC-based tools already exist now and are in fact in use for systems development. Common integrated CASE tools assist users and analysts in prototyping applications, developing program logic, and sometimes even in generating program code. Other tools let developers copy production files and databases to a PC, allowing programmers to test programs there with actual data. This transferring relieves the mainframe CPU, lessens the need for having DASD test files and databases, and protects the mainframe from inadvertent outages resulting from overzealous testing.

In addition to these advantages, using PC-based tools can provide the DP staff with further productivity-enhancing facilities. Some examples of these would be local area networks for code and data sharing, intraproject communication with electronic mail, automated task and project management reporting, and word processing facilities for documentation.

Failing to Investigate Third-party Products

One of the most common mistakes made by developers is not realizing that implementing a database management system requires implementing also all the associated security, authority, performance monitoring, and auditing systems that go with it. In general, systems used on another DBMS are not transferrable to the new one.

The most useful tools, and those most often purchased, are the monitoring and performance tools. These utilities may monitor system performance, application or transaction throughput, or other system attributes. Other tools may model the DBMS structure or access path strategies, giving analysts and programmers helpful advice for program and subsystem development.

Another set of tools handles security management and may coordinate the granting and revoking of authorities to access databases, programs, or terminals. Organizations planning to implement a relational DBMS should include in their budgets the investigation and acquisition of all these types of tools.

Failing to Plan for Future Systems Changes

Maintenance happens. DP departments recognize this fact of life by forming maintenance teams or allocating a percentage of their budget to maintaining current systems. Somehow this basic need seems to be forgotten when a new DBMS is brought in-house, however. If you begin developing systems using a relational model and a relational DBMS, you must plan for upgrades and enhancements sooner or later.

You must not only plan for how to maintain these new applications but also realize that this type of maintenance will be different from that for older systems. In general, new versions of IMS, for example, have not yet necessitated significant changes in older IMS applications. However, new versions of DB2—from V1R2 to V1R3 to V2R1 in less than two years—involved numerous performance improvements, the adding of features, and a wealth of third-party products. This degree of change meant a radical shift in the way DB2 applications had to be maintained.

One last consideration is that of distributed database systems. If you implement such a system, what mechanisms will you be in place for local DBAs to communicate performance information? How will local outages affect the whole network? And who will be in charge of maintaining, and paying for the maintenance of, distributed applications?

Processing Transactions by Using Ad Hoc Queries

The real power of relational systems lies in their ability to organize and respond to "what if" questions, which is the so-called ad hoc environment. In this environment users ask ad hoc questions directly of the system, needing no understanding of its underlying physical database structure.

Two factors have slowed the realization of this concept. First, systems designers seem to be developing in, or converting typical transaction processing systems into, the relational environment. Second, the suboptimal performance of the ad hoc environment to date has made genuine ad hoc systems perform poorly.

These two developments have led both to inefficient systems and to on-line users having the power to bring systems to their knees. Users in this environment have to fight for CPU cycles and struggle with poorly designed systems.

If you intend to implement a relational DBMS, anticipate and prevent these problems. Design the ad hoc systems with the relational DBMS, and leave the transaction processing systems on the old DBMS.

Misusing the On-line Environment

Another feature of relational DBMSs is called their set-at-a-time processing. Answers to queries may consist of an entire set of table rows where the number of rows is unknown before request submission. In an on-line environment it may not be possible to present a requester with an entire solution at once, however. The ability to do screen scrolling, for example, must be implemented either by saving the entire solution somewhere, thereby consuming DASD or other resources, or by reissuing the request for each screen, thus displaying only a portion of the entire solution at a time.

Such inefficiencies can affect other mission critical applications in an enterprise's DP environment. Keep this in mind when converting older on-line transaction processing systems.

Common Post-Implementation Mistakes

Let's say you have implemented DB2 or some other relational DBMS. Now you are ready to begin writing new applications or converting old ones. What can go wrong?

Worrying about Performance (It's Too Late!)

The problem with performance measurement is that numbers are absolute, whereas a program's perceived performance is relative. Until you define it, performance is an elusive animal—hard to catch and, once caught, difficult to tame. The basic problem is one of defining how much performance is good, and what do we measure? If performance is poor, what can we do to improve it, and by how much?

A healthy concern about the performance of relational DBMSs is justified, as few installations seem to live up to the expectations held up for them. Benchmarks do not tell the whole story. Until an RDBMS is actually installed, it may be impossible to predict its performance.

It is wise to anticipate that performance will not be quite as good as advertised. In addition, be prepared to do MVS tuning before tuning the applications. Having either insufficient DASD for paging or 95 percent CPU utilization will give poor DBMS performance regardless of the DBMS that is chosen.

Not Budgeting for Monitoring Tools and Other Tools

There are some specialized third-party software tools to complement a relational DBMS. The main subjects available are accounting, performance monitoring, change control, and systems development. These tools are essential for getting the best use out of any DBMS.

Unfortunately, certain accounting mechanisms in DB2 make it somewhat difficult with that system to charge back resource usage to specific users. In addition, relational systems may need their own completely separate change control mechanism. For example, DB2 plan updates and the associated rebind process need to be controlled.

Another area of concern is training. Operations staff must be trained to use any DBMS or system performance monitoring tools. These tools are simple to use, but they require detailed knowledge of system internals to interpret correctly their results or recommendations.

Having Insufficient DASD Space

This problem first appeared before implementation. Then, installations that planned on having additional DASD requirements before implementing their relational DBMS found that they had underestimated their requirements, sometimes by a factor of two or more.

In addition to there being simply a lack of sufficient space, some installations neglected to consider certain special DASD features. Some IBM 3350 DASD models have several fixed-head cylinders that can be accessed with no delay in head movement. Another example is the IBM 3990 DASD cache controller. This device can hold several tracks of data in a cache for later writing to the disk, while still allowing the channel to continue with data transfer.

Failing to Involve the Vendor

Too many systems departments have gurus with an "I can do it myself" attitude. Although this approach is sometimes laudable, it can lead to unacceptable system downtime while these self-styled experts attempt to solve problems. In some cases the hardware or software vendors will have already encountered such problems and be aware of solutions.

Another area where vendors should be involved is in system tuning. Vendors have a stake in system performance — they want their products to look good and perform well. Involving vendor personnel in application or system tuning will take a load off your staff and may well prove a valuable learning experience. Furthermore, if product performance remains poor, perhaps the vendor can be convinced to take their product back and offer a full refund.

Lack of Outside Technical Specialists

Businesses need to manage risk. Managers faced with a backlog of applications to develop may sometimes resort to bringing in outside services such as outsourcing facilities or consultants.

The advantages of these services are as follows:

- No permanent office space needs to be assigned.
- Such firms often warrant or guarantee their work.
- DP departments can get qualified help quickly, without resorting to a recruiting and hiring process with its corresponding learning curve.
- Outside service personnel can usually be found that have specific applications experience.

There are some disadvantages to bringing in outsiders, however. Any experience gained by these services leaves with their personnel when the task at hand is finished. And such services may cost more than some companies are willing to pay.

Implementing a new DBMS may require that developers come up to speed quickly. The best way to develop systems quickly using new technology is to begin the process with the current staff, then import the required coding and testing expertise from an outside service. With many relational DBMSs, however, few qualified personnel will exist. This shortage will make it difficult for businesses to develop new relational applications quickly.

Before committing your staff to a substantial amount of new development, check into the availability of services that can provide personnel experienced in the new DBMS. Although they may be expensive, they will help you manage risk and assist you in justifying the acquisition of the new technology.

Attempting to Fool the RDBMS

In the recent past developers have too often been forced to outthink the RDBMS optimization software. This product is the part of the DBMS that analyzes relational requests and determines the optimal database access path. The optimizers of most early versions of relational DBMSs were not very efficient. Developers thus had to structure their queries in ways they felt would be most efficient, a process called micro-optimization.

As RDBMSs evolved they became much more efficient. Unfortunately, the state of the systems developer's art has not kept pace with this trend. Except for the most recently published books, efficient relational query tactics and strategies are still being developed. Many present relational systems have embedded queries that may well become less efficient as the tricks used fool the later versions of the RDBMS, thus becoming less efficient.

Let the DBMS and the optimizer do their work. Structure relational queries using common sense, and resist the temptation to add anything to make the optimizer more efficient.

Doing Bottom-Up Performance Tuning

The first place some system programmers and DBAs look for performance enhancements in a relational system is in its applications, which is backwards. Performance in a DBMS is dependent upon the performance of the operating system and its teleprocessing subsystem; *they* must be tuned first.

The first step should be to tune the operating system. First reduce DASD device contention and CPU utilization, then check the dispatching priorities and analyze memory usage. Consider the possibility of additional DASD, expanded storage, virtual storage allocation, or of adding CPUs. Problems in these areas will greatly affect the DBMS.

Next, analyze the IMS, CICS, and TSO performance. Consider the use of IRLM and/or DBRC and their associated parameters. Investigate the available security and authorization schemes. Then check the RDBMS subsystem. Study its buffer pool allocation and usage, the DASD work space usage, and the available sort space. Determine whether any special features can be used, such as the sequential prefetch facility in DB2.

Finally, study application performance as the last area to be checked. The point is that problems in the areas just discussed may make any application performance enhancements ineffective or useless.

Allowing Disorganized Implementation and Maintenance

Implementing an RDBMS is not as simple as just hanging installation tapes and copying files. One important area often overlooked is that of performance monitoring. Any major DBMS product should come with a profusion of optional traces and performance reports. Someone must monitor these features and either make or recommend changes to DBMS parameters.

Another area often neglected is system maintenance. What happens when a new release of the DBMS comes out, with perhaps several performance enhancements? Do all the systems cut over to the new DBMS, or is it to be benchmarked first? Answers to these questions may require having a new breed of systems programming staff with specialized expertise in the RDBMS.

Lack of Standards

All development and maintenance environments require having standards to minimize confusion and control change. Bringing in a new DBMS means installing an entirely new set of standards and procedures. This process includes dealing with naming standards, change control, security and authorization control, and database design.

The new RDBMS may be so radically different from the older one it is replacing that the development of relational systems slows to a halt for lack of standards. And without standards, new applications will be impossible to maintain, but developing these standards will take some time.

Designing and Converting Hierarchical Systems

Because many developers are not familiar with the relational model they may think that conversion from, say, IMS to DB2 will require minimal programming changes. (After all, we're just converting from one DBMS to another, aren't we?)

Unfortunately, hierarchical systems are not readily convertible to relational ones. The most common problem is one of access path selection. Hierarchical DBMSs require that an application specify the access path as part of a request. This may be determined by the application at execution time. Relational DBMSs have an optimizer that resolves the access path for the user, usually at *bind* time. Thus, converting from a hierarchical to a relational DBMS may prove impossible, or at least incredibly difficult.

What Did They Learn?

Probably the most important lesson to be learned here is that a relational DBMS can in fact be implemented, but only if the implementer is willing to spend the necessary time up front. Here are two final checklists.

Pre-Implementation Checklist

- Don't forget to cost justify the RDBMS.
- Get ready for the coming staff evolution.
- Make sure that all necessary training is available.
- Analyze future DASD space requirements.
- Study current systems design practices and replace them with, or redevelop, relational design strategies.
- Take advantage of the PC environment.
- Investigate third-party software products.
- Plan for future systems changes.
- Don't do transaction processing using ad hoc queries.
- Don't misuse the on-line environment.

Post-Implementation Checklist

■ Estimate RDBMS performance and track it after installation.
■ Budget for monitoring tools and other tools.
■ Involve the vendor in the process of installation and performance measurement.
■ Investigate the availability of outside technical specialists.
■ Do not attempt to fool the RDBMS.
■ Do not do bottom-up performance tuning.
■ Organize the procedures for system implementation and maintenance.
■ Develop standards.
■ Evaluate the design and conversion of hierarchical systems.

THE FUTURE: IMS IN A DB2 WORLD

IMS in a Distributed, Relational Environment

How long will IMS hang on? Will it be able to meet organizations' needs in tomorrow's environment? If you pick up any recent data processing technical periodical and thumb through the articles you see relational databases, relational processing, relational integrity—relational is the DP buzzword for the coming decade. Another development is that future DBMS environments will be not only relational, but also distributed. Distributed data are sometimes defined as data that can be accessed by remote applications or users. This concept is then expanded to include the accessing of multiple remote and local databases or systems by a single application or user.

Many database management systems qualify as relational, to a certain degree, and there are many corresponding nonprocedural languages available to access such databases, as SQL, for example. Some installations have jumped on the bandwagon and implemented relational database management systems, intending to use them for relational distributed applications. Regrettably, there are still some common mistakes being made regarding such implementations, discussed earlier in this chapter. More conservative installations have by now taken the approach that distributed relational applications and systems are well within current DBMS technology.

Relational IMS?

Interestingly, it is sometimes possible, though rarely feasible or efficient, to develop quasi-relational systems using IMS as the DBMS. All you have to do is to follow these simple rules:

- Implement relational tables as root-only HIDAM or HDAM databases.
- Define all columns as FIELDs in the DBD.
- Create a secondary index for each field used in a data access statement.
- Use field level sensitivity to control data access.

And there you have it.

Unfortunately, data integrity must also be handled by the application, along with access path selection, and optimization must be hard coded into the programs. Further limitations are that rows are only available one at a time, subselects are unavailable, JOIN, UNION, and DIFFERENCE operations must be coded by hand, and on and on. The point is that you must go to great lengths in IMS to come even close to a truly relational system. Why, then, do some installations end up with relational systems that do interface with coexisting IMS databases or applications? The answer is simply that they must do so to survive.

Converting Applications

Typically, the first thing IMS shops do after getting an RDBMS is to convert existing IMS applications to run with the new RDBMS. This is to be expected, for an investment in something like DB2 is a large one. It includes not only the acquisition of the DBMS software but also a need for additional DASD, performance and tuning software, further staff training and education, and perhaps new systems development methodologies.

Management cannot afford to begin developing major new applications using a new and untried DBMS environment without sufficient preparation. Because staff training is a must, DP managers in such a situation usually assign selected staff to small pilot projects for converting IMS applications to the new RDBMS. This procedure usually involves rewriting many programs, since the IMS-DB environment forces developers to code access path information into applications. This process may take some time, during which IMS databases and relational databases must coexist within the same system.

This conversion process thus parallels the development of legitimate relational applications. The database environment goes through a long-drawn-out transformation process in which IMS and relational databases, perhaps having identical data, slowly appear and disappear.

Distributed IMS?

There are several levels of distributed database processing, depending upon the number of remote systems to be accessed and the type of access required. These levels are usually termed, in ascending order of their sophistication, remote request, remote unit of work, distributed unit of work, and distributed request. Some examples of distributed systems existing today are airline reservation systems, automated teller machines serving distant banks, international electronic funds transfer (EFT), and electronic business data interchange (EBDI). All such distributed systems have at least the following trait in common: they have data stored at multiple locations that is accessed by local or remote users and applications.

Many IMS systems today are distributed, at least in terms of their access by remote users and ability to communicate with remote IMS and CICS systems. This access becomes possible using the multiple system coupling (MSC) or intersystem communication (ISC) features. (For a more complete description of these features, see Chapter 8.)

Multiple System Coupling

Multiple System Coupling (MSC) enables you to have transactions that were entered in one IMS system be processed in another. With MSC, responses to messages can be returned either to the terminals that entered the transactions or to other terminals. MSC allows IMS conversational programming, by using a SPA.

MSC connects multiple IMS subsystems to each other only. These subsystems may reside in different processors, though. The processing is transparent to the user and routing is automatic, based on the system definition parameters. Such processing also permits the steps of a conversation to be distributed over multiple IMS subsystems, which is transparent both to the source terminal operator and to each conversational step or application.

Intersystem Communication

Intersystem Communication (ISC) is a part of the IMS DC feature that allows an IMS subsystem to take part in an SNA subsystem connection called an application-to-application session, using LU6 protocols. ISC can connect an IMS application either to other IMS subsystems or to a CICS subsystem. The communication is between the application programs in the two subsystems. The subsystems themselves, called session partners, support the logical flow of data between applications. Message routing sometimes requires the involvement of the application to determine a message's destination. ISC also supports Fast Path and Message Format Service (MFS). Specific routing parameters can be overridden or modified with MFS.

Both MSC and ISC permit a user to route transactions and to distribute transaction processing. MSC is used primarily to distribute conversations among two or more IMS subsystems, thereby allowing resource sharing. ISC is typically used to connect IMS to CICS or to allow an application in one subsystem to use the services in another, such as a message queue or database.

In general, the IMS-to-IMS transaction communications using either of these features are transparent to the applications. Each IMS system defines its transactions as either *local* or *remote*. When an application sends a message, IMS checks the transaction code against its internal tables. If the transaction specified is local, IMS schedules it; if remote, IMS uses a link to route it.

This arrangement is satisfactory for remote requests or remote units of work, but higher levels of distributed processing are not supported. That is, unit-of-work commits, rollbacks, or synchpoint processing must be application driven. Doing so involves a high degree of cooperation between applications among many potential IMS systems and is difficult both to design and to tune.

Typical IMS Interfaces

Distributed systems connecting multiple IMS subsystems generally implement MSC links between communicating subsystems. This procedure allows message traffic to flow through the network while also allowing conversational processing to occur. Any linking to a CICS subsystem almost always requires an ISC link. Conversational processing with a CICS transaction will thus not be supported.

IMS systems in a distributed relational environment still exist today, but their numbers are dwindling. The restrictive nature of the features mentioned earlier is only the beginning; newer relational DBMSs are appearing with advanced distributed processing facilities. It will take several years to effect a complete conversion of existing systems, but until then IMS applications must coexist with their relational counterparts.

One last related subject needs discussion here: with IMS and relational databases existing simultaneously, how are distributed systems to be tuned?

Tuning Distributed IMS Systems

With IMS systems designed today that use currently existing distributed data, applications are forced to access the data in a less-than-optimal fashion. This restriction makes the job of DBAs most difficult. Not only must they optimize multiple databases at several sites across a remote user population, but it is also necessary to plan for any future relational applications, network changes, and DBMS migrations.

Making changes to the structure of an IMS database in a nondistributed environment usually involves bringing the system down, backing up the database, doing a number of unloads and reloads, and then testing the result.

In a distributed environment, however, you must also take into account the following factors:

- While the database is being processed, network users are locked out for the interval of the change.
- Remote applications must somehow be informed of any new structure, to prevent dynamic rebind.
- Certain other remote applications may also need to be restructured.
- All changes must be coordinated with other remote DBAs.
- Network security is affected for the duration of the change.
- Relational integrity concerns may affect applications across all communicating subsystems.

These considerations make it quite difficult to tune even a single database, let alone a combination of multiple systems across several processors. To do so, distributed applications should be developed in an environment allowing designers to gather meaningful performance measurement statistics. These figures can then be used to refine DBMS access, network utilization, and overall throughput.

The DBAs also need to provide to developers information about business data models and the current operating environment, during the analysis of requirements phase of system development. The DBA and the system designer share the responsibility for system modeling during the analysis and design phases, giving them a chance to measure the impact of the various distributed database design alternatives. The DBAs then coordinate with the designers during the testing phase, allowing them access to tuning and performance measurement tools.

Summary

Can IMS-based systems meet organizations' needs in tomorrow's environment? I submit that they cannot, for the reasons just discussed and now summarized.

- IMS applications cannot perform many types of relational data manipulations, those that it can simulate are highly inefficient. Data access paths must be chosen by the programmer, relational integrity checking must be coded into the application, and true set-level processing is not feasible.

- IMS systems can indeed be distributed, but not fully. Unit-of-work commits, rollbacks, and synchpoints must be controlled by applications. And there is no central coordination of distributed units of work, resulting in possible out-of-synch conditions among databases at multiple sites.

■ Distributed relational systems containing IMS subsystems can be tuned, but not easily. Sometimes local performance requirements will force sites to do local optimization. Security considerations may also compel a site to structure its data access and retrieval rules so that they become incompatible with those of other sites.

In conclusion, IMS will be inadequate for the distributed relational environments of the future. Businesses must plan for the inevitable now by migrating to relational database management systems and by designing applications that will allow access to distributed data.

IMS-to-DB2 MIGRATION

Some IS shops currently using IMS-DB as their database management system are now considering migrating from it to DB2. This change is not as straightforward as it might seem. Replacing hierarchical databases with DB2 tables is uncomplicated, though tedious, but unfortunately DB2 does not perform well yet in a purely transaction processing environment. Furthermore, present application systems were originally designed with hierarchical or network/plex database structures in mind. As a relational DBMS, DB2 thus requires an entirely different mindset, a completely different approach to system and application design.

To understand fully the complexities involved, let us review the various features of IMS, CICS, and DB2, with the different environments in which they are used. This analysis will lead us to a projection of future IS staff makeup and how it will affect application development.

IMS, CICS, and DB2 Release Features

It is instructive to compare the features of the various releases of IMS, CICS, and DB2 (see Table 9.2).

As can be seen, recent IMS and CICS releases have concentrated on functionality, whereas DB2 has emphasized performance. The reputation DB2 had for poor performance in early releases has by now been mostly overcome. Although DB2 is designed for the ad hoc environment, as in fact are most relational DBMSs, it is now able to perform fairly well in a transaction processing environment.

As companies find that DB2 will generally perform well in most environments, they will inevitably begin to migrate their database environment over to DB2. This process may take decades, for several reasons:

Table 9.2. CICS, IMS, and DB2 release features.

CICS Version 1, Release 7: July 1985

Virtual Storage Constraint Relief (VSCR) for
     Auto-Install
     Resource Definition On-line (RDO)
Startup/Init processes made more concurrent
Files now "open on first use"
TempStore and Transient Data formatted more efficiently
Local Shared Resource (LSR) pool now the default for
     VSAM buffers

CICS Version 2, Release 1: March 1989

Extended Recovery Facility (XRF) now above the line
Future releases will be MVS/ESA
Removal of support for macro level coding, BTAM, direct
     block addressing
Special CICS internal security (RACF)

IMS Version 1, Release 3: February 1984

DASD logging
Use of LAST for checkpoint-ID
Enhancements to Fast Path

IMS Version 2, Release 1: March 1986

Enhancements to Database Recovery Control (DBRC)
Various DASD log enhancements
BKO parameter available for dynamic batch backout
Support for CICS 1.7
Use of MVS/XA for IRLM

IMS Version 2, Release 2: July 1987

VSCR for IMS-DC
OSAM Sequential Buffering (SB)
Support for CICS/MVS 2.1
Off-line dump formatting
Changes to HD locking
Future releases will be MVS/ESA

Table 9.2 (Continued)

IMS Version 3, Release 1: October 1988

VSCR for DL/I
Log reduction and compression
DB control blocks and buffers above the line
VSAM and OSAM buffer pools above the line
High Speed Sequential Processing (HSSP) for DEDBs
Time Controlled Operations (TCO)
Split into Data Manager and Transaction Manager

DB2 Version 1, Release 3: June 1987

DATE, TIME, TIMESTAMP, and associated functions
Utility performance enhancements
Optimizer enhancements
VSAM Linear Dataset (LDS) support

DB2 Version 2, Release 1: October 1988

GRANT to groups of users
Dynamic SQL governor
CICS dynamic plan selection
Optimizer and lock manager enhancements
User update of system catalog columns
DBMS-controlled referential integrity
Segmented tablespaces
"Distributed processing"

DB2 Version 2, Release 2: September 1989

Distributed processing enhancements
Optimizer enhancements
Use of Data Facility Hierarchical Storage Manager (DFHSM)

- Hierarchical and network (CODASYL) databases cannot be easily converted to relational databases.

- Most IS shops have a backlog of applications in various stages of development, so they have no staff left to do database conversion or the massive application rewriting required.

- Many common hierarchical and network database management systems have special features not available in DB2.

On the other hand, as discussed earlier in this chapter, DB2 has several features of its own that make it suitable for IS applications of the future:

- DB2 includes referential integrity, at least up to a point.
- DB2 Version 2, Release 2, includes the beginnings of distributed processing features. These advances will be enhanced in later releases.

The most common scenario will no doubt be that companies will decide to migrate their IMS databases to DB2 tables, over a period of several years. New applications will henceforth be written using DB2 whenever possible. Maintenance and enhancements to existing applications will then involve converting databases and rewriting programs.

The IS Shop Moves into the Future

The DB2 environment of the future will be quite different from the IMS and CICS DP environments of today. What will such an environment be like, and what problems will an IS staff then face? What follows is a foreshadowing of things to come (see Table 9.3).

The Future Production Environment

Today's production environment is one of transaction processing. It is here that IMS and CICS excel. Indeed, it is estimated that several trillion lines of code are currently invested in COBOL transaction processing programs alone. However, the future will see a rise to prominence of the ad hoc environment. In it packaged software and modular systems will replace standard application development. What will be left to develop will be expert systems, perhaps based on artificial intelligence, to help business planners answer "what if?" questions. Relational database management systems are specifically designed for this environment.

Future Staff Responsibilities

An estimated almost 80 percent of a DP staff's hours are spent maintaining and enhancing existing software. This will change as more and more development tools become available, shortening the system development life cycle. System designers and application analysts will use such tools as rapid analysis, logical

Table 9.3. Comparison of IMS, CICS, and DB2 Information Systems environments.

Category	CICS and IMS	DATABASE 2
Production environment:	Transaction processing	Ad hoc queries
Staff primarily doing:	Maintenance	Development
Database environment:	Static	Dynamic
Sample applications Available?	Many	Few
Third-party software available?	Much	Little
Tuning aids available?	Many	Few
PC tools and applications available?	Few	Many

data modeling, prototyping, storyboarding, and integrated CASE tools to speed development. As systems shift from transaction processing to an ad hoc environment, systems development will accelerate.

The Future DBMS Environment

Most hierarchical and network/plex database structures share a common characteristic: they are relatively static. Therefore, database structural changes or data relationship changes require system redefinition. For IMS, changing a database structure by adding or lengthening a segment, rearranging the hierarchy, and the like require something like the following procedure:

■ Define the new structure.
■ Bring the system down.
■ Unload the current database in its appropriate form as image copy, a flat file, etc.
■ Delete the original structure's definition.
■ Create the new structure's definition.

- Allocate DASD space for the new database.
- Run the required reload, reorg, and resolution utilities.
- Bring the system back up.

All these steps may not be necessary in every case; nevertheless, having them still leads shops to create standards and procedures such as "system changes will be made only every other Saturday, and only if we receive the proper paperwork by the preceding Wednesday."

The DB2 database environment is, by contrast, markedly different. In DB2, columns can be added to tables while the system is up. The ALTER and DROP statements can be used to change various parameters affecting referential integrity, indexes, and the like. This dynamic environment is essential for the IS shop of the future. Even now we hear about twenty-four-hour system availability. As more and more shops make IMS data available on-line, the need for batch programs and the corresponding batch window to run them in dwindles.

Sample Applications

Analysts designing new IMS or CICS systems have at least one great advantage over their DB2 counterparts: there are almost always other, similar applications available for comparison. Often, an existing IMS application can provide a designer with information regarding performance, development time and cost, degree of user satisfaction, skill levels of analysts and programmers, and other useful information.

By comparison, the DB2 analyst has few if any such systems to study. This scarcity makes it difficult to estimate development time and system performance. Furthermore, since the risk of making mistakes from inexperience is higher in DB2, the developer must allow for an additional "fudge factor" in development time and consider the costs and disadvantages of delivering the system late and over budget.

Third-Party Software and Tuning Aids

Over the past two decades many software and hardware companies sprang up offering tools for IMS and CICS systems that IBM did not provide. Some of these offerings later became IBM program products and others, such as Abend-AID, exist to this day. These tools and tuning aids assisted DBAs and system administrators in monitoring system performance, analyzing problems, and cataloging and organizing system information.

Until recently there were few such tools available for DB2 systems. This shortage was due in part to the rapid changes in succeeding releases. In the future, more and more such tools will appear to support the DB2 environment.

PC Tools and Applications

In today's environment there are few PC-based applications, and not many PC tools. This does not mean they do not exist, just that many companies are simply unaware of them or are unwilling to use them. Remember that IBM came out with their first PC in 1981, after IMS and CICS had been around for more than a decade.

Remember that DB2 is a relational database management system. Relational systems, based on set-at-a-time processing, are fundamentally different from transaction processing systems. As a consequence, systems analysis and design are done quite differently in relational systems. PC development tools will assist designers in carrying out this responsibility.

PC-based software, especially CASE tools, are becoming more and more common in the business environment. Some experts feel that these tools will become a necessity if businesses are to survive in the future.

The IS Environment of the Future

Based on the scenario we have just seen, what will the IS environment look like in the future?

Future Staff Profile

The IS staff of the future will need fewer technical and interpersonal skills.

DB2 isolates the analyst and programmer from many physical considerations, so knowledge of the database's structure or of the physical database's internal operations is unnecessary. Communication and presentation skills will be less important in DB2. Communication is important in today's environment as analysts meet with users to develop system requirements. In the future, however, prototyping and rapid analysis will greatly reduce this requirement.

Managing Development Efforts

Systems development in the future will have to deal with maintenance and enhancements to the "immature" systems being developed today. Many shops are now maintaining old, poorly designed systems because of the prohibitive cost of redesign. Future maintenance efforts will need to concentrate on the relational systems being built today by inexperienced staff with no sample applications experience to draw upon, designed the same way that transaction-processing systems were decades ago.

Training and Education

A completely different type of training program will be required for the future IS professional. The basic skills of reading, writing, and speaking will become less important. These abilities will be replaced by knowledge of and proficiency with PC-based CASE tools, logical data modeling, and prototyping. Such training must be hands-on, however. Lectures and reading may be fine for simple information transfer, but the tools of the future will require practice, patience, and more practice.

Hybrid Applications

Finally, many systems designed in the next decade will be hybrids containing IMS, CICS, and DB2 elements. Consider the scenario of converting from IMS-DB to DB2 and imagine yourself about halfway through the process. Production systems will still require staff attention, so maintenance will be important. Some IMS systems will need to be converted piece by piece over a long period. Some systems will therefore spend most of their existence having both IMS and DB2 databases, both IMS-DC and CICS communications, and both hierarchical and relational development methodologies. What will these systems look like? Will specific staff be assigned to IMS maintenance and others to DB2 development? Will three-year DB2 people be paid as much as or even more than fifteen-year IMS people? Only the future will tell.

Chapter 10

IMS System Tuning

GENERAL CONSIDERATIONS

Many DB2 aficionados consider themselves experts in DB2 performance tuning. What they seem to imply is that they have some expertise in adjusting SQL statements to minimize a factor such as physical I/O, page or tablespace locking, buffer contention, or CPU utilization. The same mindset occurs in some IMS DBAs, who make statements such as "all databases should be HIDAM" or "OSAM is more efficient than VSAM." This phenomenon is commonly termed micro-optimization. It ignores the bigger subsystem and system picture to concentrate instead on improving single database accesses in isolated applications. System tuning, on the other hand, concerns itself precisely with the big picture, such as how resources are to be allocated and consumed across the board.

System administrators, database administrators, and application analysts should concern themselves with the methodology described here before tuning an application.

Do MVS Tuning

The principle here is that if an operating system is tuned poorly, no amount of application tuning will help it. There are several well-known areas to investigate—and reinvestigate—once you plan to install DB2:

- *Analyze DASD device contention.* It is common to allocate a database and its index to separate DASD volumes to reduce access arm movement during random access. This practice holds true in DB2 as well. Volumes in a DB2 STOGROUP are used in sequence as DB2 needs the space. Perhaps you should consider allocating tablespaces using the VCAT option instead.

■ *Consider the latest hardware advances and where to implement them.* IBM's latest DASD version is the 3390, which is a bit bigger than the more common 3380 models. The 3390 Model 1 has a track capacity of 56,664 bytes, with 15 tracks per cylinder. It is thus possible to fit 180 control intervals on a cylinder, rather than the 150 that fit on a 3380 cylinder.

Another consideration is the 3990 cache controller. This device contains a memory cache that speeds up physical I/O. Data written to DASD are first written to the cache. The data originator is then informed immediately that the write has taken place, and the physical write follows. This procedure reduces the total apparent physical I/O time from about 20 milliseconds to about 3 milliseconds. Some 3880 controllers (Models 11, 13, 21, and 23) also have caches.

A number of uncommon, though certainly interesting, alternatives are available. Some IBM DASD models, such as the 3348 Model 70 and the 3350 Model B2F, have a small number of fixed head cylinders. These cylinders have up to eight dedicated heads per cylinder that remain motionless. They thus have extremely fast DASD access times. Shops using these DASD models usually allocate these cylinders for highly accessed databases, indexes, and data for mission critical applications.

■ *Reduce CPU usage.* A system chugging along at above 95 percent CPU utilization just can't run any faster, regardless of any application tuning you might do. Try to find ways to spread CPU consumption—either by getting more hardware, distributing the workload to other mainframes or PCs, limiting the number of concurrent users, and distributing the CPU workload across a wider span of peak time, or similar practices.

■ *Analyze dispatching priorities.* There are several priorities associated with MVS units of work. The important one here is the address space dispatching priority, which is assigned by MVS at address space creation time. MVS will update this priority when it attempts to balance out the system workload. The job of assigning the CPU to tasks is handled by the MVS dispatcher. Tasks represented by task control blocks (TCBs) and supervisory request blocks (SRBs) that have higher dispatching priorities will be allowed preferred use of the CPU.

System administrators must consider various priorities for the different address spaces of consequence in IMS, CICS, TSO, and/or DB2 environments. Some of these address spaces are, in approximate descending order of importance,

The IMS Resource Lock Manager
The Virtual Telecommunications Access Method (VTAM)
The IMS control region
DB2 Database Services
DB2 System Services
TSO performance group 1
IMS message processing regions
CICS applications
Other TSO performance groups
Batch programs

This order of decreasing priorities will vary greatly across installations, depending upon their relative degree of CPU utilization, CPU availability as a function of time, and the number of applications.

■ *Determine if there is sufficient real and/or virtual memory.* Although DB2 does not suffer greatly from virtual storage constraints, often IMS and CICS problems in this area will ripple over to DB2. Another factor to look at is the possibility of acquiring expanded storage. Although it is extremely expensive, it may be the only answer if application performance is paramount.

Do IMS/CICS/TSO Subsystem Tuning

Once the MVS system is tuned as well as is feasible, its various subsystems can then be tuned. The most common factors to consider are

■ *Buffer pool management.* There is a profusion of various pooled entities in the different subsystems, including the DB2 EDM pool, the VSAM shared resources pool, the ISAM/OSAM buffer pool, the OSAM sequential buffering pool, and so on. Each of these pools is allocated separately and must be tuned in conjunction with the others.

■ *CICS RCT entries.* The Resource Control Table (RCT) is the place in CICS where transaction connections to DB2 are defined. The most difficult part about RCT entries involves defining threads. Should you use pool threads, or dedicated threads? What maximums should be used? Should multiple DBRMs be bound into a single plan, or should we use dynamic plan allocation?

■ *IRLM considerations.* It is possible to share an IRLM among many subsystems. Probably the biggest advantage of doing so is that IRLM definition takes a long time to get right. There is one minor disadvantage, however. Part of the process of IRLM definition involves setting the "deadlock wait" time (DEADLOK, IRLMRWT). This interval is the time after which the IRLM will wake up and look to see if two or more applications are dead-locked over resources the IRLM is presently managing. Depending upon the environment, you may want applications to wait no more than, say, fifteen seconds for an IMS resource or perhaps up to two minutes for a DB2 resource. Setting up this scenario would probably require using two separate IRLMs.

- *Security and authorization systems.* Many shops have extensive, complex security subsystems or products. If these existing products are sufficient for your security needs, you may be able to dispense with IMS/CICS and DB2 security. For example, some shops use RACF security for user sign-on and GRANT privileges on resources to PUBLIC. This procedure has the advantage of streamlining DB2 authorization checking for commonly used plans. (In this case, a plan with access PUBLIC that is already in the EDM pool has a bit that is turned on indicating PUBLIC. When the next user accesses the plan, DB2 will notice this bit and bypass the authorization checking.)

- *Virtual storage constraints.* Although buying more memory may seem to be the only answer, the operations management people should consider the other various options. For example, TSO is a notorious resource hog. Limit its use by specifying a relatively low MAXUSERS parameter, which is the number of allowable concurrent TSO users. A majority of TSO usage seems to be spent in the ISPF/PDF Edit menu making program changes. Although ISPF is indeed one of the better source code editors for the IBM mainframe, consider offloading this kind of work to PCs. Many shops now use micro-computers as workstations for analysts and programmers. Program analysis, design, and coding—and sometimes even testing—can now be done on a microcomputer. This expedient saves mainframe CPU, memory, and DASD resources.

- *Consider using OSAM sequential buffering.* This feature speeds the sequential processing of databases that use OSAM as their access method. See the section on OSAM sequential buffering later in this chapter.

- *Tune the usage of VSAM.* There are many ways to tune VSAM perfor-mance, including allocation of the shared resource pool, choice of control interval size, freespace determinations, and buffer page-fixing. For more information see the section titled "VSAM Considerations in IMS/VS" later in this chapter.

Do DB2 Subsystem Tuning

Now that MVS and the subsystems have been tuned, you can address the DB2 subsystem. Part of the reason for saving the DB2 subsystem for last is that most problems with other subsystems, such as virtual storage constraints, seem to ripple over into DB2, affecting it indirectly. Most of these items are beyond the scope of this book, but some are worth mentioning here for the sake of completeness:

■ *Understand buffer pool allocation and use.* The DB2 buffer pool has several thresholds associated with it. As the buffer pool fills with buffers marked "in use" (that is, ones with changed data that have not yet been written to DASD), DB2 restricts certain activities. For example, DB2 typically waits until the buffer pool is 50 percent full before attempting to physically write buffers to disk. The pool must reach 90 percent full before the sequential prefetch function is turned off. When it is about 97 percent full, DB2 must devote almost its entire energy to writing buffers.

■ *Monitor DB2 statistics.* The DB2 Performance Monitor contains statistics that summarize data about DB2 performance.

■ *Continually analyze the need to run RUNSTATS.* Optimizer access path selection depends upon the DB2 catalog statistics. If the statistics have not been run, the optimizer uses default values. If they *have* been run, but not recently, the optimizer may end up making decisions based on faulty data.

Finally, Do Application Tuning

Now that all the system and subsystem tuning is done, application tuning may be able to make a difference. It is important to keep in mind that even though your system is finely and professionally tuned and you have thoroughly analyzed all access paths, it is still possible that application tuning will make little or no difference. In fact, the interaction of all the subsystems and their functions and subfunctions is so complex that application tuning may even have a negative effect.

Application tuners should take the following factors into account:

■ *Analyze checkpoint frequency.* Taking checkpoints is easy, but doing it efficiently is an art. There seems to be no standard way of determining exactly how often a program should issue checkpoints, although the reasons for doing so are themselves well known. (See Chapter 5 for a more detailed discussion.)

■ *Decide whether to use conversational or nonconversational programming.* This choice could be made on a subsystem-by-subsystem basis. Basically, MPPs communicate with each other, as with terminals, printers, and so forth by using messages. These units contain data for the program or terminal to act upon. Conversational programming goes one step further in allowing programs to exchange additional information not contained in the message itself. These data (up to 32K bytes) are stored in the Scratch Pad Area (SPA).

It is worth noting that conversational programming can be simulated in a nonconversational environment. One method of doing so involves using a SPA database. This database would contain the same information that a SPA would, but it would be stored here in a database segment. Programs exchanging messages would then include in their messages the SPA database key for this information.

Another method involves storing information in hidden fields. Many screens contain blank areas — even completely empty lines. These areas of the screen and hence of the screen message can contain data that would otherwise go in the SPA. This information would be displayed with the hidden or nondisplay attribute so that the user would be unaware of its existence. Obviously, the usability of this technique is limited by the amount of empty screen space available.

■ *Define databases as nonrecoverable.* This feature is available with IMS/ESA. Databases may be defined as nonrecoverable to IMS. IMS will then not attempt to log all database changes or dynamically back out database changes upon program abend. (For further discussion, see Chapter 11.)

■ *Consider using the INIT DL/I call.* This call informs IMS that you wish to receive information regarding data availability for a PCB. This notification allows an application program to determine if it has enough information to satisfy a user request or complete a transaction. (See the BA, BB, NA, and NU status code descriptions in Appendix A).

■ *Analyze access path selection.* Occasionally, an IMS program will have several available methods of retrieving a segment. Among these include using a secondary index, using a search field, using logical relationships, using path calls, and using special command codes. Each of these options must be analyzed to determine which is best in a particular situation. Regrettably, the costs of using these methods change based upon database fragmentation, buffer pool availability, the use of dataset groups, and the definition of indexes. Still, the DBAs should make themselves available during the application design process to act as internal consultants on access paths.

Another issue involves DB2 access path selection. During the bind phase, DB2 selects the access path for table access based upon the SQL statement and the DB2 catalog's statistics. Although it is possible to influence DB2's choice by tuning SQL statements, this is now less of a problem than it has been in the past. (For more information about this, see Chapter 9.)

PERFORMANCE TUNING BY APPLICATION DEVELOPERS

"Database system performance tuning, in the next decade, will be done more and more by application developers."When I heard a respected colleague utter these words, a shudder ran through my body. Too many times in the past I had dealt with well-meaning managers, analysts, and programmers trying to make easier my job as DBA. Let me share a few of these instances with you. No real names have been used.

Anecdote 1

A few years ago I worked with a manager who insisted he was "technical," by which he meant that he thought he knew as much as I did about database design. Ron loved to spend time designing IMS databases for his group's applications. He studied VSAM CI and CA splits, OSAM versus VSAM performance, buffer pool allocation, segment edit and compression routines, and the whole works.

Ron's goal was to create the most efficient database system configuration possible for his applications. The first time that I'd be notified about his database requirements would usually be during the program coding phase, well after I could have provided advice or input into the design.

Naturally, I tried to explain to Ron that what he was doing was micro-tuning. As we have seen, this involves tuning at the application or system level, ignoring interfaces to other systems or effects on other systems. "Nonsense," he would say. "When you tune each system separately for maximum performance, the entire job mix is optimized."

Sigh. Will application people never learn? The DBA's job is to optimize a diverse set of solutions to a range of business problems, some of which have mutually contradictory objectives. Some may require instant response time, others lots of CPU usage. Balancing and tuning these factors is a full-time job that requires knowledge of all the systems, devices, and users and how they interact.

Anecdote 2

Another acquaintance of mine also considered herself DBA material. In this case, however, Millie decided to optimize her system's batch access to their databases. Fine, I thought; after all, she doesn't report to me, and what she does with her own time is her concern.

Then one evening the IMS Master Terminal Operator called to tell me about a system outage: some program had apparently caused the system to crash. A quick investigation disclosed that the program in question was doing massive database updates without doing any checkpoints (i.e., database commits). This process caused the system to enqueue all the update database information. Eventually, when it ran out of disk space to enqueue, the database manager died, bringing all the other applications down with it.

I asked Millie, whose program it turned out to be, why the program did no checkpointing. "We didn't need it," she replied. "The program is built to rerun from the beginning if it abends. Remember that class you gave us on restart versus rerun? I decided that this would be more efficient." A short explanation of enqueuing followed, after which Millie promised to install checkpoints immediately.

That evening I received another call from the MTO, again about a system outage. This time, however, the problem was even more interesting. It seemed that some program (guess which?) was taking checkpoints too often — so often, in fact, that the checkpoint messages printed on the operator's console filled the screen, then the buffers for the console. With the console's buffers full, the system had no buffer space to put any other messages and therefore abended.

Good grief. How difficult can it be to follow simple rules? Besides, if Millie had only followed our standards and procedures and had reviewed her program's checkpointing strategy with the DBA staff (me), all of this could have been avoided.

Anecdote 3

Bart was an analyst who concerned himself with the big picture. He studied his company's business data model and made a special effort to understand our data communications network. He familiarized himself with the various customer and user groups and learned whatever he could about system interfaces. After a while he began to consider himself an expert on the way we did data processing.

Unfortunately, Bart began to suffer from analysis paralysis. Whenever his group was designing a new system, he worried that it would not interface correctly with existing applications. He studied all the possible database designs, trying to develop plans to integrate the new database into the business. He spent a lot of time poring over system flow diagrams trying to optimize data flows, access paths, and user turnaround.

I tried to explain to Bart that this was not his job: he was an application designer, not a data administrator. After all, a lot of the things he was worrying about had been studied and in most cases solved by our DBA staff. "But our systems need to be tuned!" he would say. "Our users expect optimal performance from our new applications."

Bart could not see the trees for the forest. His awareness of the big picture caused him to lose sight of his immediate objectives.

Turnabout

These anecdotes, and countless other possible ones, at one time led me to believe that allowing applications people to do tuning was absurd. They simply don't have the perspective needed to evaluate system designs and integrate them into an existing environment.

Yet lately I have come to believe that there may be a grain of truth in what my colleague said. With the arrival of relational databases and distributed processing, I think the time has come for database administrators to swallow their pride and admit that their jobs are becoming too complicated. It may be time for some of this tuning to be given to application developers.

Here is where I think we as DBAs are going, and some of the problems we will be facing.

Future Environments

Articles in recent data processing technical periodicals are concentrating on relational databases and relational processing. It is also becoming clearer daily that the DBMS environment of the future will be not only relational but distributed.

Some of the distributed systems that exist today include those mentioned earlier such as airline reservation systems and electronic business data interchanges (EBDI).

There are several levels of distributed database processing, depending upon the number of remote systems to be accessed and the type of access needed for each. These levels are usually termed (in ascending order of sophistication) remote request, remote unit of work, distributed unit of work, and distributed request. An explanation of each type appears in Table 10-1.

DBA Responsibilities

In a distributed data environment, how is a DBA to do any kind of reasonable performance tuning? There are two conventional methodologies appropriate here: microtuning, a local tactic, and macrotuning, a global strategy.

Table 10.1. Levels of distributed processing.

Remote Requests

Remote requests permit users to read and/or update data residing on a single remote system. Each SQL statement used is considered a unit of work (see below) in that an implicit commit is performed after each request.

Remote Units of Work

A Remote unit of work permits an application or user to group several requests into a single logical unit of work (LUW). This allows an application program to request that the system either commit or roll back an entire group of updates. It also enables an application program to read or update data at more than one location. However, all data that the program accesses within a given unit of work must be on the same computer system.

At this level each local or remote system usually has its own relational database management system that participates in processing the request.

Distributed Units of Work

A distributed unit of work enables a user or application program to read or update data at multiple locations. SQL statements in such a transaction are restricted to referencing data in a single system. Multiple SQL statements are grouped into a single unit of work, which may then be committed or rolled back.

Distributed Requests

Distributed requests are the most sophisticated level of processing. They let a user or application program issue a single SQL statement that can read or update data on multiple systems simultaneously. Relational database technology has only recently advanced to this level of sophistication, at least as far as multisite updating is concerned.

Microtuning

Certainly each database, or set of databases, at a single location can be structured and/or configured for best performance on a single system. Examples of this type of tuning could include VSAM CI and CA allocation, the apportioning of datasets among multiple volumes, assigning of free space, choosing appropriate access methods, and normalization and denormalization.

Other considerations might include the choice of a DBMS (IMS, IDMS, or DB2); the choice of a run-time environment (CICS, IMS-DC, TSO, or VM); the type of connections to other systems (ISC, MSC, or a hybrid); and hardware configuration.

Macrotuning

Here the DBA is concerned with relationships among remote databases and how applications access them. This process involves network communications through servers, gateways, connection facilities, and communication lines, using the available hardware and software (such as workstation tool kits and access security), and DBMS interfaces like SAA.

The Basic Assumption

Although each of these tuning methodologies is useful, the basic assumption underlying each of them is that applications are developed to make the best use of tuned systems. This was not always the case, for historically it has been the design of the application that determined the structure of the data. With systems designed today using currently existing distributed data, applications are forced to access the data in a less-than-optimal fashion.

This restriction makes the DBA's job quite difficult. Not only must they optimize multiple databases at several sites across a remote user population, but it is also necessary to plan for future applications, network changes, and DBMS migrations.

To get a feel for this situation, imagine yourself to be the DBA in charge of changing the structure of a particular database in a distributed environment. The usual sequence might involve bringing the system down, backing up affected databases, doing various unloads and reloads, then testing the result.

The distributed environment requires, however, that you also take into account the following considerations:

- Locking out network users from database access for the interval of the change
- Informing remote applications of the new structure and thus preventing dynamic rebind
- Restructuring other, possibly remote, applications for efficiency
- Coordinating the changes with other, remote, DBAs
- Considering the effects on network security
- Examining relational integrity changes across multiple systems.

These considerations make it almost impossible for one DBA to tune a single system, let alone a combination of multiple systems across several computers. What then is the answer?

Developer Responsibilities

The burden must shift to the application developer. It then becomes the developer's responsibility to design applications that are tuneable independently of the DBMS and the network. This procedure is easier in fact than it sounds.

First, the analysis of new systems should consider the local processing of transactions, if possible. This step is a good idea in any case, as most on-line systems should include some mechanism for processing, in case of hardware or system failure.

Second, the design of distributed applications should encourage use of the lower levels of distributed processing. For example, do not use distributed units of work if a remote unit of work is feasible. Again, use remote requests rather than remote units of work, to reduce the complexity of the application and decrease the workload of the DBA attempting to do the performance tuning.

Third, coding and testing of prototypical distributed applications should be done in an environment where developers can gather meaningful performance measurement statistics. These statistics can then be used to refine DBMS access, network utilization, and overall throughput.

These suggestions are fine—if they can be implemented. But what if the system's design precludes such intrusions? What if the developer must use highly sophisticated distributed processing?

The Final Answer

The answer is that developers must become aware of available optimizing techniques in the distributed environment. The only practical way to do this is to share responsibility with the DBA for application system performance. This involves

- Having DBAs provide information during the requirements phase of system development so that developers are aware of the business data model and the current operating environment

- Sharing responsibility, during the analysis and design phases, for system simulation, thus giving developers and DBAs a chance to measure the impact of database design alternatives

- Coordinating activities during the testing phase, to allow developers access to tuning and performance measurement tools

- Using a standard approach to production system monitoring, thus permitting DBAs and developers to anticipate all needed tuning requirements.

Summary

The best answer to how to tune systems that are evolving into relational, distributed environments is to require both the DBA and the developer to share the responsibility for application performance. Only in this way will businesses be able to adjust to their users' needs, while retaining the flexibility to adapt and tune systems in a changing world.

VSAM CONSIDERATIONS IN IMS/VS

Tuning Outside of IMS/VS

To understand the pros and cons of selecting VSAM as an access method, let us first concentrate on those aspects that would affect an IMS/VS database application but that are not directly IMS/VS-related. Later we will discuss the major alternative to VSAM, ISAM/OSAM.

Two types of VSAM datasets occur in IMS/VS full-function database applications: Key Sequenced Data Sets (KSDS) and Entry Sequenced Data Sets (ESDS). A KSDS has two parts: its index component and a data component. Data may be accessed either directly by key or sequentially in key sequence. In contrast, an ESDS consists of only a data portion. Data access to an ESDS is by physical byte displacement from the beginning of the dataset. (The other types of VSAM datasets—Relative Record Data Sets or RRDSs and Linear Data Sets or LDSs—are not used in any IMS/VS database organization.)

Control Intervals and Areas

The physical unit for data transfer corresponding to the block is the VSAM Control Interval (CI). One or more VSAM logical records may fit into a CI. The dataset definer controls the size of the CIs of both the index and data components, by using the Access Method Services (AMS) DEFINE command. Control intervals are in turn grouped into areas called Control Areas (CAs). VSAM usually controls the size of the CA.

If CI sizes are poorly chosen, application efficiency may be affected. Choosing a large CI size may decrease physical I/O, but it may also waste unused buffer space. Conversely, a small CI size may cause more physical I/O to occur, thus slowing data access.

VSAM Buffers and Physical I/O

VSAM I/O uses buffers in the VSAM Shared Resource Pool. Buffers in this pool may have only a few fixed sizes. If a CI is to be read from DASD, an available buffer is chosen with the same or a larger size. Should the buffer size be greater than that of the CI, the remainder of the buffer will go unused and be wasted.

VSAM can detect if two or more records are being inserted in sequence into a dataset. In such a case VSAM uses a technique called mass sequential insertion. This procedure reduces physical I/O operations and conforms to control interval and control area freespace specifications. The dataset definer may specify that mass sequential insertion is to be considered during dataset processing.

Optimization

Several options of the Access Method Services DEFINE facility may affect VSAM's processing efficiency. The IMS DBA must make several choices regarding free space, buffer usage, and key usage. Some of these options appear in Table 10.2, along with their ramifications.

VSAM maintains certain control information within the control interval itself. This information includes one or more Record Descriptor Fields (RDFs) describing record attributes. It also includes a Control Interval Descriptor Field (CIDF) containing, among other things, the amount of free space left in the CI. The VSAM dataset definer must take this control information into account when defining control interval size. It must coexist with data in data records.

The VSAM Shared Resource Pool

In IMS/VS, buffers for VSAM datasets reside in the VSAM shared resource pool (SRP). This pool is divided into subpools constructed during IMS/VS system initialization. All buffers in a particular subpool have the same length.

Subpool attribute definitions are assigned in one of two places, depending upon the IMS/VS region type. For message regions, subpool descriptions occur in the members of the IMSVS.PROCLIB dataset. The member names are of the form DFSVSMxx, where xx is the region ID. For batch regions, subpool descriptions occur in the dataset with DFSVSAMP as the DD-Name.

Table 10.2 VSAM DEFINE options and their effect on processing.

Option	Considerations
CONTROLINTERVALSIZE or CISZ	The length of the control interval. For a data component this must include 7 bytes of VSAM overhead. Data component CISZ must be a multiple of either 512 or 2,048. Index components must be 512, 1,024, 2,048, or 4,096.
RECORDSIZE or RECSZ	The average and maximum record lengths. VSAM uses three bytes of overhead per record in the data component.
BUFFERSPACE or BUFSP	The minimum space to be provided for buffers. VSAM will require at least enough space for two data component CIs, and one index component CI for a KSDS.
RECOVERY or RCVY	Whether or not on initial load of a data component the data areas are to be pre-formatted. This is the default. The alternative is SPEED, which makes a load faster but not restartable.
REPLICATE or REPL	Forces index records to be repeated on a track as many times as will fit. More space for the index is required, but rotational delay is reduced. (KSDS only).
IMBED	Forces the lowest level of the index to be placed in the data component. This speeds keyed access. (KSDS only).
FREESPACE or FSPC	The amount of space left unused after cluster load. You may specify the percentages of CIs and CAs to be left empty. Free space will speed update by delaying CI and CA splits. (KSDS only).

There may be 1 to 11 VSAM buffer subpools, with 3 to 255 buffers in each subpool. The buffer sizes may be the following lengths, in bytes: 512, 1,024, 2,048, and multiples of 4,096 up to a maximum of 32,768. If more than one subpool is defined with buffers of a particular length, the subpools are combined into a single subpool.

During IMS/VS database OPEN, IMS/VS selects a subpool from the SRP, based on CI size. Sometimes there will be no available subpool with buffers that have the same length as the CI. In this case IMS/VS chooses a subpool with buffers large enough to contain the control interval. Any remaining space in the buffers selected is not used.

Buffers in a VSAM subpool are chained using pointers. Empty buffers are placed at the bottom of the chain, with accessed buffers placed at the top.

When a buffer is needed to satisfy an I/O request for retrieval, VSAM searches the chain to see if the CI has already been accessed. If not, VSAM chooses the least recently used buffer, at the bottom of the chain. If that buffer is not empty and the data in it have been updated, VSAM writes the buffer to the database before use. It then places the buffer at the top of the chain.

The mix of buffer lengths and subpool sizes defined for an IMS/VS region affects I/O performance. Table 10.3 contains some considerations for VSAM buffer definition.

The ISAM/OSAM Alternative

For most databases in IMS/VS, the alternative to VSAM is some combination of ISAM and OSAM. (See Table 10.4 for a chart of the various choices.) In IMS/VS, buffers for ISAM/OSAM datasets reside in the ISAM/OSAM buffer pool.

The ISAM/OSAM Buffer Pool

Buffers in the ISAM/OSAM buffer pool may be of the following lengths: 512, 1,024, or multiples of 2,048 bytes up to a maximum of 32,768. There may be 4 to 255 buffers in each subpool, with a maximum of 18 subpools. Buffer descriptions are placed similarly to those for VSAM subpool descriptions.

Each buffer subpool contains a number of buffer prefixes. Each such prefix, which corresponds to a buffer with data, has an entry in the subpool hash table, which records buffer prefixes. When the buffer handler receives a request for I/O retrieval, it uses the buffer subpool hash table to choose a buffer. Locating one in this manner is much quicker than having to search a chain.

Unlike VSAM's, the ISAM/OSAM subpools may be assigned to specific database datasets. This practice allows the DBA to tune applications using their own particular I/O requirements.

Table 10.3. Considerations for VSAM buffer subpool definition.

The buffer size used by the database must be at least as large as the CI size. In addition, IMS/VS overhead in segment prefixes must be taken into account.

Several buffers should be allocated for a database. Having more buffers means data will be available more often, reducing program wait time. The disadvantage is that more real storage is used.

VSAM buffers are shared among database datasets with a common CI size. Allocate enough buffers for all active databases to share them.

When inserting large amounts of keyed data, use the mass insert facility. This will use VSAM sequential mode PUT processing and not consume free space.

Page-fixing buffer subpools and/or their prefixes will speed buffer access but consume real storage.

Table 10.4 Allowed access methods for IMS/VS full function databases.

IMS/VS Database Organization	Access Method Choices	
DEDB	VSAM (KSDS)	
GSAM	VSAM (ESDS)	BSAM
HISAM	VSAM (KSDS + ESDS)	ISAM/OSAM
HDAM	VSAM (ESDS)	OSAM
HIDAM	VSAM (ESDS + KSDS)	ISAM/OSAM
Secondary Index	VSAM (KSDS or KSDS + ESDS)	

Table 10.5 contains some of the keywords used to define the VSAM shared resource pool and the ISAM/OSAM buffer pool. Table 10.6 specifies some additional options that may affect VSAM I/O performance. The parameters in these tables should be used during job execution to tune programs that use VSAM files.

Table 10.5. Buffer pool definition statements.

VSRBF=*n,m*   **Define VSAM subpool**
n = Buffer size in bytes.
One of 512; 1,024; 2,048; 4,096; 12,288; 16,384; 20,480; 24,576; 28,672; 32,768
m = Number of buffers of size *n* (3 to 255)

IOBF=(*n,m,f1,f2,id*)   **Define ISAM/OSAM subpool**
n = Buffer size in bytes. From 512 to 32,768. Will be rounded up to 512; 1,024; or a multiple of 2,048 up to a maximum of 32,768
m = Number of buffers of size *n* (4 to 255).
f1 = Y if buffers and buffer prefixes are to be long-term page-fixed; N otherwise (default).
f2 = Y if buffer prefixes are to be long-term page-fixed.
id = A 1- to 4-character identifier for the subpool. Used with the DBD statement.

DBD=dbdname(*ds#,id*)   **Define dataset, assign to subpool**
ds# = The index number of the dataset.
id = The subpool identifier assigned to the dataset.

Table 10.6. Additional VSAM buffer pool options.

OPTIONS,*opt1,opt2,* ...   Define additional pool options.

     BGWRT: If (YES,*n*), *n* is the percent of VSAM buffers in each subpool that are candidates for Background Write.
     INSERT: If SEQ, VSAM will use mass sequential insertion to add records.
     VSAMFIX: Buffer subpools and I/O-related blocks will be page-fixed.
     VSAMPLS: If GLBL, the VSAM shared resource pool is placed in the CSA. If LOCL, the SRP is built in the IMS/VS control region.

One last comment before leaving ISAM/OSAM. IMS/VS Version 2, Release 2, introduced a new concept called OSAM sequential buffering. The new OSAM buffer manager can now, if requested, analyze the read access patterns of OSAM datasets and prefetch blocks it believes will be read soon. OSAM sequential buffering is covered later in this chapter.

VSAM Datasets in IMS/VS

Some ways of organizing databases have special characteristics that are important to know when choosing VSAM as the access method.

HISAM Databases

HISAM databases consist of two datasets that implement VSAM using a KSDS for the primary dataset (the prime area for storing data) and an ESDS for the secondary dataset, used for overflow.

The deletion of a root segment will result in its logical record being erased, if the root and its dependents did not participate in any logical relationships. This space then becomes available in the primary dataset. Logical records in the overflow dataset that contain dependents of the deleted root will not, however, be available.

If a large number of root segments is inserted within a narrow key range, many control interval splits can occur. These splits may degrade VSAM performance. The DB monitor statistics reports contain the counts of such splits. The VSAM buffer pool report gives information about the VSAM subpools, including the number of write requests issued and the presence of any permanent write errors. The VSAM statistics report includes the number of retrievals and insertions made of logical records. The DBA should monitor this information over a period of time, using the information it provides to schedule a required database reorganization.

A steadily increasing number of physical I/Os on the VSAM statistics report for a database may indicate an unusually high number of CI or CA splits. In addition to these user-requested reports, the access method services LISTCAT command may be used for VSAM datasets. It contains the high used relative byte address (HURBA) and high allocated relative byte address (HARBA) of a VSAM dataset. When HURBA and HARBA become equal, the dataset will have no remaining available unused control areas.

Hierarchical Direct Databases

HDAM databases implement VSAM with an ESDS. For the data portion HIDAM databases use an ESDS, and use a KSDS for the index portion. When defining control interval sizes, you must consider the various pointer options used and how much space you will need for anchor points and other control information. Free space can also be set aside during dataset definition of the KSDS. This step is accomplished using the FREESPACE parameter of the DEFINE command. Freespace considerations are discussed later in this section.

IMS/VS HD databases may be defined by using a number of different logical and physical pointers. Although a complete discussion of these options is beyond the scope of this book, some general comments are appropriate. For one thing, the DBA must analyze an application's functional logic to determine database access paths. This analysis should include how often segments are retrieved and updated, which paths are used to access segments, and whether access is on-line. With this information the DBA can select appropriate pointer options. Because pointers reside in the data portion of the dataset, they must be included in any calculation of the necessary CI size.

HDAM databases also use certain CIs to store control information. VSAM reserves the use of CI zero. IMS/VS uses CI 1 to contain a bit map n bytes long. This bit map shows which of the following n CIs has space available. Should there be more CIs than bits in the bit map, additional maps will be created in later control intervals.

The DBA must consider control information when designing a randomizing module for an HDAM database. Most such modules use the root segment key as input to a hashing function that determines the desired position of the segment in the database. Root segments with different keys will occasionally "randomize" to the same position. In this case IMS/VS will chain the roots together. A poorly designed randomizing module will cause many roots to be chained together in this way, creating additional processing overhead with possible additional physical I/O.

Roots that randomize to a CI containing control information, such as pointers, may be chained and placed into another CI, thus requiring two physical I/Os for access. This redundancy degrades performance correspondingly.

Secondary indexes must be VSAM datasets. If the keys are unique, use a KSDS. If they are not unique, add an ESDS. (Although it is possible to specify the /SX or /CK fields as subsequence fields to make a key unique, just adding an ESDS has the advantage of being simpler to understand, implement, and recover.) As with HD databases, a secondary index logical record contains certain control information. This factor must be considered when defining control interval size.

VSAM Tuning Tips

Here are some general tips for tuning VSAM datasets in IMS/VS applications. These arise from observations discussed earlier.

■ *KSDS definition.* In general, use the IMBED and REPLICATE options to decrease the seek time for keyed retrieval. Although some additional DASD space will be so consumed, data access will be appreciably faster. Note that the value of this advice depends upon the particular DASD environment. When using devices with fixed-head cylinders (optional on the IBM 3344, 3348 Model 70, and 3350 Model B2F), using IMBED and REPLICATE can significantly reduce rotational delay for sequence and index sets.

Regrettably, the issue becomes somewhat clouded in an environment including DASD using cache controllers (e.g., the IBM 3990). Access Method Services commands do exist, though, that can be used to select or in some cases bypass certain cache management modes (see the SETCACHE and BINDDATA commands). In some cases, using IMBED can actually decrease performance. The best advice at this point would be to try VSAM dataset definition in several ways and compare the resulting performance. One measurement is worth a thousand expert opinions.

■ *Specify FREESPACE (KSDS only).* Doing so will create apparently empty control intervals. VSAM will load the database, allocating some control intervals as empty. This device will defer some CI splits during regular database processing, until the free space is used.

Free space is defined using the FREESPACE parameter in the DEFINE command. It is usually specified as FREESPACE (n,m) where n is the percentage of CIs to be left empty and m is the percentage of CAs to be left empty on initial database load. After the load the free space is consumed by inserting additional logical records. The amount of free space to be defined will depend upon the processing requirements.

In general, allocate sufficient free space to allow for insertions until the next expected database reorganization. Although specifying a generous amount of free space will serve to minimize CI and CA splits, it will also make the dataset physically larger. This expansion may increase data access time, because of the greater number of cylinders now used by the dataset.

■ *Specify SPEED.* This parameter may be used if restartability is not required for a database load. This process will prevent VSAM from having to preformat control intervals and will improve load performance.

A VSAM database load using the Utility Control Facility may be restarted from the point at which the process abnormally terminated. However, in this situation you cannot specify SPEED. In cases where the recoverability of the load is required you must specify RECOVERY for the VSAM dataset. In this case VSAM will preformat CIs with control information, allowing for a load program restart.

■ *Specify INSERT=SEQ* in the DFSVSAMP dataset during database load. VSAM will then leave free control intervals as defined in FREESPACE.

■ *Consider allocating VSAM index and data components* to different direct access volumes. Doing so will prevent excessive DASD head movement during data access.

■ *Experiment with page-fixing of buffers and buffer prefixes* to find a good combination. Page-fixing effectively makes certain control blocks memory resident.

   Some systems have limited memory capacity and page-fixing may not be possible in this case. Other systems having sufficient available real storage will allow the residency of buffers or buffer prefixes. Because memory access is orders of magnitude faster than DASD access, buffer prefix searching and buffer usage are extremely fast. Page-fixing is more efficient in systems where the load is not constant or where insufficient real storage exists.

■ *Consider allocating dedicated buffers* for highly active databases that must use ISAM/OSAM. Use the DBD parameter in buffer pool definition statements for this.

■ *Different segment sizes* can allow the DBA to define VSAM index and data portions of clusters with different control interval sizes. This procedure may require additional buffer allocation but will nonetheless allow for more efficient use of buffer space.

   Typically, the DBA will allow VSAM to calculate the CI size of the index portion of a KSDS. This value may then be changed afterward (before database load, of course) with the ALTER command. In general, the CI size of the index portion of a KSDS must be large enough to contain VSAM index entries for each of the CIs in a CA. If it is smaller, then some CIs in the CA will not be used. If the CI size is too large, use of the IMBED and REPLICATE parameters discussed earlier may not be possible.

■ *Monitor the VSAM Buffer Pool Report and VSAM Statistics Report.* These reports are produced by using the appropriate options in either the DFSVSAMP dataset or the appropriate DFSVSMxx member of IMSVS-.PROCLIB. These options allow the DBA to monitor control interval and control area splits. These reports may reveal the need for database reorganization.

■ *Specify free space in a HISAM KSDS,* by using the FREESPACE parameter of the DEFINE CLUSTER command.

■ *Specify free space in HDAM* by overallocating the root addressable area. This practice will allow the randomizing module to work effectively.

■ *Specify free space in HIDAM databases in the DBD,* by using the FRSPC= parameter of the DATASET statement. Defining free space in this way is necessary for HIDAM because a VSAM ESDS is used. The parameter is specified as FRSPC=*(fbff,fspf)*. The free block frequency factor *(fbff)* specifies how many CIs will be left as free space during initial load. The default is zero.

Specifying *2* would result in every other CI's being left free, a *3* would result in every third one being left free, and so on. A value of *1* is not allowed. The free space percentage factor *(fspf)* is an integer from zero to 99 that specifies the percentage of space within each CI to be left free during initial database load.

Summary of VSAM Considerations

In an IMS/VS environment the DBA and the application manager share a common goal: overall system efficiency. This shared responsibility sometimes brings them into conflict. For instance, tuning a particular application for maximum throughput may have an undesirable effect on other systems. Degraded response time, excessive I/O, and a poor use of direct access storage may be the result.

This conflict can best be resolved only by sharing responsibility. Typically, the DBA has primary responsibility for system tuning, and the application manager has the chief responsibility for application tuning. It may seem impossible to reconcile these two duties, but the DBA can assist in application tuning. With specialized training and knowledge, they can educate application personnel in methods that will harmonize with the DBA's job.

These relatively simple concepts should afford the DBA the opportunity to share with application designers appropriate techniques for good database design. These shared techniques will assist both parties in their common goal of maximizing total system efficiency.

OSAM SEQUENTIAL BUFFERING

IMS system programmers and database administrators must make several key decisions during the process of IMS database design. Among these are the choice of access method (HISAM, HIDAM, MSDB, etc.), the DASD space allocation needed, database structure, the creation and maintenance of indexes, the designation of dataset groups, whether or not to use logical databases, and various other system performance items. One of the most frequently considered alternatives is whether to use VSAM or ISAM/OSAM as the database access method.

The ISAM/OSAM Alternative

The usual alternative to VSAM for choice of access method in IMS databases is some combination of ISAM and OSAM. HIDAM and HISAM databases may use either two VSAM datasets (a Key Sequenced Data Set, or KSDS, and an Entry Sequenced Data Set, or ESDS) or a combination of ISAM and OSAM. HDAM may use either a VSAM ESDS or OSAM.

Typically, the choice between VSAM and OSAM revolves around performance issues. Some of these factors are the buffer pool sizes obtainable, database freespace definition, dump options and trace parameters, and available performance reporting. Sometimes the choice between the two is simply a matter of convenience.

With IMS/VS Version 2, Release 2, a new option for OSAM processing appeared called Sequential Buffering (SB). This feature now enables the OSAM buffer manager to achieve a significant performance improvement in reading (but not writing) blocks in databases that use OSAM. This section describes the characteristics of sequential buffering and gives helpful hints on its installation and monitoring.

First, let us take a brief look at how OSAM database processing is done without sequential buffering.

The ISAM/OSAM Buffer Pool

In IMS, buffers for ISAM/OSAM datasets reside in the ISAM/OSAM buffer pool. This pool is subdivided into smaller units called subpools. The subpools' attribute definitions occur in one of two places, depending upon the type of IMS region. For message regions, subpool descriptions occur in the members of the IMSVS.PROCLIB dataset. The member names are of the form DFSVSMxx, where xx is the region ID. For batch regions, subpool descriptions occur in the dataset having DFSVSAMP as its DD-Name.

Table 10.5 contains some of the keywords used to define the ISAM/OSAM buffer pools.

During IMS database Open for ISAM/OSAM databases, IMS selects a subpool from the ISAM/OSAM pool, based on block size. Sometimes there will be no available subpool with buffers of the same length as the block size. In this case IMS/VS chooses a subpool with buffers large enough to contain the block. The remaining space in the buffers selected is not used.

Each ISAM/OSAM buffer subpool contains a number of buffer prefixes. Each such prefix, corresponding to that of a buffer with data, has an entry in the subpool hash table, which is a table of buffer prefixes. When the buffer handler receives a request for I/O retrieval, it uses this buffer subpool hash table to choose a buffer. Finding one in this manner is much quicker than having to search a chain.

An ISAM/OSAM subpool, unlike VSAM, may be assigned to a specific database dataset. This then allows DBAs to tune applications using their own particular I/O requirements for certain databases. ISAM/OSAM buffers can also be page-fixed in storage.

When DL/I requests a data block for a database, using OSAM, the OSAM buffer pool manager first searches the OSAM buffer pool to see if the block already exists in the pool. If so, the request is satisfied. If not, a read request is issued for the block.

OSAM Sequential Buffering Read Requests

When OSAM sequential buffering is active, an additional step becomes possible. If a read request is not satisfied by a search of the OSAM buffer pool, the OSAM buffer pool manager checks with the SB buffer handler.

If the read can in fact be satisfied from the SB buffer pool, the block requested is copied from the appropriate SB buffer to an OSAM buffer. If, however, the read request is not satisfied, the SB buffer handler then has the option of issuing a sequential read for the next ten blocks from the database. Upon completion of this phase, the first block is copied to the OSAM buffer.

Let us proceed to a description of SB buffer pools.

Defining SB Buffer Pools and Buffer Sets

SB buffer pools and buffer sets (explained below under "SB Buffer Processing") are defined in much the same way as ISAM/OSAM buffer pools. For message regions, SB buffer pool descriptions occur in the members of the IMSVS-.PROCLIB dataset. The member names are of the form DFSVSMxx, where xx is the region ID. For batch regions, pool descriptions occur in the dataset having DFSVSAMP as its DD-Name.

SB buffers may be defined for any database PCBs that occur in the application's PSB. If a database has multiple dataset groups, a separate buffer set is defined for each group. Each of the DB-PCB/DSG combinations requires its own separate buffer sets and is activated individually.

SB buffers are page-fixed, and occur above the 16-megabyte line in the MVS/XA operating system. You may need to increase the batch or message region size, or perhaps the size of the ECSA or CSA, when implementing SB.

Activating Sequential Buffering

OSAM sequential buffering is requested either during PSBGEN, through using an SB Initialization User Exit Routine, or by using JCL. The PSB parameters are as follows:

PCB TYPE=DB, ...,   **SB={COND or NO}**

COND   SB to be conditionally activated.
NO   SB should not be used.

This parameter can be overridden in batch regions by specifying the SBPARM parameter in the //DFSCTL DD statement. Some of the subparameters for this statement are given in Table 10.7.

Specifying SBPARM subparameters will override the specification in the PSB, and both of these will override any parameters specified using the SB Initialization Exit. Additional SB parameters may be included in the //DFSCTL dataset. These parameters are described in the IMS/VS System Definition Manual.

Specifying SBPARM subparameters makes it possible to choose SB activation for a particular database or dataset or for all databases referenced by a PSB for an application.

When a database PCB specifies SB=COND, or if the //DFSCTL JCL statement overrides the PSB, the application informs IMS that OSAM sequential buffering is requested for this PCB. However, SB will not be immediately activated. When SB is requested, IMS monitors the application's I/O reference pattern and activity rate for each DB-PCB/DSG combination. If IMS then deems that the application's performance can benefit from SB, it activates it conditionally.

After this activation, IMS continues monitoring the I/O activity and reference pattern of the DB-PCB/DSG in what is called a periodic evaluation. After any such evaluation IMS may temporarily deactivate SB. Its purpose in doing so may be either to unfix and page-release the SB buffers, or simply result from a decision that SB is no longer beneficial for the application.

SB Buffer Processing

When activated, SB buffers are allocated in n buffer sets of 10 buffers each. There are always 10 buffers in each buffer set, although the number of sets itself may be overridden.

If a request for a data block cannot be satisfied from the OSAM buffer pool, a request is sent to the SB buffer handler. If the requested block exists in the SB buffer pool, the block is copied to an OSAM buffer. If not, the SB buffer handler decides whether to issue either a random read (meaning it sends the request back to OSAM) or a sequential read (if it does the read itself). If it is a sequential read, when it has been completed the SB buffer handler will copy the appropriate SB buffer to an OSAM buffer.

The IMS Master Terminal Operator may override SB at any time with the /START SB and /STOP SB commands.

Table 10.7. SBPARM parameters.

//DFSCTL DD *	(overrides PSB parameters)	
SBPARM	[ACTIV = {COND or NO}]	[,BUFSETS=nn]
	[,DB=dbdname]	[,PCB=pcblabel]
	[,DD=ddname]	[PSB=psbname]

where BUFSETS is the number of buffer sets

The following parameters specify to IMS which databases, datasets, PCBs, or PSBs are to have SB activated.

DB	is a DBD name
PCB	is a PCB name
DD	is a DD name
PSB	is a PSB name

Additional Features

This feature of being able to read multiple consecutive blocks from the database with a single I/O operation can go one step further. For batch and BMP regions, SB can overlap sequential reads with the CPU processing and I/O operations from the same application. Other programs, applications, and utilities that do large volumes of sequential database block reads can also benefit from SB. Some of these are

- Data Extract Facility (DXT)
- On-line DB Image Copy
- HD Reorg Unload
- Database Scan
- Database Prefix Update

Note that SB has high initialization overhead. It is thus not recommended for short-running MPPs, Fast Path programs, CICS/VS programs, or programs that do primarily random access.

Performance Monitoring of SB

To determine whether IMS has activated sequential buffering for an application, include the following statement in the JCL:

//DFSSTAT DD SYSOUT=A

The existence of this JCL statement will cause the following IMS reports to be printed:

- PST Accounting Report
- VSAM Buffer Pool Report (batch regions only)
- OSAM Buffer Pool Report (batch regions only)
- Sequential Buffering Summary Report
- Sequential Buffering Detail Report

The last two of these display statistics regarding SB.

The SB Summary Report

This self-explanatory report summarizes SB activity for an application. Some of the fields it contains are

- Number of Search Requests Issued by OSAM Buffer Handler
- Number of Random Read I/O Operations
- Number of Sequential Read I/O Operations
- Number of Blocks Read Randomly
- Number of Blocks Read Sequentially
- Percent Read per Search Request

The SB Detail Report

This report is a highly detailed report for each SB buffer pool used by an application. It includes average I/O wait times for random and sequential reads, control block usage, activation statistics, and an analysis of the I/O activity rate. Although most of these fields will be of interest only to systems programmers, they give a complete picture of SB activity, making performance analysis a simple task.

Summary

Using the new OSAM sequential buffering feature in IMS/VS 2.2 can significantly affect the database's read performance. Database designers and systems programmers should thus consider using ISAM/OSAM as a viable alternative to VSAM whenever the clear majority of database read access is sequential.

Chapter 11
IMS/ESA

In mid-1989 IBM announced that it was coming out with a new release of IMS called IMS/ESA Version 3, Release 1. (The term IMS/ESA stands for Information Management System/Enterprise Systems Architecture). This release is currently the latest one of IMS, and became available in March 1990. It consists of two programs: the IMS/ESA Database Manager and the IMS/ESA Transaction Manager. IMS/ESA executes only with MVS/ESA to take advantage of several MVS/ESA characteristics. Some of the more important features of IMS/ESA are now described.

THE DATABASE MANAGER

The IMS/ESA Database Manager handles the interface to IMS databases and the data manipulation language DL/I. DL/I is used to create and access IMS databases. Database administrators can create nine different types of IMS databases, including seven kinds of full-function databases and two types of Fast Path databases for Integrated Fast Path applications (see Table 11.1). The Database Manager provides the following database-related features:

- *Logical relationships.* Logical relationships let an application program access a logical database record. A logical database record can consist of segments from one or more physical databases. A logical database record thus lets an application program view a database structure that is different from the physical database structure.

  One advantage of using logical relationships is that programs can access data even though it may exist in more than one physical hierarchy.

Table 11.1. Database types supported by IMS/ESA.

Type of Database	IMS Access Method
HSAM	Hierarchical Sequential Access Method
SHSAM	Simple Hierarchical Sequential Access Method
HISAM	Hierarchical Indexed Sequential Access Method
SHISAM	Simple Hierarchical Indexed Sequential Access Method
HDAM	Hierarchical Direct Access Method
HIDAM	Hierarchical Indexed Direct Access Method
GSAM	Generalized Sequential Access Method
DEDB	Data Entry Database
MSDB	Main Storage Database

If you did not use logical relationships and two application programs needed to access the same data simultaneously through different paths, you would have to store the data in both physical hierarchies.

■ *Secondary indexing.* Secondary indexing allows you to access database records in a sequence other than that defined by the root key. If you do not use secondary indexing, accessing a segment that is qualified by anything other than the root key can be inefficient, because DL/I must search through several segments to find the correct one. With secondary indexing, DL/I can access a segment directly, based on a field value that is not that of the key field.

■ *Variable-length segments.* Variable-length segments allow the data portion of a segment type to be variable in length. You would want to use variable-length segments when the size of the data portion of a segment type varied greatly from one segment to the next. With variable-length segments you define the minimum and maximum length of a segment type. This practice saves space in the database whenever a segment is shorter than the maximum length.

■ *Field level sensitivity.* Field level sensitivity allows an application program to use a subset of the fields that make up a segment, so that it doesn't have to process fields it doesn't use, or to use fields from a segment in a different order. This technique also allows an application program to access only selected fields in a segment for security purposes, or to add fields to a segment without affecting the processing of fields that already exist in that segment.

■ *Segment edit/compression.* Segment edit/compression provides an exit to permit you to compress data when a segment is written to the device, so that the direct access storage device space is better utilized. It also allows you to encrypt or edit data so that application programs can receive it in a format other than the one in which it is stored.

■ *Multiple dataset groups.* Having multiple dataset groups allows some of the segments in a database record to be put in datasets other than the primary one. This option can be used without destroying the hierarchic sequence of segments in a database record. Doing so permits you to separate seldom-used database segment types from those used often. Thus, an application program can quickly access the segments it is interested in and bypass those it is not.

   Multiple dataset groups might also be used to save space by putting segment types whose sizes vary greatly from the average into a separate dataset group.

■ *Data partitioning.* Data partitioning allows you to divide a DEDB into several areas, each containing a different collection of database records grouped by a randomizing algorithm. The areas are independent of each other, so that an error in one area will not affect other areas in the DEDB. Areas may be of different sizes and stored on different types of devices. This makes it possible to store the most frequently accessed data in an area stored on a fast type of device.

■ *Data replication.* Data replication allows you to make as many as seven copies of each area dataset in a DEDB, thus further increasing the data availability of a DEDB. If there is an error in one area dataset and a copy of that dataset exists, application programs may continue to process the data in the copy.

The IMS/ESA Database Manager also provides the following features:

■ *Database recovery control (DBRC).* Database recovery control permits easier recovery of IMS databases. DBRC keeps track of and controls IMS logging, including that of on-line and system logs. It also controls three types of database recovery:

Full recovery, which results in the recovery of an IMS database or database dataset to its condition before it failed.

Time-stamp recovery, which results in reconstructing a database dataset to an earlier condition, perhaps as it was when a log dataset was closed or an image copy was made.

Track recovery, which results in restoring a failed track of a VSAM database dataset.

For each type of recovery, one command to the DBRC recovery control utility generates the JCL and any control statements needed to perform the specified recovery.

The DBRC stores information about events that might affect recovery in two recovery control (RECON) datasets. IMS uses this recovery control dataset information (such as dataset names, volume serial numbers, and times of creation) to determine what datasets will be needed as input during a restart or recovery. The DBRC also supports the sharing of information among IMS applications. Recovery control datasets hold authorization control information to assist IMS in controlling and serializing application programs' access to and display of information from IMS databases.

■ *Sharing databases among multiple subsystems*. When several application programs run at once in a DB/DC environment, the IMS control region makes it possible for them to read and update IMS databases concurrently. It does so by preventing one program from accessing data that another is updating until the updating program indicates to IMS that its changes are valid (i.e., committed). This form of data sharing is called program isolation (PI).

For convenience, let us use the abbreviated term *data sharing* to refer to the process of sharing data among multiple subsystems instead of the term *program isolation*. Data sharing extends the functions of the control region by making it possible for application programs in separate IMS subsystems, running in the same or separate central electronic complexes (CECs), to access databases concurrently, both for reads and for updates. Batch and on-line programs can both share IMS databases. CICS systems can participate in data sharing, and CICS on-line programs can share databases with IMS on-line and batch programs. Data sharing is not supported for MSDBs or GSAM databases.

Database Manager Environments

There are two environments provided by the IMS/ESA Database Manager: IMS batch, and database control (DBCTL).

In the batch environment a program runs by itself and does not compete with other programs for DBMS resources. Programs that run in a batch environment do not process messages from message queues, insert messages to the queues, or access on-line databases. Typically, these programs process large amounts of data or even an entire database. They are initiated using JCL and are usually scheduled for specific times. They are probably not scheduled during the prime shift, but when demand for system resources is lowest.

In a DBCTL environment, in contrast, transaction management subsystems other than the IMS Transaction Manager, such as CICS, have on-line access to full-function databases and DEDBs. BMPs that do not access message queues can also concurrently access DBCTL-supported databases. Full-function databases and DEDBs can be accessed from one or more transaction management subsystems through the facility known as the database resource adapter (DRA). The DRA and the transaction management subsystem are together known as the coordinator controller (CCTL).

A DBCTL environment has several advantages over a batch environment:

- The database resource adapter interface permits DBCTL and transaction management products to be developed, installed, and maintained independently of each other.

- A failure of the DBCTL will not affect the transaction management subsystem, nor will a failure of the transaction management subsystem usually affect DBCTL.

- One or more transaction management subsystems, each with multiple users, can connect to the DBCTL environment simultaneously.

THE TRANSACTION MANAGER

The Transaction Manager handles activity relating to messages, transactions, and message queues. It manages the network of IMS terminals, routes messages between terminals and applications, queues input and output messages, schedules application programs, and provides other system control facilities, described below.

Managing the Terminal Network

The Transaction Manager supports the attachment of many types of terminals, including remote subsystems. For on-line processing it uses the network facilities of communications managers such as BTAM and VTAM.

During the process of IMS system definition the system definer describes the physical network. In addition, they also define logical terminals (LTERMs). These terminals are simply logical devices associated with physical terminals. A physical terminal may have one or more logical terminals associated with it. Messages sent and received in IMS are associated with the names of these logical terminals. This practice frees the application designer from needing to know the physical network. Application programs need not then be concerned with terminals' addresses, device availability, or the geographic locations of hardware.

Another advantage of such an arrangement arises if a physical terminal should become inoperative. In such a case the logical terminals associated with the physical one can be dynamically reassigned, perhaps by the IMS Master Terminal Operator, to another physical terminal. Then messages that were waiting to be sent to the now-inoperative physical terminal may be rerouted to another physical destination. This concept of the logical terminal enhances IMS security, because each logical terminal can have its own unique security parameters.

Routing Messages

IMS processes three basic categories of input messages. The first few characters of an input message indicate the type of message it is and identify the destination of the message. The categories are as follows:

- *IMS commands.* IMS commands begin with a slash (/). These commands are usually requests for IMS to display the system status or alter a system parameter. Some commands are restricted to certain classes of users but others, such as those affecting system security, are limited to use by the Master Terminal Operator.

- *Message switches.* If the first one to eight characters of an input message are the name of an IMS logical terminal, the message text will be sent directly to that LTERM.

- *Messages.* If the first one to eight characters of an input message are a transaction code, the message text will be processed by an IMS application program.

Queuing Input and Output Messages

When IMS receives a message, it determines the message's destination and places it in an input queue for that destination. Message queuing lets a terminal user enter transactions into a system even though the application program that is needed to process the transaction may not be immediately available. The transactions entered while IMS is busy processing a previous transaction are queued for later processing.

Once an IMS application finishes processing a transaction, it places an output message in an output queue. The output message will then either be routed to the originating terminal or an alternate destination. The alternate can be prespecified when originally defining the transaction to IMS. If the output is being returned to the originating terminal, IMS places it in a queue for that terminal. That terminal's operator may then request the message when convenient.

During the process of IMS system generation, two message queue datasets are defined: the long message queue dataset and the short message queue dataset. Messages of up to a certain length are stored on the short message queue dataset, and the remainder go to the long message queue. This division of messages has implications for system performance.

Another feature of how messages are defined at IMS system generation is whether or not a message is recoverable. When a message defined to be recoverable is placed on a queue, it can be recovered if the IMS system shuts down, on either a scheduled or unscheduled basis.

IMS Fast Path (IFP) is a facility that provides its own expedited message handling. Messages to and from an IFP program bypass the IMS message queue processing system, thereby reducing the time that a message must wait to be processed. After they finish processing, IFPs remain in virtual storage and wait for the next message. This technique reduces the time required by the application program to process the next message.

Scheduling Messages

As a part of the process of IMS system definition the system definer associates application programs with the transactions they are to process, using the APPLCTN and TRANSACT macros. When a transaction is entered on an LTERM, IMS uses the transaction code in the message to determine which application is associated with the transaction. IMS then schedules the application program to process the message.

Transactions can be assigned many attributes, including normal priority, limit priority, processing limit count, and a message class. Based on these and other parameters, IMS schedules the application programs. It is able to balance its workload, if necessary, by scheduling an application that processes a single type of transaction into more than one IMS region.

Message Format Service

The IMS Message Format Service (MFS) facility is one of several message editors that an application can use to format IMS messages as they pass from devices to applications and vice versa. MFS allows application programs to deal with logical messages instead of device-dependent data. An application program that uses MFS can interact with different devices or types of devices without needing multiple versions of program logic.

A program using MFS need not be concerned with the physical characteristics of the device it is interacting with unless it wants to use such specific device features as highlighting or form feed. And even when these features are used, the application program will request them by using logical functions through MFS. The application does not send or receive device control characters directly.

Alternatives to MFS include Basic Edit, a generic message editor, and the option of bypassing editing altogether. Most on-line IMS applications use MFS simply because it is so convenient.

Multiple Systems Coupling

Multiple Systems Coupling (MSC) connects multiple IMS systems to each other. These systems may reside in the same central electronic complex (CEC) or in different ones. MSC provides processing that is transparent to the terminal operator; it appears to be occurring in a single system.

MSC does not require that the terminal operator or application program know the routing information unless what is known as directed routing is being used. Routing is automatic, based on the parameters supplied during the process of system definition. Individual system definitions describe the routing for all messages. Message routing is automatic unless the programmer uses a routing exit routine to alter a message's destination.

MSC directed routing allows different IMS systems in the same MSC network to use the same logical names for their terminals and transaction codes. The application program is able to determine the system identification of the system that scheduled it. It can directly specify not only the system identification of the system designated to process the message but also a destination within that system.

MSC does support conversational transactions, but it cannot connect IMS to unlike subsystems such as CICS or user-written subsystems. MSC does not permit the use of Fast Path expedited message handling between IMS subsystems, nor does it permit the use of the Message Format Service (MFS) to assist in routing and formatting messages between subsystems.

Multiple Systems Coupling lets a user enter transactions in one IMS subsystem for processing in another one. IMS then returns the results to the originating terminal without the operator's even being aware of this processing. To the operator, the processing will seem to have occurred within a single system. MSC also permits users to configure multiple IMS systems so that processing loads and system databases are distributed among them to satisfy particular geographic and business requirements.

Intersystem Communication

Intersystem Communication (ISC), like MSC, permits operators to communicate with and exchange data among multiple IMS systems. In addition, ISC allows communications between IMS and CICS or a user-written subsystem, provided that all the subsystems involved have implemented the ISC protocols.

ISC provides a unique message switching capability that lets message routing occur without involving an application. ISC allows the use of Fast Path expedited message handling between IMS subsystems and permits the use of MFS to assist in routing and formatting messages between subsystems.

Extended Recovery Facility

The Extended Recovery Facility (XRF) increases the on-line availability of an IMS system by providing an alternate IMS system to monitor the active IMS subsystem so that it can be ready to take over if necessary. A similar facility exists in CICS.

XRF acts like a shadow IMS. It waits in the wings, monitoring the IMS system. Should an outage occur, XRF will take over for the failing system. It will then become the active IMS system.

The usability of XRF is based on the assumption that a problem causing a failure in one environment may not cause the same failure in another. Regrettably, many customers feel that anything severe enough to cause IMS to fail will probably also cause the XRF to fail soon after.

DATABASE CONTROL

Database control (DBCTL), described earlier, is a new environment that allows applications running in it to access DL/I full-function databases and data entry databases (DEDBs). The DBCTL/CCTL (coordinator controller) interface provides access to IMS/ESA from transaction management subsystems like CICS/ESA, except for the IMS/ESA Transaction Manager. The DBCTL environment consists of three address spaces: the DBCTL address space, a DL/I address space, and a DBRC address space. (If IRLM is used, it occupies a fourth address space.) CICS/ESA Version 3, Release 1, supports the DBCTL environment for access to IMS resources through CICS/ESA.

The DBCTL environment allows the use of the On-line Change Facility and the On-line Image Copy utility (OLIC) for full-function databases, and the Concurrent Image Copy (CIC) facility for HSSP/Image Copy for DEDBs. DBCTL has its own log dataset and participates in database recovery. Locking is provided either by IMS program isolation or IRLM.

DBCTL Structure

The DBCTL environment is similar to a DB/DC control region, but without its data communication, message management, and transaction manager support. DBCTL does support non-message-driven BMPs. BMP regions can access DBCTL databases concurrently with other transaction management subsystems like CICS/ESA. DBCTL does not support program-to-program message switching.

Batch jobs that access DL/I databases through IMS/ESA data sharing can be converted to run as BMPs accessing the DL/I databases through DBCTL. This ability should provide a simpler operations environment when compared with the environment introduced with data sharing in the batch environment. Applications running as BMPs using DBCTL can make calls to DB2 by using the Extended Subsystem Attach facility.

DBCTL uses PCBs to process DL/I calls accessing its databases. The database processing requirements of the application programs that access the databases are described via PCBs.

VIRTUAL STORAGE CONSTRAINT RELIEF

The DB/DC and DBCTL environments will experience virtual storage constraint relief (VSCR) for the DL/I address space and the common storage area (CSA) because many buffers, blocks, and modules have been moved above the 16-megabyte line. (This 16-megabyte line refers to addresses in real memory that were previously not accessible because of 24-bit addressing.) OSAM and VSAM dataset buffer pools and VSAM control blocks are moved above the 16-megabyte line in CICS, local DL/I, and batch environments. VSCR supports application programs above the 16-megabyte line. An application program's DL/I calls, parameter lists, and I/O areas can also reside above this line.

Common Storage Area

Extended CSA (ECSA) resides above the 16-megabyte line. The buffers, control blocks, and modules shown in Table 11.2 have been moved into the ECSA. The trace tables listed in Table 11.2 record diagnostic information in the system. Virtual storage constraint relief for trace tables can be experienced only if you used the tables in previous releases.

The specifications you choose for databases will determine the size of the Partition Specification Tables (PSTs). You can specify a mixed full-function database and Fast Path database installation, as well as a full-function-only installation. The size of the PSTs depends on whether you use Fast Path and/or IRLM. If you choose Fast Path facilities for your system, each dependent region

Table 11.2 Blocks, modules, and buffers moved into ECSA.

Trace Table	PSB Work Pool
PST	Resident PSBs (CSA portion)
PDIR	Resident intent list
DDIR	Save area prefix (SAP)
SMP	Some Fast Path modules (DBFxxxxx)
PSB Pool (CSA portion)	

generates a larger PST. Similarly, using the IRLM increases the PST size for each dependent region.

To take advantage of the increased availability of virtual storage now available for performance enhancements, you may want to increase the size of the PSB pool, as well as of the DMB pool and database buffer pools. Even though VSCR provides relief from existing virtual storage constraints, an increase in these pools should be backed up by providing increased real storage. If this is not done, page faults could adversely affect performance.

The dependent region ECB pool is new, residing below the 16-megabyte line. It serves as an interface between the routines and pools residing above the line. This pool contains one DECB for each PST.

Access Method Support

Even though ISAM is no longer supported in IMS/ESA, ISAM datasets can be converted to VSAM key sequence datasets (KSDSs) for database access methods using ISAM. Doing so will require unloading and reloading the database, then defining VSAM buffer pool entries.

HIGH SPEED SEQUENTIAL PROCESSING

Data entry databases (DEDBs) are generally used in IMS when there is a large amount of data being updated or read. This activity usually produces a sizable amount of log data and consumes a lot of CPU time and other IMS/ESA resources. High speed sequential processing (HSSP) is a feature of IMS/ESA designed to improve the sequential processing of DEDB areas. HSSP reduces elapsed DEDB processing time by using private buffer pools to perform updates and make image copies.

The HSSP image copy option permits multiple applications to update the DEDB while image copying is in process, including updates to the area being copied. Because of this feature the HSSP image copy is called a "fuzzy" image copy. The image copy facility is invoked through control statements supplied in the HSSP DFSCTL dataset.

HSSP executes in the control region. As an on-line program it can access on-line buffers for the DEDB area, area control list, and other information contained in the second VSAM control interval for the area. HSSP writes all these areas as part of its regular processing.

A separate buffer pool is allocated for each area being processed by HSSP. A pool is allocated for an area when the first VSAM CI in the area is accessed, then deallocated when the HSSP job is completed or when processing for the next area begins. The area's pool is page-fixed in extended CSA. A sequential read will allocate a single set of buffers, whereas a sequential update will allocate two sets. The buffers in the private pools correspond to a unit of work and include space for dependent overflow control intervals.

Programs must request HSSP processing for a DEDB by using a new PCB processing option H. A PSB can have none to several DEDB PCBs with PROCOPT=H, but only one PCB with a PROCOPT=H activated is permitted per database area per PSB. A program with a PSB having multiple PCBs for the same database can reach completion successfully if PROCOPT=H is deactivated for the additional PCBs. In a PCB, PROCOPT=H can be deactivated by the SETO function.

The locking of database CIs is slightly different when using HSSP. Applications accessing DEDBs without using HSSP will lock on a CI basis, assuming that no HSSP application is then processing against the same DEDB area. However, if an area is being processed by both an HSSP application and a non-HSSP one, the non-HSSP application will first issue a unit-of-work lock followed by a CI lock. This style of locking prevents block level data sharing of DEDBs, which was allowed in previous releases of IMS.

An important advantage to using HSSP during image copy is its reducing of log records. Under HSSP updates made by application programs doing sequential processing of the DEDB are not logged. Instead, they are written to the image copy dataset. Applications making nonsequential updates do continue to have their updates logged. If an application completes successfully, the log records will not be needed, because the HSSP image copy will have produced the latest image of the database records. If, however, the application program does not complete successfully and the updates are in fact needed for an emergency restart or database recovery, the partial changes are available on the HSSP image copy and in the area used for log input.

TIME-CONTROLLED OPERATIONS

The Time-Controlled Operations (TCO) facility allows IMS/ESA messages to be sent automatically at IMS start-up, at certain times of day, and after designated time intervals. It replaces the former Time Initiated Input Facility (TIIF). It can also be used with the Automated Operator Interface (AOI) to intercept commands and messages from IMS applications for later processing. TCO and TIIF cannot coexist—because TCO is implemented in IMS/ESA, TIIF must therefore be excluded.

TCO is implemented by using *scripts* describing messages or requests for TCO to process. Each script should be checked by the off-line verification utility for errors. This utility provides an error report, a time schedule request report, a message report, a statistics report, and a summary report.

Scripts are collected in a script library containing script members. Each member contains time schedule requests for timer services. A time schedule request specifies the name of an exit routine and a given time of day, a regularly scheduled time interval, or a specified delay after the completion of IMS initialization. At the requested time the exit routine is invoked and can then load a new script, enter operator commands, send messages, or invoke transactions.

Members can also contain message sets, which are optional. They are associated with time schedule requests and are passed to the exit routine.

TCO, which is driven by the script, invokes various exit routines that use DL/I calls to retrieve script data and insert any required messages. Requests to be issued at IMS start-up time are distinguished from those that are simply time delayed. The latter requests are sorted according to their time delay required, whereas start-up requests are issued immediately.

LOG SIZE REDUCTION

IMS/ESA uses several means to reduce the volume of log data associated with database updates.

Reduced Logging for REPL Calls

In IMS/VS, whenever a segment was replaced using the REPL call the image of the entire segment was logged, even though much of the segment had not changed. However, IMS/ESA attempts to log only the changed parts of a segment. The size of the logged data depends upon the amount and location of the data in the segment that has changed. In addition, IMS/ESA is sometimes able to log multiple changes to the same segment by using a single log record.

Nonrecoverable Databases

IMS/ESA allows the system definer to declare any full-function DL/I database to be nonrecoverable. Choosing this option for a database by registering it with

DBRC makes IMS/ESA log only the before images of database changes. After images are not logged. The before images are required for backouts, including a dynamic backout following deadlock or program abend. If before images are deleted during log archiving, IMS/ESA may not be able to back out a non-recoverable database successfully. Note that database changes for non-recoverable databases may be dynamically backed out, provided that the log records are on the on-line log dataset, that is, have not been archived.

Batch backout will back out nonrecoverable databases only if the non-recoverable database's log records can be found on the log created by an IMS batch job. The batch backout facility will not back out nonrecoverable databases for input logs from DBCTL or CICS subsystems that use local DL/I.

Log Compression

After the log reduction process takes place, as described, IMS/ESA uses a data compression algorithm to compress repeated single characters in the segment data portions of log records. This process applies to updates resulting from ISRT, DLET, and REPL calls.

LANGUAGE SUPPORT

IMS/ESA supports the languages shown in Table 11.3. The newest additions to this list are the Ada and C languages. C, usually associated with microcomputers, is now available on the mainframe.

SUMMARY

The acceptance of and migration to IMS/ESA will be slow—but inevitable. Although some of the features described in this chapter are significant improvements in the way IMS works, most IMS shops will remain content with IMS/VS. Because having MVS/ESA is a prerequisite for installing IMS/ESA, IS shops must cost justify the new operating system first.

Table 11.3. Languages supported in IMS/ESA.

Assembler H, Version 2	VS COBOL II Version 3, Release 0
OS/VS COBOL	OS PL/I Version 2, Release 2
PL/I Version 1, Release 5.1	PL/I Version 1, Release 6
Pascal Version 1, Release 2	C/370 Version 1
Ada Version 2, Release 11	

Appendix A
Common IMS Status Codes

What follows is a list of the most commonly received IMS status codes. In each case the code's probable cause is listed, along with a short explanation of it and a description of possible solutions.

AA   CHNG or ISRT for Response Alternate PCB must specify LTERM, not Transaction Code

In this case the program attempted to use a response alternate PCB to send a message to a transaction or application program. To do this is invalid. Response alternate PCBs are used to send messages to terminals, not to do message switching to other programs. When you use such a PCB during response mode or conversational mode, the LTERM specified in the PCB must represent the same physical terminal as that of the originating LTERM. Response alternate PCBs are defined by specifying ALTRESP=YES in the PSB. Also, LTERM names, transaction codes, and MSNAME link names must be collectively unique.

AB   No I/O area specified in DL/I call – required

This code typically indicates a programming error. The DL/I call issued requires an I/O area in the parameter list. Although some DL/I calls specifically prohibit an I/O area from being present (such as CHNG, SYNC, and ROLL), most require it. One other remote possibility is that the program is written in PL/I and the parmcount parameter was omitted.

AC   Hierarchic error in SSAs, or segment not in PSB

This error usually indicates an SSA problem. Such an error is commonly caused by misspelling a segment name in an SSA. IMS searches the DB PCB that was specified in the DL/I call for the segment name specified in the SSA. If IMS cannot find the segment name there, it generates an AC status code. Another possibility is that the call may have specified two SSAs for the same segment. IMS will be unable to find the segment name for the second SSA because it will assume that the second segment is a hierarchic dependent of the first one.

AD   Invalid function code in DL/I call

This error is commonly caused either by misspelling a function code (CKPT instead of CHKP, for example), or having a programming error overlay the definition of the function code in Working Storage. Other, more remote, possibilities include 1. specifying a DB PCB where an I/O PCB is called for; 2. issuing a Get call that references an alternate PCB; or 3. issuing a GU call to the I/O PCB in a transaction-oriented BMP without specifying the IN= parameter in the JCL.

AH   SSA required for ISRT, or RSA not supplied for GSAM GU call

This error indicates that either 1. the ISRT call requires an SSA; otherwise, how is IMS to know what type of segment is being inserted? or 2. the program issued a GU call for a GSAM database without specifying an RSA.

AI   Data management open error, or database not allocated

This very common error is usually caused by incorrect JCL or by using the wrong PSB. Some of the possibilities are

- A BMP referenced a database that 1. did not have corresponding DD-statements in the JCL; 2. had the appropriate DD statements but misspelled the DS-Names; or 3. had the correct DS-Names, but the datasets had not yet been allocated. The DBD for the database contains a DATASET statement specifying the DD-statements for the database. These statements must be present in the JCL.

- A program attempted to load a nonempty database (i.e., the PCB PROCOPT was L or LS). Once a database has been loaded, it cannot be referenced by a PCB with a load PROCOPT.

- A program attempted to access a database with a PROCOPT other than L or LS when the database had not yet been loaded. Empty databases must always be loaded initially before they can be accessed, even if the load process consists of nothing more than inserting and then deleting a dummy segment. (This method of loading a database is, by the way, quite common. The DFSDDLT0 utility is used to insert a segment with High Values as the key, then delete the segment.)

- The buffer pool does not have a buffer big enough to hold the database record requested. Physical I/O in IMS is done in chunks called blocks. The sizes of these blocks correspond to those of the buffers in the buffer pools. In addition, IMS almost always deals in database records, which each consist of a root segment and all its dependents. A request for a segment requires IMS to access the entire database record and store the record in a buffer. The VSAM and ISAM/OSAM buffer pools are defined in the //DFSVSAMP dataset.

- The record format and block size specified in the JCL do not match those in the database definition (DBD). Alternatively, incorrect or missing information is preventing IMS/VS from determining the block size or the logical record length.

- RACF was used to protect an ISAM or OSAM dataset and the control region has no authorization to update it.

AJ   Invalid SSA qualification format, invalid parameter in RSA, or error in subset command codes

This message usually indicates a problem in SSA or RSA structure. The most common errors include missing parentheses, invalid command codes, or relational operators, boolean connectors, or pointer numbers. One frequent mistake is that of having an SSA that is either too long or too short. If too long, IMS looks for either a right parenthesis or a boolean operator but finds instead part of a search field value. If too short, IMS will use the trailing right parenthesis as part of the search field value and continue scanning memory to try to find the ending ")".

Another, less common, error would be to use a qualified SSA with either DLET, REPL, or ISRT. Check the SSA or RSA and correct it, then verify that the DL/I call can in fact use the SSAs specified. This sometimes happens because the programmer misunderstands path calls.

AK   Field name in SSA not found in corresponding DBD

This error is usually caused by a misspelled field name in a qualified SSA or by the DBA's forgetting to include a search field in the DBD. Another, remote, possibility involves using field-level sensitivity in the PCB when the program is not authorized to access that field.

AM   Function code not compatible with processing options, segment sensitivity, transaction definition, or program type

This condition is usually caused by the program's attempting to issue a DL/I call that is inconsistent with the PROCOPT specified in the PCB. Some customary mistakes include 1. the DB PCB PROCOPT=L, but the program attempted a call other than ISRT; 2. the program attempted an ISRT, REPL, or DLET call and either the PROCOPT=G or the program was defined to IMS as INQUIRY=YES; or 3. the program attempted a path call (command code of D in the SSA), but the database PCB processing options did not include P.

AO   Physical I/O Error

This error is usually caused by a GSAM database DD-statement having an incorrect or missing LRECL or BLKSIZE designation. (Note that the O in AO is the letter "oh", not a zero.)

A1   LTERM name not defined to IMS/VS

The usual cause of this error is that the program attempted to issue a CHNG call with an LTERM name that was unknown to IMS. Another common error is that of issuing a CHNG call in an MPP before the program has retrieved its message from the I/O PCB. Note that message switching is invalid if a program is Fast Path exclusive.

A2   CHNG invalid for PCB, or ISRT has already been done

This condition is usually caused by attempting to issue a CHNG to an alternate PCB that is not modifiable (i.e., MODIFY=NO in PSB). Another possibility is that the PCB was already being used to route a message and had not yet been PURG-ed.

A3 ISRT/PURG attempted for PCB with no destination set

Before doing an ISRT or PURG, the program must set the destination for the PCB. This can be set either by specifying the destination in the PSB, using the NAME= parameter, or by issuing a successful CHNG call specifying the destination.

A4 Security violation

This error is usually caused by attempting a program-to-program message switch where the originating LTERM has no authorization to use the switched-to transaction. It is also possible if you do a CHNG call and RACF gives you a nonzero return code.

BA Data unavailable

This status code, along with the next, BB, was new in IMS/VS 2.2. Both codes indicate that one or more databases were not available at the time of the call.

BB Data unavailable, databases backed out to prior commit point

See the previous, BA, status code. Note that this status code is BB (Bee-Bee). Some IMS shops use a standard naming convention for IMS status code values (e.g., IMS-STATUS-GE for a GE status code). Unfortunately, these same shops often use the variable IMS-STATUS-BB to mean a status code of blanks or spaces (commonly referred to in IBM manuals as bb). Be careful not to confuse these two status codes.

DA Segment key field changed

The program did a DLET or REPL for a segment after changing the key field specified in the DBD. Alternatively, the PCB specified field-level sensitivity and the program changed a field it was not allowed to modify.

DJ DLET/REPL attempted with no prior Get Hold call, or too many SSAs

Most programmers do not realize that you can do multiple REPL calls after a single GHU or GHN. Only one DLET is allowed, however. A common programming mistake is to have checkpointing logic that performs a checkpoint call between a DLET/REPL and the previous corresponding Get Hold call. Another, rare, possibility is that incorrect SSAs may have been included with the call.

DX   Delete rule violated

Delete rules for a segment are specified in the DBD. In this case the program attempted to DLET a segment and violated one of these rules.

FA   Arithmetic overflow in MSDB during commit interval

This condition is usually caused by a bad FLD/CHANGE call.

FD   Deadlock occurred. DB updates have been backed out to previous SYNC or CHKP

This problem occurs most often in IMS BMPs that use DB2. There are several types of deadlock situations, the most common being the deadly embrace. In this case a program has already allocated one IMS or DB2 resource (A) and is attempting to allocate another one (B). Meanwhile, some other program has done just the opposite, having allocated (B) and attempting to allocate (A).

The FD status code indicates that, through some process such as the IMS Resource Lock Manager (IRLM), IMS has determined that your program was involved in a deadlock situation and, furthermore, that your program was selected to be the *victim*. All database updates made by your program have therefore been backed out.

For more on deadlock processing, see Chapter 9.

FE   FLD call received nonblank status code in RSA

This code indicates that the Fast Path program should check the status code in the RSA.

FF   No free space in MSDB for ISRT

This error is caused by running out of free space in an MSDB. Unfortunately, the status code may not be returned to the program until well after the out-of-space condition has occurred. Specifying MSDB free space requires performing an IMS SYSGEN.

FG FLD call received nonblank status code in RSA; program has used up normal buffer allocation

This error is usually caused by not doing checkpoints frequently enough.

FH DEDB area inaccessible

This error is commonly caused by failing the authorization check when first accessing a DEDB.

FN FLD call contains field name in FSA not defined in DBD

This error is usually caused by misspelling a field name in an FSA.

FP Invalid packed decimal field or hex field in MSDB REPL, ISRT, or FLD/CHANGE I/O area

This situation usually indicates an invalid field in the I/O area.

FT Too many SSAs in call

The maximum number of SSAs allowed in a particular IMS call depends upon the call and the database access method. A call to an MSDB, for example, is allowed to contain only one SSA.

FV FLD verify operation failed, databases backed out to previous SYNC or CHKP

This condition happens when one or more verify operations in a FLD call fail when a Fast Path program reaches a commit point.

GA GN/GNP retrieves segment at higher level

This notification is an informational status code. Whether it is also an error depends upon the application program's logic. The GA status code means that an unqualified GN or GNP has successfully retrieved a segment whose level is higher than the previous one. This condition can be verified by checking the segment level field in the PCB.

GB   GN call reaches end of database

This status code causes problems because programs simply do not get it. This code can occur only for GN calls. Some programmers code a qualified GU call as part of a loop that processes many segments, expecting to get a GB status code after they have processed the entire database. *This will not happen*—the program will most likely get a GE status code instead.

GC   Attempt to cross unit-of-work boundary

This status code is strictly informational, notifying the program that it has crossed a unit-of-work boundary.

GE   Segment not found, or parent not found on ISRT of child

This status code is commonly caused by IMS's being unable to satisfy a request for a segment. Another common occurrence is that of issuing an ISRT call for a dependent segment and specifying SSAs for its parents. If one of the parents does not exist, the ISRT fails, with a GE status code.

GG   Invalid pointer found for Gxxx call with PROCOPT of GOT or GON

Programs attempting to access databases using a PROCOPT of GOT or GON are here specifying that they wish to read a segment without intending to update. IMS also allows other applications to update such segments at the same time, however, sometimes causing the read request to fail because the database is in a state of flux.

Program logic must handle this situation either by terminating the program, continuing with another request, or reissuing the same call. (The call may by now succeed if the updating program has finished its processing of the database record.)

GK   GN/GNP retrieves different segment type at same level as previous

This status code is returned if a GN or GNP retrieves a different segment *type* that is at the same *level* in the database as the previous one.

GP No parentage established, or segment not a dependent of specified parent

This strictly informational status code is caused by issuing a GNP or GHNP call without first establishing parentage. This situation is usually accomplished by first issuing a successful GU or GN call for the parent segment.

II Segment already exists

The most common cause of this status code is attempting to ISRT a segment whose key already exists. Other, less likely, possibilities involve logical database processing or database pointer options.

IX Insert rule violated

Insert rules for a given segment are specified in the DBD. In this case the program attempted to ISRT a segment and violated one of these rules. Other possibilities include attempting to ISRT a segment to a GSAM database after having received an AI or AO status code or attempting to ISRT a duplicate segment when a unique secondary index exists.

LB Segment already exists

This status code occurs only in load programs. Either the program attempted to ISRT a duplicate segment or, in an HDAM or HIDAM database, attempted to ISRT a segment with a key of High Values.

LC Load out of sequence

This status code also occurs only in load programs. It is caused by attempting to ISRT a segment with a key field that is out of sequence.

LD Parent not loaded

This status code is another that occurs only in load programs. It occurs when attempting to ISRT a segment whose parent has not yet been loaded.

LE   Hierarchic error in load sequence

This status code, which occurs only in load programs, arises when the sequence of segments being loaded does not match the hierarchic sequence specified in the DBD.

NA   INIT with DBQUERY says at least one DB not available

The INIT call is new with IMS V2.2. It requests IMS to inform the program whether any of the database resources specified in the PSB are unavailable to the program. The NA status code specifies that at least one of the databases specified in the PSB is not available.

QC   End of input messages

Either there are no more messages in the queue for this program or the number of messages already processed equals the limit specified in the IMS SYSGEN for this transaction.

QD   Last segment retrieved of multisegment message

This informational code is self-explanatory.

RX   Replace rule violated

Replace rules for a segment are specified in the DBD. In this case the program attempted to REPL a segment and violated one of these rules.

V1   Invalid variable length segment

This status code is usually caused by the program's specifying an invalid or incorrect length for a variable length segment. The length must be valid, large enough to contain the reference field if any, and be less than or equal to the maximum length specified in the DBD.

XA   Attempt to message switch conversation after responding to originating terminal

In this situation a conversational MPP had already responded to the terminal that originated the conversation, then tried to pass the scratch pad area on to another program. The SPA should instead have been returned to IMS.

XB   Attempt to respond to terminal after message switching conversation

This condition is in a way the opposite of the XA status code. In this instance a conversational MPP passed the SPA to another program via a message switch, then tried to respond to the originating terminal.

XC   Z1 bits in message have been changed

The Z1 field in the message prefix is reserved for use by IMS. A common programming error is to initialize a message area by moving spaces to it. When doing so, be sure to move spaces to the area actually containing the message, not to the LL and ZZ fields preceding it.

XD   IMS terminating with CHECKPOINT FREEZE or DUMPQ

This status code is usually caused by having the IMS Master Terminal Operator issue a /CHECKPOINT FREEZE command. BMPs receive an XD status code when they issue a CHKP or SYNC call. Programs should then terminate immediately, for this indicates that IMS is coming down.

bb   (spaces) Successful call

This status code is usually caused by IMS's successfully completing what you *told* it to do. Unfortunately, this is sometimes different from what you *wanted* it to do.

Appendix B
Common IMS User Abends

The following is a list of the user abend codes for the most common IMS program abends. In each case the probable cause is explained and possible solutions to it are discussed.

U002   Control region abnormally terminated

This condition is typically caused by a dependent region's attempting to start up after normal IMS control region shutdown, perhaps even a scheduled one. Other possibilities can be lumped under the category *program problem*. Some program — possibly yours — caused the abend.

U102   Checkpoint records not found: no //IMSLOGR DD, or invalid checkpoint-ID

This message is the usual result of trying to restart a batch program without including a log file, or including the wrong log file. Another possibility is that of attempting to restart a program that has terminated normally, or of specifying the incorrect checkpoint-ID in the restart JCL. One last possibility is of issuing a second XRST call that includes a checkpoint-ID.

U103   Invalid parameter passed in CHKP call

This error is usually caused by having an invalid length for one of the seven user areas than may be passed to IMS in the CHKP call. Verify that all length parameters are valid.

U206   **Unable to open IMSVS.PSBLIB or IMSVS.DBDLIB**

This situation usually indicates a JCL error. Verify that the //IMS DD statement is present and contains the correct DS-Names for the PSB and DBD libraries.

U240   **MPP exceeded allowable execution time, or BMP execution exceeded CPUTIME=**

This situation is the IMS equivalent of a timeout condition. For a BMP the CPUTIME= parameter in the JCL specifies the total allowed elapsed CPU time in minutes for the program, not including time for IMS/VS initialization. For an MPP the PROCLIM parameter of the TRANSACT macro in the IMS SYSGEN specifies the total CPU time allowed for the MPP to process a single transaction or message and the number of messages the transaction can process in a single scheduling. This parameter can be overridden by the Master Terminal Operator's using the /ASSIGN command.

U251   **Unable to open dataset – message printed to //PRINTDD DD**

In this case the utility DFSDDLT0 was unable to open a dataset. It prints the dataset name on the //PRINTDD data set.

U260   **More than 18 parameters in DL/I call, or too few or mismatched parameters on CHKP or XRST call**

The most probable cause of this error is a mismatch between the parameters specified on the XRST and CHKP calls. Other possibilities include invalid addresses in the parameter list, caused by omitting a length field or having an invalid parameter's count for PL/I.

U261   **Invalid parameter in IMS call, invalid PCB, or incorrect DCB subparameters for GSAM input**

This message commonly occurs when IMS detects an invalid PCB address. This happens when the list of PCBs in the PSB and in the program ENTRY statement do not match. If there are too many PCBs in the ENTRY statement, the extra PCB addresses not matching ones in the program PSB will be invalid. (Note that having these extra PCBs in the ENTRY statement is not invalid, as long as the program does not refer to them during its execution.) Other, less common, causes of this particular abend include an invalid parmcount parameter or invalid DCB information for a GSAM input dataset.

U273 **GSAM DCB discrepancy on restart, or error repositioning GSAM dataset during XRST**

This condition is caused by restarting a program that uses a GSAM database. In this case IMS was unable to reposition the GSAM database, probably because the DCB of the dataset in the restart JCL differs from that in the original job.

U427 **Error encountered while processing VSAM database**

This error usually indicates that a database using VSAM as the access method has not been properly loaded.

U428 **PSB not defined for attempted BMP execution**

This message indicates that the PSB name specified in the JCL for the program was not known to IMS. This situation is usually caused by misspelling the PSB's name.

U432 **Attempt to execute BMP, PSB not defined as BMP**

This message is usually caused by attempting to run an MPP in batch or by misspelling the PSB's name.

U437 **Application Group Name or resources specified are not valid for this dependent region**

This error can be caused by specifying the incorrect Application Group Name on the AGN= parameter of the BMP execution JCL.

U451 **I/O error on database dataset**

This error can be caused by misspelling the DS-Name in the JCL for a database. Alternatively, the database dataset may not be the same access method as defined in the DBD. For an excruciatingly complete description of the various possibilities, reference the DFS0730I message in the *IMS/VS Messages and Codes Reference Manual* (SC26-4174).

U454   A BMP or MPP was started after all active regions were stopped

This message indicates that a program attempted to begin execution after IMS had begun to come down, perhaps as part of a normal shutdown. If the program was a BMP, resubmit the job when IMS comes up.

U456   PSB for Batch or BMP is stopped

This message is probably the most frequently occurring IMS error. This error most commonly happens because a prior program abend caused IMS to mark the PSB for the program as being STOP-ed. To rerun the program, the PSB must first be START-ed. Another cause might be from attempting to run a BMP referencing a PSB that is not in the ACBLIB.

U457   BMP started for PSB already scheduled in another region

Multiple copies of an MPP, as specified by its PSB, are allowed to execute simultaneously, as are BMPs. This situation is possible only when the APPLCTN macro specifies SCHDTYP=PARALLEL for the program in the IMS SYSGEN. The default setting is SCHDTYP=SERIAL. This error is typically caused by submitting a BMP defined as SCHDTYP=SERIAL for another execution while it is already running in another region. Another possibility is a misspelling of the PSB's name in the JCL.

U458   Database stopped or locked on attempted BMP execution

This message is usually caused because a Fast Path database required by a BMP is STOP-ed.

U462   MPP terminates without doing GU to message queue

This message points to an on-line program logic error. MPPs must process at least one input message from the message queue before being allowed to proceed to normal termination.

U474   /STOP REGION issued

The /STOP REGION command can be issued by the Master Terminal Operator to terminate application execution.

U499   Maximum ISRT call count exceeded

When an MPP is defined to IMS, the TRANSACT macro specifies the maximum number of segments that can be inserted by the program during a single scheduling. If this count is exceeded, the program receives an A7 status code. However, if the program continues and attempts another insertion, this U499 error occurs.

U688   Operator enters CANCEL in response to DFS690A. (DFS690A CTL PGM NOT ACTIVE, REPLY 'WAIT' OR 'CANCEL')

This message means that an MPP or BMP began executing when the IMS/VS control program was not active. Note that the user can specify OPT= on the IMSBATCH JCL procedure to specify what to do if the BMP starts when no control program is active. OPT=N (default) says "ask the operator," OPT=W says "wait," and OPT=C says "cancel."

U775   Enqueue space exceeded

This error does not necessarily indicate a program problem. It shows instead that the program attempted to enqueue a database record and failed. This failure is usually due to some program, usually a BMP, having enqueued many database records without reaching a commit point. When the enqueue space is exhausted in this fashion, all active programs are terminated with a U775. Recognize that it may not be your program that caused the problem.

U777   Application terminated due to deadlock

This message is commonly termed a *pseudoabend*. In this situation IMS has determined that the program, an MPP, was involved in a deadlock situation (see the full discussion under FD Status Code). IMS terminates the application, then places the input message that is being processed back at the top of the queue.

U844   No space available in database

This message is a common database full condition. Either 1) the database can in fact hold no more data; 2) the database is a HISAM one that needs to be reorganized to reclaim lost space; or 3) the database was defined in the JCL as DD DUMMY.

U929   DBD or PSB not found in library

This common error is typically caused by one of the following: 1) misspelling the DBD or PSB library name on the //IMS DD statement; 2) misspelling the PSB name in the JCL; 3) a PSB's referencing a DBD name that did not exist or was misspelled; or, 4) the IMS system is not yet aware that a newly GEN-ed DBD or PSB exists.

U949   Unable to open //SYSPRINT DD

This message is caused by forgetting or misspelling the //SYSPRINT DD statement in the JCL. Another, remote, possibility is that of including COBOL DISPLAY or EXHIBIT statements in an MPP. When the program attempts to write these to //SYSOUT, no DD-statement is to be found. The system then attempts to print a message on //SYSPRINT indicating that no DD-statement exists for //SYSOUT.

Glossary

This glossary contains short definitions of the most misunderstood IMS and DB2 terms. Terms that refer particularly to one or the other area are prefixed with an indicator such as "(IMS)." More complete lists can be found in some IBM manuals, especially the *IMS/VS Version 2 Master Index and Glossary* (SC26-4182).

abend. Abbreviation for "abnormal end." Do not use this word in speaking to a user. Also avoid such terms as *abort, bomb out,* and *blew up.*

ad hoc. Latin for "to this," meaning "for this specific purpose." An ad hoc query is typically a one-of-a-kind question rather than one that is regularly entered.

APPLCTN macro (IMS). A macro instruction used during IMS/VS system generation. One such macro is used for every application program to be defined to IMS.

application control block (ACB) (IMS). A combination of a PSB and all of its associated DBDs. Required for all IMS application programs.

application plan. *See* **plan.**

back out. The process of undoing changes to a database. Usually accomplished by reading the log file, in reverse order. All database updates performed by an application are hereby removed.

batch-oriented BMP. A BMP that has access to the IMS/VS message queues for output only, while performing batch-type processing. It can access on-line databases, GSAM databases, and OS/VS files for both input and output.

bind (DB2). The process of merging several database request modules (DBRMs) into a single **plan**. The DB2 **optimizer** is invoked to analyze access paths for SQL statements in the DBRMs.

buffer pool. A set of buffers that are all the same length.

change accumulation. The process of creating a condensed version of one or more IMS/VS log datasets. This procedure is done by eliminating records not needed for recovery and by combining multiple log records that record multiple changes to a single segment.

checkpoint (IMS). A point in the execution life cycle of an application when the program commits that the changes it has made to the database are consistent and complete. Checkpoints therefore provide points at which a program can be restarted.

commit point (DB2). The point in the execution life cycle of an application when the program commits that a unit of work is complete and that the data it has either modified or created is consistent and complete. A commit point occurs when a program terminates normally or when it issues a checkpoint or synchpoint call or command. *See also* **synchronization point, synchpoint**.

connection (DB2). A set of control blocks associated with an attachment between DB2 and another subsystem. Analogous to a railroad right-of-way, the connection specifies the characteristics of the path between DB2 and, say, IMS. The so-called thread, corresponding to the railroad tracks, is a specific pathway. *See also* **thread**.

control region (IMS). The operating system's main storage region, in which the IMS/VS control program executes.

conversational processing (IMS). An IMS facility allowing an application program to amass information obtained through multiple interchanges with a terminal, even though the program terminates between interchanges. Note that this is an IMS/VS definition that does not refer to generic conversational programs.

cursor (DB2). A DB2 object that is used by an application program to point to a particular row that is of interest within a result table and to retrieve rows from that table, possibly making updates or deletions. Cursor processing includes open, fetch, and close.

database record (IMS). An IMS database root segment along with all of its dependents, if any.

database record enqueuing (IMS). As database segments are updated, IMS locks the corresponding database records by using an enqueue table.

database repositioning (IMS). When an IMS program issues a checkpoint call, the positioning on all non-GSAM databases is lost. This forces IMS programs to reestablish their current position, if required.

database description (DBD). A collection of statements describing an IMS/VS database, including its hierarchical structure, IMS/VS access method, device type, segment lengths, sequence fields, and search fields.

dataset group (IMS). A dataset containing a subset of an IMS/VS database. Each dataset group contains one or more unique segment types. At least one dataset group is required for an IMS/VS database.

deadlock. A situation where a required resource is not available because it has been allocated to another user.

deadly embrace. A special case of **deadlock**. In its simplest form, two users each allocate a resource and then attempt to allocate the other's resource. Whichever product is the one managing locks (for example, the IMS Resource Lock Manager) must then recognize this situation and take appropriate action.

debugging. The process of proving to yourself that your program has no errors. (You can never prove this to anyone else.) Note that debugging demonstrates the presence, not the absence, of bugs.

delete byte (IMS). A byte not accessible by an application that is associated with a database segment on DASD indicating whether the segment has been logically deleted. Logical deletion consists of setting the delete byte, rather than physically removing or overwriting the segment. Many programmers become confused when they discover through independent means (for example, the IDCAMS PRINT function) that a segment seems to exist on a database but cannot be retrieved by an application.

distributed processing. A method of arranging processing power in a network so that several processors are each available to nodes on the network.

DLT0 (IMS). Abbreviated form for DFSDDLT0. A general purpose IMS utility typically used for testing IMS database call sequences. May also be used to load segments to a database or produce a formatted print.

dynamic backout. A situation where IMS undoes database changes because of a program failure.

expedited message handling (IMS). A facility for IMS/VS Fast Path programs that bypasses normal IMS/VS transaction message queuing and application scheduling. Only single-segment messages are allowed.

EXPLAIN (DB2). A facility used to analyze the access paths DB2 may choose for a query.

extended recovery facility (XRF). A facility in IMS/VS or CICS designed to minimize the impact of various failures on users.

foreign key (DB2). A key that is specified in the definition of a referential constraint. Because of this key the table becomes a dependent table. The key must have the same number of columns, with the same descriptions, as the primary key of the parent table.

image copy. The process of creating a backup copy of a database's dataset.

Intersystem Communication (ISC). An extension of IMS/VS **Multiple Systems Coupling (MSC)**. It allows connecting IMS/VS to another subsystem, provided both subsystems use ISC. Connections to another IMS/VS or CICS/OS/VS are also possible.

limit count (IMS). If the number of transactions enqueued and waiting for an application is equal to or greater than this number, the priority value assigned to the next transaction during scheduling will be the **limit priority;** otherwise the **normal priority** will be used.

limit priority (IMS). A transaction's priority when the number of transactions enqueued and waiting to be processed is equal to or greater than the **limit count**.

line response mode. A variation of **response mode.** All operations on a communication line are suspended while an application program output message is being generated.

load. In IMS, any process that inserts the initial segments into an IMS database. In DB2 it refers to the execution of the LOAD utility.

logical unit of work. The processing a program performs from one synchpoint to the next.

logical terminal (LTERM) (IMS). A logical destination, usually either a physical terminal or a printer. Each logical terminal has a name related to one or more physical terminals.

master terminal. The IMS/VS logical terminal that has complete control of IMS/VS resources during on-line operations.

message class (IMS). An identifier associated with a message processing region that identifies which MPPs may execute within that region.

message-driven program (IMS). A type of IMS/VS program that uses expedited message handling in a Fast Path region.

multiple system coupling (MSC). An IMS/VS facility that allows IMS/VS systems to communicate with one another.

nonresponse MPP (IMS). A message processing program that does not respond to the originating terminal. Usually used to process messages stored on the IMS message queue.

normal priority (IMS). The priority given to a transaction when the number of such transactions enqueued and waiting to be processed is less than the **limit count.**

off-line database (IMS). An IMS database not defined in the IMS control region JCL.

on-line database (IMS). An IMS database that is defined in the IMS control region JCL.

optimizer (DB2). The DB2 component that processes SQL statements and selects access paths.

physical terminal (IMS). A device attached to the computer and supported by IMS-DC as a terminal.

plan (DB2). A structure created from database request modules (DBRMs) during the **bind** process that specifies physical access paths for SQL statements.

primary key (DB2). A unique, non-null key that is part of the definition of a table. A table cannot be defined as a parent unless it has a primary key.

processing limit (IMS). The number of messages an application program is permitted to process during one execution.

randomizing module (IMS). An assembler language program that converts a root segment key into a physical position in a database. Used for HDAM databases and DEDBs.

referential integrity (DB2). The enforcement of referential constraints on LOAD, INSERT, UPDATE, and DELETE operations.

rerun. To begin execution of an abended program at the beginning. Contrast with **restart.**

response mode (IMS). When IMS/VS receives an input transaction defined as being in response mode, no more input is allowed until the application program response has been transmitted back to the terminal. *See also* **line response mode.**

restart. To resume execution of an abended program at a given synchpoint, usually the one immediately preceding the point of the abend. *See also* **rerun.**

roll back. The process wherein IMS or DB2 undoes any database or table changes made in the current unit of work.

scratchpad area (SPA) (IMS). In IMS/VS a work area used to store information from an application across interchanges with a terminal, even though the program terminates between interchanges.

standard work unit. A nebulous term usually meaning a measurement of the work that may be done by an application before it is required to commit resources.

synchronization point, synchpoint. A point in time in the execution life cycle of either an application or of the IMS/VS system. At this point IMS/VS or the application can start over if a failure makes recovery necessary. There are two types of synchpoints: 1. system checkpoints done by IMS/VS itself; 2. application program synchpoints (also known as **commit points**) done by individual programs.

system checkpoint (IMS). A point in the execution life cycle of the IMS/VS system when the system records control information to the log and restart dataset, allowing IMS/VS to reconstruct its condition if later required. IMS/VS monitors the log dataset and performs a system checkpoint after a certain number of records are written to the log.

temporary destination (IMS). Messages sent using a non-EXPRESS PCB are not sent to their destinations immediately, but are held pending a synchpoint. Should the program issue a ROLL or ROLB call, the messages may be deleted. During synchpoint processing such messages are then released and sent to their destinations.

thread (DB2). A DB2 structure that describes an application's connection, traces its progress, provides a resource function processing capability, and delimits the application's accessibility to DB2 resources and services. Most DB2 functions execute under a thread structure. *See also* **connection.**

TRANSACT macro (IMS). A macro instruction used during IMS/VS system generation to define a transaction. One such macro is used for each transaction defined to IMS/VS.

transaction-oriented BMP (IMS). A BMP that gets its input from the IMS/VS message queues.

two-phase commit. A process whereby two systems such as DB2 and IMS cooperate in the commit process.

wait-for-input (IMS). An option for some MPPs and BMPs that allows the transaction to be read into memory once and remain resident.

Index

RDE Services Quick Reference Cards
Summary of Features

DB2 Quick Reference Card Summary

The RDE Services Quick Reference cards contain a wealth of useful and practical information not easily found in any single manual. Here is a summary of their contents:

* All SQL Return Codes
* SQLCA Layout
* List of Reserved Words
* IMS Operator Commands
* CICS Commands
* DB2 Operator Commands
* Data Types
* Column Functions
* Complete SQL Syntax

* EXPLAIN Table Layout
* DB2 System Limits
* SQL Limits
* List of DB2 System Tables
* Layouts of Selected Tables
* Correlated Subquery Example
* Operators
* Scalar Functions
* Summary of Normal Forms

IMS/VS Quick Reference Card Summary

* List of applicable IBM Manuals
* DL/I DB Call Format
* DL/I DC Call Format
* DL/I XRST/CHKP Call Format
* IMS Access Method Comparison
* Common Status Codes
* Possible Status Codes for DL/I Calls
* Common User Abend Codes
* Processing Options

* Command Codes
* Data Base PCB Mask
* I/O PCB Mask
* Alternate PCB Mask
* SSA Qualification and Usage
* PSB Generation Parameters
* IMS Program Type Comparison
* Terminal Operator Commands
* FSA Status Codes and Operators

PREFERRED CUSTOMER ORDER FORM

Yes! Rush me my IMS and DB2 Quick-Reference Cards, as indicated below:

Description	Quantity
IMS/VS Quick Reference Card, Version 2.2	
DB2 - DBA Quick Reference Card	
DB2 - Programmer Quick Reference Card	

TOTAL QUANTITY   └──────┘

UNIT PRICE   └──┴──┴──.──┴──┘

Volume Discounts Available   **TOTAL PURCHASE PRICE**   └──┴──┴──.──┴──┘

QTY	PRICE
1-5	3.25
6-24	2.85
25-49	2.50
50+	Write

4% Sales Tax (Michigan only)   └──┴──.──┴──┘

$1.50 Shipping & Handling
(Orders of 6 or more)   └──.──┴──┘

TOTAL AMOUNT ENCLOSED   └──┴──┴──.──┴──┘

Quick Reference Cards
are available with your
company logo! Write for
more information.

Make checks payable to: **RDE Services**

SHIP TO: _____

_____

_____

_____

DATE: _____/_____/_____

Most orders shipped
within 48 hours!

PHONE: (_____)_____-_____

RDE Services * 3580 Warringham, Suite 401 * Waterford, MI 48095